36/24    GS LIT    £12.00    9

# JANE ELLEN HARRISON

Portrait of Jane Ellen Harrison by Augustus John, Newnham College. Reproduced by permission of the Principal and Fellows of Newnham College, Cambridge.

# Jane Ellen Harrison

## The Mask and the Self

Sandra J. Peacock

Yale University Press

New Haven and London

The author wishes to thank the following for permission to
quote from unpublished sources: Christopher F. Cornford,
for permission to quote from the Cornford-Darwin Family
Papers, British Library, London; the Principal and Fellows of
Newnham College, Cambridge, for permission to quote from
the Jane Ellen Harrison Papers, Newnham College Archive;
Mrs. Jean Pace, for permission to quote from the Jessie
Stewart Papers, Newnham College, Cambridge; Mrs. T. S.
Eliot, John Saunders, and Margaret N. Ellis, literary
executors for Hope Mirrlees, for permission to quote from
the Hope Mirrlees Papers, Newnham College, Cambridge;
and the Brotherton Library, University of Leeds.

Designed by JoAerne and set in Trump type by Huron
Valley Graphics, Inc., Ann Arbor, Michigan. Printed in the
United States of America by Halliday Lithograph
Corporation, West Hanover, Massachusetts.

*Library of Congress Cataloging-in-Publication Data*
Peacock, Sandra J., 1955–
Jane Ellen Harrison: the mask and the self / Sandra J.
Peacock.    p.    cm.
Bibliography: p.
Includes index.
ISBN 0–300–04128–4 (alk. paper)
1. Harrison, Jane Ellen, 1850–1928.  2. Classicists—Great
Britain—Biography.  3. Archaeologists—Great Britain—
Biography.  4. Newnham College—Biography.
5. Civilization, Ancient—Historiography.  6. Ritual—
Historiography.  7. Mythology— Historiography.  I. Title.
PA85.H33P43 1988
292'.08'0924—dc19
[B]    88–109    CIP

10  9  8  7  6  5  4  3  2  1

For Thomas W. Africa,
with affection and gratitude

... what other dungeon is so dark as one's own heart! What jailer so inexorable as one's self!

—NATHANIEL HAWTHORNE,
*The House of the Seven Gables*

# CONTENTS

# Illustrations

# PREFACE

IN AN ERA in which social history dominates historical scholarship, writing a biography may seem hubristic. Social history's emphasis on the living conditions of the masses seems incompatible with a study of the life of a highly educated, upper-middle-class academic who aspired to membership in Edwardian Britain's intelligentsia. Yet one of the dangers contemporary historical study faces is that of losing sight of its most valuable source: the individual whose actions, for better or worse, make up history. The recent burgeoning interest in biographies of women, moreover, promises a new understanding of women's lives by encouraging us to look beyond a limited gallery of prominent figures.[1]

Jane Ellen Harrison—daughter, teacher, scholar—was in some ways an ordinary woman leading an ordinary life. But in many other ways, she was an extraordinary woman leading a fascinating life. Her journey from Yorkshire's merchant class to the Cambridge intelligentsia illuminates many trends in British culture of both the Victorian and the Edwardian eras, and her scholarly work provides insight into some complex issues, such as the character of the female experience in a male-dominated world, the influence of gender on scholarship, and the course of women's intellectual history.

In the first half of this biography, chapters 1–4, I offer a chronological account of Jane Harrison's life from her childhood to her decision to leave Cambridge in 1922. Chapters 5 and 6 examine her relations with her closest colleagues: Gilbert Murray and Francis Cornford. Chapter 7 weaves together the personal and intellectual strands by focusing on how her relationships influenced her major scholarly works. The final chapter deals with the last years of her life, notable mainly for a four-year sojourn in Paris and the writing of her autobiography.

One of the thorniest problems in biography centers upon how to address the subject. During the four years I spent researching and writing on Jane Harrison's life, I grew to believe that to refer to her by her last name would impose an artificial and unwarranted distance. Moreover, it seemed pointless to create this distance out of scholarly "objectivity" on the one hand while revealing painful, intimate evidence on the other. I decided to refer to her as "Jane" throughout most of the text. I made one exception by referring to her as "Harrison" when discussing her work in chapter 7. Because that is conventional practice when referring to a published author, it seemed fitting in that case. I do not by any means intend to appear disrespectful, overly familiar, or casual. To the contrary, I take Jane and her work very seriously. Part of her appeal as a scholar, though, is her intensity and engagement with her work. I have tried to present a portrait of a flesh-and-blood human being, and calling her "Jane" seemed the best way to do so.

I then decided to refer to the other principal players by their first names as well, reserving the formal use of last names for those characters who play small parts in the drama of Jane's life and for secondary references. Thus, I refer to Francis Cornford, Gilbert Murray, Mary Murray, Jessie Stewart, Hope Mirrlees, and Frances Darwin by first names. D. S. MacColl also played a central role in Jane's life. She called him "Sutherland," his middle name, in the few letters to him that survive, and I followed her example. Jane herself recognized the importance of the magical. She created names for her friends that captured their essence and gave her a primitive feeling of control over them. These names were playful in part, but also represented a means of bestowing or withdrawing approval.

Much of this book is based on the personal correspondence of Jane Harrison as well as revelatory passages in her printed works. Unfortunately, about 1922 Jane destroyed a good deal of the correspondence that she had received over the years. What remains of this primary material is largely in the archives of Newnham College. Her correspondence overflows with eccentric spelling and punctuation, which I have chosen not to correct or to burden with a cumbersome *sic.* Her grammatical idiosyncrasies usually do not interfere with the meaning of what she said; furthermore, they convey the sense of familiarity that permeated her relationships with her closest friends.

So far, little has been written about Jane's life. Two of her students tried to write about her: one succeeded, but the other did not. Jessie Stewart, who had been one of Jane's first archaeology students at Newnham, edited and published a collection of some of Jane's letters to Gilbert Murray interspersed with personal commentary. This brief sketch, *Jane Ellen Harrison: A Portrait from Letters,* appeared in 1959.[2] Jane and Jessie were close friends for nearly thirty years, and although their relationship lacked the same intensity as that between Jane and her other favorite pupil, Hope Mirrlees, it seems to have been in many ways equally satisfying.

Hope Mirrlees arrived at Newnham in 1909, studied Greek with Jane, and remained her faithful companion until Jane's death in 1928. Hope then began to gather materials for a life, but put the notion aside, feeling disqualified as a biographer by her admiration for her subject. Her extensive notes reveal both her bias against most of Jane's friends and her reluctance to face the full implications of Jane's personal history, but they survive to provide a great deal of information.

More recently, Robert Allen Ackerman has written on the Ritualist circle's theory of the ritual origin of myth and religion, but without exploring Jane's life in depth.[3] Harry Payne has recognized the intellectual importance of the Ritualist circle in relation to fin-de-siècle aestheticism and discussed the circle's contributions to the study of ancient drama.[4] The Swiss classicist Walter Burkert has led the revival of interest in Ritualist theory by reconsidering their work in the light of structuralist method.[5] Feminist scholars such as Martha Vicinus have lately taken an interest in Jane, whose independent and intellectually exciting life makes her a fine subject for such an approach.[6]

My quarrel with the scholarship on Jane to date lies in its refusal to explore her personality and work in depth. Scholars have largely ignored her early years. Yet the events of her childhood decisively shaped her unique vision of the past, and to ignore them is to ignore compelling evidence. Feminist scholars particularly, wishing to see in her a model of a successful female intellectual, have failed to understand how much her scholarly success cost her. By taking her words literally, they have subscribed to Jane's own view that she lived a happy, satisfying, fulfilled life. In many ways she did, but in some critical ways she did not. She lived a life too marginal and beset by conflict to be entirely carefree. Her periodic bouts with illness and depression and the complexity of her work attest to a fundamental sense of unhappiness about the world. Rather than being defeated, however, she held her own against this great sadness by using her inner anger to fuel a lively, vital creativity. She was most emphatically not a victim, but one can live a reasonably satisfying day-to-day life while still sensing the terror and tragedy of the human experience. I contend that this is exactly what Jane did and, furthermore, that this duality determined the nature of her work.

Jane once told Gilbert Murray that all her life she had wanted to be a Buddhist and that, when she found out what Buddhism was, she discovered she had been one all along without knowing it.[7] I always wanted to be a disciple of Freud, and when I discovered his work I reacted as Jane had. I felt as if I had finally arrived home. I found Freudian theory personally satisfying, but felt reluctant to rely on it as a guide in writing a biography.[8] Once I started to examine Jane's life closely, however, I saw that Freudian theory worked perfectly: not only because it appealed to my own thought, but also because Jane shared an intuitive kinship with it herself. Critics attacked her for allowing emotion into her scholarship. They complained about the nature of her theories, but one suspects that it was her emotions, rather than her theories, that made them uneasy. Most Victorian classicists strove to equate their age with the serenity of classical Greece. Jane refused to accept that interpretation and insisted on exposing the darker side of both eras. Like Freud, she sensed the turbulent emotion constantly threatening to break through the veneer of civilization. Contemporary male scholars often rejected her work because she refused to play by their rules. She did not pore over tragedies or pay homage to the Olympians and the triumph of reason. But neither did she set out to glorify her own age. She wrote, like one of J. H. Plumb's "true creators, to ease the ache within."[9] Because she trusted her intuition, she often saw with extraordinarily clear vision.

In a delightful and compelling examination of modern German classical scholarship, *The Tyranny of Greece over Germany*, Eliza M. Butler compares the Continental classicists to children at play on an imaginary island. Her characterization of the German romantics captures the essential difference between traditional scholarship and genius. When the Germans plunged into the sea of classical study, "they dug deeper, but built less securely; they swam faster, but not so far; they made larger boats which capsized sooner; they grew angry and created confusion and uproar; they either could not or would not assimilate the rules of the various games. And yet they knew something the others did not, something about the nature of the sea."[10] Jane also refused to play by traditional rules. Her passion for and intuitive understanding of the past enabled her to see very clearly. Present-day scholars may reject her theories, but that is irrelevant. The best history teaches us more than something about the past; it teaches us something about ourselves. Jane reminded her readers that we run grave risks by ignoring the emotional life, and the world of scholarship has been enriched by her efforts.

## Acknowledgments

A WORK SUCH as this has an extended family, not just one parent. I may have been primary caretaker, but the book would not have flourished without the help of its large family and stimulating environment. It gives me great pleasure to thank everyone who helped me write it, for working on Jane Harrison's life brought me into contact with many wonderful people. It is not often that one has the chance to honor one's family publicly, for reunions are all too rare; so I want to take full advantage of the opportunity to thank all who have played critical roles in the last five years.

Even before I began to write, some of them were rehearsing the supporting roles they would play in this production. From its earliest days, my friends Teresa Jenkins Butchko, John Butchko, Sharie Harless, and Naomi Lockwood Barletta helped me struggle with my ideas, cheered me up when I despaired, and made several different parts of the Northeast feel like home.

Ann Phillips, reference librarian at Newnham College Library, Cambridge, and her assistants, Julia Rowe Chadd and Tricia Lacey, made my three months of research there in 1983 and 1987 a richly rewarding and enjoyable experience. They provided not only superb research assistance but also genuine kindness and hospitality in the days when I was a student thousands of miles from home. I also thank the Inter-Library Loan staff at the Glenn G. Bartle Library, State University of New York at Binghamton, especially Diane Geraci and Carol Clemente, who cheerfully deciphered my scribbled requests and tracked down obscure texts.

During the years in which this work grew from a doctoral dissertation to a book, my friend Tracy Mitrano read every page of every draft and offered boundless intellectual and emotional support. Her keen insights into Jane Harrison's life and her critical comments on my interpretation of it clarified my thinking and kept me from intellectual fuzziness. For her generosity, friendship, and encouragement, I owe a debt that can never be repaid.

I found a new group of supportive friends when I moved to Newcomb College of Tulane University, and they helped see me through the final stages of turning a dissertation into a full-fledged book. Nancy Anderson of Loyola University in New Orleans, a fellow British historian who also shares my interest in psychohistory, gave me much valuable advice, especially on the theoretical framework. Karen Kingsley, Tulane University School of Architecture, took an interest in Jane Harrison's life and encouraged me to explore other aspects of it, especially her travels to Greece, that I had not had time to focus on in the dissertation. Beth Willinger, director of the Newcomb College Center for Research on Women, gave encouragement and assistance, and understood when my distraction over the work made me a less than congenial colleague. Sylvia Collins typed the manuscript and introduced me to the wonders of word processing. The support I received from this group of friends has been invaluable, and I could not have asked for better company.

Peter Green read the manuscript and made many excellent suggestions, based on a lifetime spent brooding about ancient Greek culture. His tolerance for diverse interpretations of the past made him a delightful critic. I am especially grateful to him for gently reminding me that Jane Harrison was disappointed with Greece when she visited there. Frank Turner also read the manuscript and offered both generous encouragement and several constructive ideas for improvement. Both of these men gave me a great deal of excellent advice; that I did not follow all of it attests more to my own stubbornness than to the validity of their insights.

Ellen Graham, my editor at Yale University Press, offered valuable advice and assistance throughout the publication process. My research was funded in part by a National Endowment for the Humanities Travel to Collections grant, which enabled me to study the Cornford-Darwin family papers housed in the British Library in London.

Finally, I must acknowledge two people above all others: Elizabeth Fox-Genovese and Thomas Africa. Elizabeth Fox-Genovese took me on as a graduate student at SUNY-Binghamton and directed my dissertation with grace and good humor, believing in its value from the very start. Years ago, when I felt too unprepared and ill equipped even to complete my graduate course work, she encouraged me to continue. She gave freely of her vast knowledge of and insight into the female character, the nature of female experience, and intellectual history. She strengthened my ideas by constantly challenging me to be more precise and improved my work by editing my entire dissertation. For these reasons, and many more, I am in her debt.

Thomas Africa introduced me to Jane Harrison in a research seminar in 1980, somehow sensing that she and I would be compatible. Such perceptive matchmaking is rare. He followed my progress eagerly, reading chapters as they appeared and patiently pointing out their indiscretions. Jane Harrison has long been a special favorite of his, and I dedicate her story to him with gratitude for sharing her with me and entrusting me with a subject so close to his heart. I suspect there were times when he questioned the wisdom of his decision, but if there were, he kept his doubts to himself. His passion for history has opened up new worlds for me, and for that I am more grateful than I can say.

I could not have written this book without the help of the people named above, and their existence serves constantly to remind me how important friendship is in an academic world that often creates more chasms than bridges. In a sense, all my teachers have had a hand in shaping me and thus in shaping the book. I offer it to all of them as a gift of thanks for their efforts to make a good historian of me. They did their best with an often stubborn and recalcitrant pupil. What I have done with their fine training in the following pages is, of course, my responsibility.

# ABBREVIATIONS

Titles given are of works by Jane Ellen Harrison. Abbreviations occur both throughout the text and in the notes.

*A&O*   *Alpha and Omega: Essays from Experience* (London: Sidgwick & Jackson, 1915; reprint. New York: AMS Press, 1973).

CDP   Francis Cornford–Frances Darwin Family Papers, British Library, London.

*ISGA*   *Introductory Studies in Greek Art* (New York: Macmillan & Co., 1892).

JEH   Jane Ellen Harrison Papers, Newnham College Archive, Newnham College, Cambridge University.

*PSGR*   *Prolegomena to the Study of Greek Religion* (Cambridge: Cambridge University Press, 1903).

RSL   "Reminiscences of a Student's Life" (*Arion* 4 [Summer 1965]; originally published London: Hogarth Press, 1925).

*TH*   *Themis: A Study of the Social Origins of Greek Religion*, 1st Amer. ed. (New Hyde Park, N.Y.: University Books, 1962; reprint of 2d ed. rev. Cambridge: Cambridge University Press, 1927; originally published Cambridge: Cambridge University Press, 1912).

# JANE ELLEN HARRISON

# PROLOGUE

IN OCTOBER 1928, Virginia Woolf traveled to Cambridge to deliver the two lectures that later became *A Room of One's Own*. She spoke at Newnham and Girton, the two women's colleges at Cambridge. One of the lectures included a description of a ghostly scene glimpsed at Newnham, to which she gave—for the purposes of her talk—the mythical name of Fernham. Woolf painted an eerie portrait, for Fernham, it appeared, was haunted.

Somebody was in a hammock, somebody, but in this light they were phantoms only, half guessed, half seen, raced across the grass—would no one stop her?—and then on the terrace, as if popping out to breathe the air, to glance at the garden, came a bent figure, formidable yet humble, with her great forehead and her shabby dress—could it be J—— H—— herself?[1]

The ghostly scholar was Jane Ellen Harrison, a Newnham teacher whose life had been entwined with Newnham's for the first quarter of the twentieth century. She had died the previous April, but Woolf still sensed her presence. One might wonder about a personality that could so interest Woolf, a rather formidable personality herself. Who was Jane Ellen Harrison, and why did her presence infuse both Newnham's atmosphere and Woolf's memory?

Jane Harrison was a British classical scholar whose life spanned both the Victorian and Edwardian eras—she was born in Yorkshire in 1850 and died in 1928. She was one of the earliest students at Newnham College, which had been founded at Cambridge in 1872. She studied classics there, against the advice of most of her teachers, who encouraged women to study the more genteel and suitable field of moral science. After receiving a second in the classical tripos in 1879, she spent nearly twenty years in London, first studying archaeology under Sir Charles Newton and then lecturing at the British Museum. During these years, she published works on *Myths of the Odyssey in Art and Literature* (1882), *Introductory Studies in Greek Art* (1885), and *Mythology and Monuments of Ancient Athens* (1890). These early works showed the influence of the aesthetic movement and reflected her close engagement with London intellectual culture in the 1880s. Had she remained in London, perhaps her vision of the ancient world would have continued in the same vein. She wanted to return to academic life, however, and finally got her chance in 1898 when she was awarded Newnham College's first research fellowship.

Jane Harrison's return to Newnham set the stage for her greatest scholarly achievements by nurturing her increasing fascination with ancient Greek religion. Two years after her return to Newnham, she met the two figures who most influenced the course of her subsequent career: the Oxford classicist Gilbert Murray and the Trinity College philosopher Francis Cornford. Together, these three formed a remarkable scholarly circle known as the Cambridge Ritualists. Their collaboration brought an entirely new perspective to classical scholarship. Following the lead of Sir James George Frazer, William Robertson Smith, and Edward Burnett Tylor, they incorporated the new evidence of anthropology and its theoretical framework into the study of the ancient world. To varying degrees, their work rejected traditional Victorian interpretations of ancient Greek culture. They challenged old ideas by extending the scope of scholarly inquiry beyond the classical age of Greece, back to the archaic period. Although Gilbert Murray's and Francis Cornford's studies have traditionally been cited as the important work of the Ritualists, Jane Harrison actually stood at the center of the circle. Her major works, the *Prolegomena to the Study of Greek Religion* (1903) and *Themis: A Study of the Social Origins of Greek Religion* (1912), constitute the most detailed and passionate defense of Ritualist theory. In them, she argued for the ritual origin of mythology, religion, theology, and drama.

Her work, as well as that of her Ritualist colleagues, places her in the vanguard of what H. Stuart Hughes has called "the revolt against positivism."[2] For many complex reasons explored in the following pages, she objected to the triumph of cold rationality in scholarship and used her work to create a more emotionally satisfying historical past. To some degree, she and the Ritualist circle were influenced by Frazer's monumental work, *The Golden Bough*. The Ritualists' vision of the past reflects a debt to Frazer's radical break with previous scholarship. But Jane Harrison, at least, argued that Frazer did not go far enough. As Robert Ackerman has pointed out, despite Frazer's important role in popularizing a kind of ritual theory, he can be identified as a Ritualist for only a short time in his distinguished career.[3] Like many other Victorian scholars, Frazer preferred to maintain distance between himself and the past; he also preferred the tragic but orderly death and rebirth embodied in fertility rites to the sheer terror in the face of a hostile universe that inspired it. Jane Harrison disagreed with Frazer on fundamental principles, writing to Gilbert Murray, for instance, that "Frazer was somehow all wrong when he would keep on saying that magic was the beginning of science—magic never proceeds by experiment but by imagined relations."[4] Although Frazer spent his career at Trinity College, not far from Jane Harrison at Newnham, they seem not to have crossed paths often.[5] Ultimately, Frazer rejected the work of the Ritualist circle, so he himself does not receive much attention in this book. Nevertheless, Jane Harrison acknowledged his achievements and influence, and any discussion of the Ritualist circle must acknowledge them as well.

Jane took Frazer's work several steps farther and tried to get at the core of human emotional experience, finding in the religious impulse and its expression in ritual the center of that experience. Rather than internalizing Victorian scholarly views of classical Greece as the model for nineteenth-century Britain, she explored the archaic period in order to understand the intense emotional experience that underlay both cultures. She looked not to classical Greece to glorify the achievements of Victorian Britain but to the archaic period to explain its failures.

Most Victorian classicists generally agreed that the glory of Victorian Britain's political accomplishments had been equaled only by the classical period in Greece.[6] They based their perceptions of the ancient world on that premise, thereby enhancing the image of both eras. Historians such as George Grote created a past, allegedly grounded in indisputable proof, that made their own era look remarkably—and equally—enlightened. So long as Victorian classical scholarship remained mired in studies of political and military exploits, it had no room for innovation and speculation. As the traditional intellectual playground of upper-class male scholars, the field of classics neither tolerated nor encouraged diversity of opinion. It required a revolution in classical scholarship—the integration of new anthropological theory—to break down the intellectual walls. This biography explores Jane Harrison's part in that revolution.

As scholarly debate over Ritualist theory grew more heated, Jane found herself in a position not shared by many women of her generation: at the center of an academic controversy. Women had earned the right to a university education in the mid-nineteenth century but with the general cultural expectation that they would use this education to become better wives and mothers, not academics who challenged their (male) elders. Jane Harrison's experience as a female intellectual alone would make her an interesting figure, but her impressive scholarly achievements and the controversy surrounding them make her even more fascinating.

Jane Harrison's experience provides a different perspective on one of the liveliest and most exciting periods of intellectual achievement. She shared her Cambridge years with some of the most interesting figures in its long and distinguished history. At Trinity College, Bertrand Russell, Alfred North Whitehead, and George E. Moore broke new ground in philosophy as she struggled with the development of Ritualist theory. She traveled to Sweden with Lytton Strachey and Pernel Strachey in search of an efficacious rest cure.

On a more personal level, she shared an enduring friendship with the art historian Dugald Sutherland MacColl, whose role in her life has not received much attention to date. Jessie Stewart and Hope Mirrlees, two of Jane's favorite students and her closest young female friends, played siblings locked in a rivalry for their surrogate mother's affections. Frances Darwin, granddaughter of Charles Darwin and daughter of Jane's closest friend, found herself in the pivotal role of ingenue.

Virginia Woolf, who spoke so eloquently for a generation of female intellectuals, knew Jane Harrison because of her own Cambridge connections. One can imagine that she would have responded enthusiastically to a woman whose experience clearly embodied some of the issues with which Woolf herself wrestled. How do women perceive the world? How do they create? Why is their work valued less highly than men's? All these questions, which so vexed Woolf, might be asked with regard to Jane Harrison's life. She might have mulled them over as she walked, "formidable yet humble," through Newnham's garden at twilight. In her case, she dealt with them by turning her attention to the ancient world.

My goal here is to flesh out Woolf's ghostly figure. The self that Jane Harrison tried to conceal shines through her scholarship, illuminating a particular episode in women's intellectual history. This self, however, also illuminates the process by which the creative imagination transforms personal experience into scholarship. As Frank Turner noted in *The Greek Heritage in Victorian Britain*, "writing about Greece was in part a way for the Victorians to write about themselves."[7] His observation holds true for Jane Harrison as well, who was certainly a Victorian by temperament if not strictly by chronology. The most important difference between her and her contemporaries is that she wrote about an entirely different kind of self than they did. She experienced her culture far differently from her colleagues for many reasons, not the least of which was that she was female. Her achievements alone are noteworthy, but deciphering the story behind them enriches our understanding of both their significance and the construction of the female self.

Any biographer faces many dangers. The worst of these is to make the subject seem larger than life. When viewed as a totality, Jane's experiences read more like a Victorian novel than a real life. But the challenge of biography lies in its reliance on the actions of people who once existed. The characters are all real people and, as such, often unruly and recalcitrant. Their unpredictability makes them fascinating, for real life is always more absorbing than fantasy. Jane literally acted out her life rather than merely live it, and her penchant for conducting her life as if it were a Greek tragedy may well be the most interesting thing about her. Her friends complained of this tendency. She skillfully, albeit unconsciously, designed a persona with which to protect herself from the world. She was a mass of contradictions: a woman who craved affection yet feared intimacy; a passionate woman who cultivated rigid self-control; a conservative provincial who donned the trappings of eccentricity to hide her uneasiness among the intellectual elite; a student of the past who denied its importance and power in her own life. But both sides are equally compelling and revealing—the mask as well as the self it conceals.

# A Yorkshire Childhood and
# the Education of a Young Lady

*To know people well is to know their tragedy: it is usually the*
*central thing about which their lives are built.*
> —Bertrand Russell to G. Lowes Dickinson, July 19, 1903

JANE HARRISON'S entry into the world was not exactly the stuff of
tragedy. Born on September 9, 1850, in Cottingham, near Hull, she
was the third daughter of Charles Harrison and Elizabeth Hawksley
Nelson Harrison. Her father was a Hull timber merchant and her mother
a member of the gentry, the daughter of Thomas Nelson of Timber
Grange, Lincolnshire.[1] A month after Jane's birth, however, her mother
died. In many respects Jane built her subsequent life around this decisive
event, which in her eyes was indeed the stuff of tragedy.

It is difficult to piece together a coherent picture of Jane's family
because she rarely mentioned them directly. Her general denial of her
past consigns them, like so much else about her, to obscurity. Yet they
inevitably shaped the woman she became. The class differences between
her parents' families and the influence of those differences on her played
an important role in determining the course of her life. Moreover, her
immediate family's ideas about woman's role, education, and work set
the standard against which she finally rebelled.

When Hope Mirrlees began to collect information on Jane's background
in preparation for her attempt at a biography, she received some details
about the family from Jane's cousin, Marion Harrison. Marion's reminiscences depict the Harrisons as a fairly typical mid-Victorian middle-class
merchant family, which included its share of eccentrics. The Harrisons
descended "from seventeenth century farmers near Rudstone," near
Bridlington. Jane's grandmother, a "very low-church" woman, bore
twelve children, and "she and the sons rode rough-shod over the daughters." She may have controlled some of her daughters, but she provoked
rebellion in others. She kept two of Jane's aunts, Kitty and Harriet, on a
small allowance until they were over forty years old. Kitty and Harriet
both married late in life, Harriet a warden of the family's church. Another, unnamed daughter ran away with a blind poet named Lambert. Yet
another, Charlotte, married a "clergyman near Cheltenham." The youngest, Jessie, an adventurous woman who enjoyed hunting and amateur
photography, nevertheless always "had breakfast in bed" because of "a

bad heart" and died at only thirty-four years of age. According to Hope, Jessie, "Jane's first passion," "seemed to her a very romantic figure," although she never summoned enough courage to reveal her feelings to Jessie.[2]

The timber business prospered in mid-nineteenth-century Hull, and so did the Harrisons. Jane's uncles believed that their sisters had married "rascals" who were interested only in their money. These uncles were an intriguing group themselves. Crowther, the eldest, worked in the family business and also owned racehorses. He dabbled in the classics and in languages, and had "lived several months with the Gypsies to study Romany"—hardly the typical undertaking of a Victorian business-man. He lived in Melton, Yorkshire, and was educated, like his brothers after him, at Kingston College, Hull. His first wife died in a carriage accident that occurred when he was driving. Thereafter he became "temporarily insane" and had to be institutionalized for a short period. Joseph, the next in line, became a doctor, but abandoned his practice immediately after losing his first patient. Jane considered her uncle Edward, a classical scholar and aspiring architect, a "clever & cultivated man." Hope Mirrlees also mentioned an uncle named Arthur, but revealed nothing about the remaining two siblings.[3]

Charles Harrison made enough money in the timber business to retire early. Both Jessie Stewart and Hope Mirrlees described him uncharitably. In her *Portrait from Letters*, Stewart characterized him as "a silent serious man with deep prejudices: against Rome, against noise, against all things modern."[4] Hope Mirrlees wrote still more unkindly of him, describing him as "handsome & timid like a deer, entirely without intellect & yet w/a certain sensibility of his own . . . silent, with more than his share of the Harrison obstinacy & this tendency to brood over imaginary grievances." Jane's cousin Tetenka redeemed him by admitting "there was something about him one couldn't help liking." Significantly, Jane herself had little to say about her father, but her feelings about him colored every aspect of her life.[5]

Although the Harrisons engaged in respectable business and attempted to raise sons and daughters who would fulfill their expectations, evidence shows that the family comprised many unusual characters. The domineering grandmother, the rebellious daughters, and the neurotic sons sharpen the differences between the Harrisons and the more refined Nelsons.

Hope Mirrlees described the Nelsons as "people of property but not armiger." She related an incident Jane described to her that demonstrated an early awareness of class distinctions and family pride. A playmate taunted Jane with her own father's being a lord while Jane's was not. When Jane confronted her father and demanded the truth, he "solemnly produced the pedigree of her maternal grandmother Hawksley, in which there is a royal strain, & told her never to forget that she had as good blood in her veins as anyone in England."⁶ His tracing of Jane's lineage back two generations on her mother's side is significant: the Nelson side had better blood, and the marriage, like so many others in the nineteenth century, probably allied money and status. In her "Reminiscences of a Student's Life," Jane ignored the schoolmate incident, but she recalled wanting very much to be "Lady Jane." Her governess dashed this hope by informing her that she could never be Lady Jane "unless they made my father an earl, which seemed somehow unlikely" (RSL, 315). Jane considered her mother's family superior to her father's, and perhaps Charles Harrison encouraged her by identifying more with the Nelsons than with his own family.

The Harrisons liked Elizabeth Nelson, although they, as good merchants, considered her love of poetry "odd."⁷ Jane worshiped her dead mother's memory and suffered terribly from the knowledge that her birth had caused her mother's death from puerperal fever. When her Russian friend Prince D. S. Mirsky lost his mother in 1926, Jane wrote to console him. She urged him to be thankful that "thro' those last troublous years" he had been "her mainstay and comfort." She added, "I have always wondered what it was like to have a mother for I sent mine out of the world—but one has to pay the price in losing her." The pain of having grown up motherless was compounded by guilt over having been the cause of her death.⁸

Jane had good reason to construct such a loving memory of her mother. Her death had allowed her daughter to have her father to herself, and guilt over such an effortless Oedipal victory drove her to create an image of a mother good enough not to punish Jane for having won. Jane's recognition of her role in her mother's death represents more than simple adjustment to a horrifying fact; it also represents a tenuous reconciliation of her culpability with her satisfaction in achieving an Oedipal victory. She used her family's memories of her mother to create an all-forgiving figure and to relieve herself of a very heavy responsibility.

Elizabeth Harrison's death marked all three of her daughters. Lucy Harrison, the middle daughter, remembered her mother's suffering with puerperal fever and her own "horror on one day finding a basin of blood in the lavatory," left from when "mother had been 'bled.'" She also recalled that her father could not stand pain, for "it always made him faint." Hope Mirrlees recounted Lucy's "feeling that her father had a 'complex' about deaths" and her belief that "it must have been more than a coincidence that each time a member of his family died in a place, he left it shortly afterwards." The family left for Wales soon after Elizabeth's death and then moved to Filey in Yorkshire in 1855. They remained there for only one year, however, and spent 1856–58 in Barmouth, Wales. They returned to Filey in 1858 and then moved to Scalby in Yorkshire, where they remained until 1875, except for another year in Wales in 1870–71.[9]

Despite the pain of Elizabeth's death, Jane's early years passed happily. She exercised selective memory in her "Reminiscences," saying little about her early childhood, but Lucy Harrison spoke more freely about it. As they grew older, the girls enjoyed freedom to roam around the Welsh countryside. They had a series of nurses and governesses who, if not very intelligent, were at least amicable.[10] Lucy remembered and recorded the happier times, whereas Jane remembered the bad times and wrote about them in unlikely places. Nonetheless, both concur that Elizabeth's death created enormous changes. For Jane, the subsequent course of events etched the unhappy memories more indelibly in her mind than the happy ones.

In many middle-class families, an aunt often assumed the role of nurturer in the event of a mother's death. In the Harrisons' case, Charles's unmarried sister Harriet, or "Auntie" as she was known to the children, came to care for the house and the three young girls. Lucy remembered that "during 'Auntie's' reign Jane used to sit on her lap with her head on her shoulder—she called this 'dudding' (loving)." In those days, Charles Harrison "used to help them with their little garden-plots, & their Sunday treat was to walk over to their Uncle Crowther's with him to see the horses." Auntie treated the girls as their mother had done, dressing them, for instance, "exquisitely" in their mother's style. Interestingly, Jane never mentioned this apparently tranquil period. Yet these years, by providing her with a fine model, allowed her to construct an ideal mother. Harriet set the standard for a good and loving mother while, like Elizabeth Nelson, not threatening Jane's ties to her father. Despite this advantage, Jane's first memories seem to coincide with the arrival of the Welsh governess who completely changed the little girls' lives.[11]

This upheaval occurred when Auntie Harriet decided, late in life, to marry. Jane was five years old at the time. Psychologically, Harriet's departure proved to be a more significant event than Elizabeth Nelson's death. On one hand, Harriet's marriage heralded another easy victory in Jane's battle for her father's affections at a critical time in her development. Just as Jane's interest in her father became more proprietary, Harriet left the scene. On the other hand, the change came at a time when Jane was extraordinarily vulnerable. An Oedipal victory could not quite compensate for the sense of abandonment she felt when her aunt left to create a home of her own. A brief excerpt from the 1914 essay "Crabbed Age and Youth" reveals how deeply Jane suffered at the disintegration of the circle in which she had felt so secure.

This being the centre of your own . . . universe is best seen in the extreme case of the megalomania of young children, as yet untaught by life. . . . I had as a child—I was about seven—a very kind and much-adored aunt, aged about forty. At forty-one she quite unexpectedly married. I can never forget the shock her marriage gave me. My whole universe was deranged. . . . I had been at the centre of my own universe, my aunt gently and protectively hovering over that centre. Suddenly she had made a centre of her own, and I was at the circumference, with no tendency at all to hover sympathetically round her. . . . At seven years old one cannot analyze, so one must agonize. That is why it is so terrible to be a child, or even a young thing at all. One sees things, feels them, whole. There is no such devastating, desolating experience as to have been at the centre, warm and sheltered, and suddenly to be at the outmost circumference, and be asked to revolve as spectator and sympathizer round a newly-formed centre.[12]

There is a discrepancy in ages here, but clearly Jane referred to her aunt Harriet's marriage. To be "untaught by life" meant to expect events to conform to one's wishes; experience taught one, however, to expect nothing and to live a more orderly life by gaining control over one's emotions. This passage exposes the roots of some central themes in Jane's life: the image of the circle, with her at the center, as emblem of security; the hatred of marriage as an institution that destroys more personal bonds than it creates; and the apparent indifference she evinced toward other people's children resulting from her own knowledge, gained through bitter experience, of what they faced in their lives. These themes coalesced to become the central thesis of her scholarly work and directly influenced how she lived her life.

Before leaving to start her new circle, Auntie engaged a young Welsh woman, Miss Gemimi Meredith, as governess through the recommendation of a friend. She herself never met Miss Meredith until her arrival at the family home, when the new governess turned out to be a lovely young woman. A school friend of Jane's, Caroline Dutton Mitchell, later described Miss Meredith as "very odd-looking—just like a Gypsy, with jet black corkscrew curls."[13] Beauty notwithstanding, "the narrowness of her provincialism was only equalled by that of her Evangelicalism." She had been brought up near Barmouth in Wales and educated at a Birmingham boarding school. "Jane adored her at first," Hope stated, but Jane's cousin Tetenka, daughter of the classical scholar Arthur, said "she was always nicer to the children when their father was there." The beautiful Miss Meredith angered Charles Harrison by attracting many suitors, but within six months he himself proposed marriage. Five years after Jane lost her mother, and only months after Auntie's abandonment, she lost her father to a second wife.[14]

Scholars have been reluctant to discuss Jane's relationship with her parents. Enough evidence exists, however, to conclude that Jane adored her father and felt the perceived loss of his love to his second wife very keenly. She related his less serious foibles with genuine understanding and love, and hinted at a deep attachment between them that survived even his betrayal. Jane described him as "the shyest man I ever knew, and terribly absentminded" (RSL, 325). The family remembered with amusement the day two years after his first marriage when he "rode up to Timber Grange, my maternal grandfather's house, and asked to see Miss Elizabeth Nelson [his wife]" (RSL, 325). Jane could testify that the presence of "unexpected visitors in the drawing-room" might prompt him to "give a frightened look round, shake hands courteously with his embarrassed wife and daughters, and disappear like a shot deer" (RSL, 325). She spoke more charitably than Hope Mirrlees and Jessie Stewart of her father's distrust of all things modern. Granted, she remembered that he "left Yorkshire because of the threatened approach within a mile of our house of a small branch railway connecting Scarbro' and Whitby" and his fear that "it would bring with it tourists, char-a-bancs, gas lighting, and all the pollution of villadom." But she commented only "I think he was unduly anxious" (RSL, 326).

Two poignant remembrances of her father stand out in Jane's autobiography. She fell in love with Russia at an early age because of her father's extensive business dealings with Russian timber merchants, and one of her fondest memories was of a Russian sledge in which he sometimes took her for drives. Describing these outings, Jane remarked, "thank God it held only one, so I could dream undisturbed of steppes and Siberia and bears and wolves" (RSL, 312). Thank God too, no doubt, that it allowed her time with her father by herself. Much later in her life, she tried to share her work with him.

I always sent a copy of every book I wrote to my father, and he always
acknowledged them in the same set words: "Thank you for the book
you have sent me, your mother and sisters are well. Your affectionate
father." I am sure he never read them, and I suspect his feeling towards
them was what the Freudians call *ambivalent*—half shame, half pride.
Years after his death I learnt, and it touched me deeply, that, on the rare
occasions when he left home, he took with him a portmanteau full of
my books. Why? Well, after all, he was a Yorkshireman, it may have
been he wanted a "bit o' coompany." (RSL, 325)

This passage evokes a marvelous image of the young Jane trying to please her father, who was, however, a taciturn man unable to show his approval directly.

Despite their shared pain, Jane stood in a special relationship to her father. As the youngest daughter of his first wife, her birth intimately connected to her mother's death, she remained his last link to that part of his life. Understandably, then, father and daughter felt conflicting emotions toward each other. For his part, Charles Harrison must have often experienced a twinge of sadness when he glanced at the daughter whose birth had cost him his first wife. For her part, Jane could not have helped resenting what she perceived as his rejection of her in favor of a stepmother. The other side of such pain, however, was closeness and fierce attachment based on a common regret over Elizabeth Harrison's death and their attempts to atone for having inflicted such pain on each other.

As the figure who turned Jane's tiny circle into a triangle, Miss Meredith played a decisive role in Jane's life. Religious, class, and temperamental differences between the two created conflict in the home and shaped Jane's intellectual and personal life. Miss Meredith's background and her treatment of her stepdaughter also contributed to Jane's lifelong abhorrence of and flight from provincialism.

Deborah Gorham asserts in *The Victorian Girl and the Feminine Ideal* that "only a limited number of families ever employed" a governess and that "presumably they were upper-middle-class and upper-class families." The expense of paying and supporting another member of a household could be prohibitive, so the Harrisons must have been at least upper middle class in status. Governesses tended to be genteel women whose families' inability to support them in leisure forced them into service. Normally this arrangement might work out to each party's benefit and provide a proper middle-class home for a young woman turned out on her own. Such, initially, may have been the case in the Harrison household. But the children of an upper-middle-class family would have found it very difficult to accept a former employee as stepmother, a figure of authority and superiority. Thus, many conflicts arose between the former governess and her charges in the Harrison family.[15]

First, Elizabeth Nelson and Gemimi Meredith differed in temperament. Although Jane could not remember her mother, she idealized her as "a silent woman of singular gentleness and serenity" (RSL, 320). Regardless of Elizabeth's true nature, Jane needed an idealized image of her to compensate for her anger at her mother's abandonment. The garrulous Miss Meredith, in contrast, could (as her own son remembered) "talk the hind leg off a donkey" (RSL, 320). She treated the girls decently while serving as their governess, but "as soon as she was married, a great change came over her attitude to the three little sisters." Hope Mirrlees recorded that Jane was raised "*entirely* without love [after the second marriage], though, as she often told me, she was, by nature, an unusually affectionate child." Aunt Harriet concurred; she told one of her great-nieces, Hilda Lane, that Jane had been called "the Professor of Dodoism because she had such loving caressing ways & as a little girl seems to have used the word dodo as a term of affection."[16]

The second Mrs. Harrison was strict, perhaps at times unduly so, with the girls. Even as governess she had been "severe on Jane," who had trouble with her consonants, "for her babyish way of talking & soon got her out of it." After her marriage, she also refused to allow the girls their Sunday walks with their father to visit Uncle Crowther's horses. She objected to these excursions as a breach of the Sabbath, although Lucy later saw it as an attempt at "keeping them away from their father." These rules probably reflected Mrs. Harrison's adherence to Evangelical precepts more than a dislike of her stepdaughters. Nevertheless, the girls interpreted her actions as a deliberate attempt to deny them their father's attention.[17]

The status difference between the Harrisons and Gemimi Meredith exacerbated their temperamental difference. Theoretically, it must have been difficult for the daughters to accept a woman who had formerly worked for a wage as their equal in status. Not even Jane's eccentric aunts were so unconventional as to hold a job. They married men who could support them and presumably lived middle-class lives. Jane's mother, with her roots in the gentry and her love for poetry, could not have differed more radically from her provincial, Evangelical stepmother. Since the Harrisons exhibited some upper-class pretensions, the gulf between mother and stepmother must have seemed enormous. But economic issues also struck home at the practical level, as Charles Harrison and his new wife began a second family.

The size of the new family, which eventually numbered seven daughters and two sons, exacerbated financial worries. But concerns left over from the first marriage plagued Charles Harrison as well. He brooded for many years over the terms of his first father-in-law's will, "which he considered a reflection on himself." Thomas Nelson had arranged for his daughters to hold the money he left them independently of their husbands. To make matters worse, Elizabeth Harrison in turn left this money solely to her daughters, once again allowing it to slip from Charles's hands.[18] He held a grudge against "the Law for granting his children the right to their own money."[19] In fact, the prospect of his daughters' gaining financial independence so disturbed him that when Jane's eldest halfsister, Gemma, inherited some money separately and decided to use it to train as a nurse, Charles "forbade her the house for years."[20] At age twenty-three, Jane composed a tract for the Religious Tract Society to earn money to contribute to a Cheltenham fund. She received three guineas for her effort, but "dared not tell" her father about it. "He held old-fashioned views as to women earning money. To do so was to bring disgrace on the men of the family" (RSL, 324–25). But his disapproval would seem ironic, since he could not afford to support his numerous children anyway.

Hope Mirrlees provided a more sinister account of the financial woes caused by the second marriage. From Lucy's memories, Hope concluded that Miss Meredith "evidently was working towards her final triumph—the disinheriting of the first family." Hope implied that the Harrisons lived comfortably before Miss Meredith appeared on the scene. The rapid succession of children depleted Charles's resources, though, and the girls were fortunate to have inherited from their mother approximately a hundred pounds apiece that Charles could not touch. Hope cited one example of the second Miss Harrison's profligacy. She owned a piece of land in Wales whose value Charles increased from three hundred pounds to eight thousand pounds, but at his death she used profits from its sale to pay off her oldest son's debts. How she came to own the land or what Charles did to increase its value so enormously remains unclear, but it provides the most tangible accusation against her. The incident also hints that at least one of Jane's half brothers was not as financially responsible as the parents would have liked.[21]

Hope asserted that Gemimi Harrison was not "actively unkind" to the daughters, "but they were neglected, & she evidently grudged every penny their father spent on them."[22] Charles Harrison left virtually all his money to the second family, even some he had inherited from his sister Harriet on the condition that it would go to Elizabeth's daughters.[23] Eventually, Gemimi's behavior forced the daughters either to marry or to support themselves. Lucy, the middle daughter, chose the first path in order to get away from home, but Jane took the harder road of an independent life.[24] For a woman of the upper middle class this was not a common choice, but the need to work for a living directly influenced Jane's decision to attend Newnham College and study the classics. She determined that if such a pursuit was acceptable labor for upper-middle-class men, it would suit her equally well. And, too, pursuing an academic career would restore, albeit through the back door, the status of which her stepmother had deprived her. The experience with a stepfamily also influenced Jane's perceptions of family in general, and she projected her ideas about family life back into the ancient world through her scholarly work.

Religious differences also plagued Gemimi's relationship with the Harrisons. Jane believed her Nonconformist father "incapable of formulating a conviction," but felt "he really would have sympathised with the eminent statesman who 'had a great respect for religion as long as it did not interfere with a gentleman's private life' " (RSL, 316). She recalled that he "attended church with fair regularity," although the family "noticed that on what used to be called 'Sacrament Sundays' he was apt to have a slight attack of lumbago" (RSL, 316).[25] But Gemimi Harrison "was made of quite other metal. She was a Celt and her religion was of the fervant semi-revivalist type" (RSL, 316). When the family visited London in 1861, she showed her true colors. On this trip, Jane's only visit to London until she moved there in 1880, the Harrisons made just one purchase: a copy of a German Bible.²⁶ The clash of Charles Harrison's tepid Nonconformism with his wife's passionate Evangelicalism only emphasized their differences in status and temperament, as well as in religious conviction.

Little evidence exists to illuminate Gemimi's life, but enough survives to suggest that her family and religious background aroused both attraction and repulsion in her youngest stepdaughter. A wave of Evangelical revivals had swept Wales throughout the first half of the nineteenth century, culminating in 1840 and 1849 with powerful movements fueled by a visit by American evangelical Charles Finney and the threat of a cholera epidemic, respectively. Welsh Evangelicalism combined rational, Calvinist nonconformity with a passionate, emotional sense of mystery and superstition. Gemimi Harrison seems to have exhibited both traits. In everyday life, her compulsive propriety clashed with Jane's high spirits, but intellectually, her "fervent semi-revivalist" faith stimulated her stepdaughter's imagination. Its effect became apparent decades later, when Jane turned her attention to the wild emotion of the Greek chthonic cults, Gemimi's religious fervor having contributed to her passion for the emotional element of religion.

Evangelical attitudes toward the family also influenced Jane's thought, although in a more negative way. Evangelicals took seriously their responsibilities to their families, which accounts for their somewhat rigid views on proper behavior. Parents stood in relation to their children as God to mortals and exercised (or attempted to exercise) comparable control over them. They exalted the family as the ideal unit since it mirrored this relation. Above all, they rejected celibacy as verging on popery.²⁷ Jane rebelled against the established order by rejecting the family as an ideal and remaining celibate. Although she would undoubtedly have justified this rebellion on grounds of intellectual incompatibility with Evangelical precepts, its real root must have lay in her fury at her father and stepmother for creating a circle that she felt excluded her.

However dubious the reliability of personal recollections, the vituperation of Jane and other members of her family on the subject of Gemimi Harrison merits attention. Despite their class and religious differences, the daughters' greatest complaint against her was simply that she was their stepmother. They resented her for seducing their father, drawing his attention from them, and consolidating her position by bearing so many children. At best, Jane grudgingly admitted that she was "a conscientious woman and tried to do her duty . . . to the three rather dour little girls who had been her charges and were later presented to her as step daughters" (RSL, 316).

Helene Deutsch's *Psychology of Women* offers some insight into the problem of stepmothers in general and Jane's case in particular.²⁸ After cautioning readers that the image of the wicked stepmother found in fairy tales is much more damning than flesh-and-blood stepmothers deserve, Deutsch examines why children and stepmothers so often clash. She perceptively points out that women who take over a mother's role as nurturer and homemaker, such as governesses and housekeepers, are more acceptable to children, for they are perceived to be more interested in the children than in their father and therefore do not compete for his attention. If a woman assumes the role of stepmother, however, their response changes, "for it is the sexual character of the relationship that principally stirs up the infantile protest and the hate impulses of the children of both sexes against the stepmother" (439). A good stepmother tries to restore the family unity "broken by the mother's departure" (447), whether through death or divorce. "But as long as the stepmother is merely the father's wife, or even worse, the father's sexual object, the woman who sleeps with him, she must remain the wicked stepmother" (447). Extrapolating from Deutsch's theory, one could surmise that the worst possible case would be one in which a female figure originally brought into the house to care for the children suddenly becomes the father's sexual object: a case perfectly illustrated by Jane's childhood experience.

Deutsch focuses on another obstacle, potentially more damaging because of its effects on a little girl's later life. "It is harder to overcome the infantile Oedipus complex with regard to a stepmother than with regard to the natural mother," she claims (444). "The little girl can more easily tolerate the renunciation of intimacy with her father when the presence of the mother as a rival no longer spurs her fantasy activity. When she has a new rival in her stepmother, she feels betrayed and deserted by her father" (445–45). Whatever disadvantages the young girl suffers through the loss of her mother, she can substitute for the mother-daughter bond the rich closeness of a father-daughter bond, unencumbered by the negative aspects of a rivalry with her mother. Certainly the father-daughter bond is illusory since it is grounded in unrealistic although unspoken expectations, but the little girl can reconcile herself equally well to her father's inaccessibility if her mother is present or absent. Problems arise when an intruder threatens the little girl's security.

Deutsch also recognizes and sympathizes with the stepmother's hardships. Such a woman suffers especially if the child has lost its mother by death; for unlike the case of divorce, where the mother can be openly perceived as having abandoned the child, a child whose mother has died "must often remain loyal to her out of his own guilt feelings, and hates the stepmother who woos him, because she thus exposes him to the danger of disloyalty" (444). Deutsch's study illuminates Jane's tenacious clinging to her mother's memory and her steadfast refusal to accept her stepmother. Gemimi Harrison's character clearly hurt her efforts to

court the children's approval: Deutsch emphasizes that the least successful stepmothers are "women whose personalities are rigid, congealed
under a definite formula, aplastic, unintuitive" (447). By all accounts,
these characteristics describe Gemimi Harrison perfectly. At age five,
Jane was too old to accept any proffered benevolence gratefully and
without qualification, and in any case she had already been indulged by
an aunt whose sole responsibility had been caring for her and her sisters.
Deutsch's observation that "orphaned children are often pampered by
friends and relatives and their narcissistic demands are reinforced" (444)
applies here, as does its inevitable corollary. The children's "emotional
attitude toward a reality that must gradually limit their demands is full
of disappointment and hatred. Since the stepmother often personifies
this limitation, she comes to be regarded as invidious" (444). For better
or worse, Jane exemplified this phenomenon.

She perceived her father's remarriage as yet another abandonment. In
1914, sixty years after the fact, she discussed his betrayal of her in an
essay. "Homo Sum" purports to address the suffrage question, but it is
in fact a thinly disguised criticism of her father. It attacks the "sex
egotism" that makes lovers useless to society as a whole because their
interest in each other blinds them to the needs of those around them.
She uses her father and stepmother, in hypothetical terms, of course, to
show how completely lovers are lost to the world. Her discourse on the
subject, although lengthy, is absorbing enough to quote in full.

Take a simple instance, constantly occurring, almost always misunderstood. A man loses his wife early in life; his daughter grows up; they
live in constant companionship, in close sympathy. She helps him with
his work. They are "all-in-all" to each other. In middle life the father
falls in love and marries again. Father and daughter still love each other,
but the daughter wakes up to find herself wounded, inwardly desolate.
The father is too intensely happy to mind anything very acutely, but in
a dim way he is irritated with his daughter for her obvious uncontrolla-
ble misery, and conscious that, if she, who used to be his only earthly
joy, were out of the way, things would be for him more comfortable.
    What has happened, and what does the father say?
    If he is an early Victorian father, now is the time for him to revel in a
perfect orgy of self-deception. "My love," he will begin, "at your age
you need a woman's guidance. Putting aside my own inclinations, I
have formed new ties, I have sought and found for you a new mother.
Welcome her, love her, and obey her, as your own." Nowadays, however, public opinion is barely tolerant of self-delusion so besotted. The
father is more likely to feel uncomfortable than complacent, and he will
take refuge by gliding into the nearest and safest moralizing rut. "My
dear, be reasonable. The love I feel for my new wife has nothing to do

with my affection for you, my daughter, and cannot conflict with it. It is impossible that I should take from you what was never yours." Perhaps even, warming to his subject, he will add: "My love for my new wife makes me a better and a nobler man. Instead of loving you less, I love you more. Some loss there may be, but much gain. We should both of us be thankful to her who—" etc., etc.

The father is, of course, with the best intentions, talking rubbish, and rather insulting rubbish at that. In the daughter's heart anger at his stupidity is added to desolation. She knows him to be the prey of his own strong, blinding sex delusion. His life *is* richer and happier, so he demands that hers should follow suit. His horizon *is* enlarged and brightened, so he fondly expects that hers, too, will glow with a new light. She, unexcited—nay, depressed with the sense of imminent loss— knows quite well the source of his delusion, the impossibility already pointed out, of a strong double emotional focus. What one gains, the other loses. If the father is a man who cares for truth, he will know, and—if he has also the keen instinct of the surgeon's knife—he will perhaps say, "Everything *is* different. In the old days, when life left *me* cold and desolate, *you* were the focus, the fire at which I warmed my frozen hands. On my hearth a new fire is lit now, by the side of which your flame is pale and cold. By it you cannot stand. Face facts. You are young. Go out into the cold and rain, make for yourself no false shelter; for my sake and yours, flinch as little as may be." And the girl, if she is wise and brave, accepts the inevitable. She will stretch out no appealing hand; she will silence the reproach upon her lips. How should she blame her father? He cannot help himself or her.[29]

Since Jane was only five years old when her father remarried, she clearly did not recognize these feelings as events unraveled. Equally clearly, she brooded over her father's betrayal for more than half a century.

Before "Homo Sum" was published, Jane sent a copy to Mary Murray, wife of fellow Ritualist Gilbert Murray and one of Jane's closest correspondents, for comment. Mary Murray objected to her inclusion of such sensitive material, and Jane agreed in her response. She was "sure" that she was right and claimed that she "accepted" Mary's criticisms. She admitted that the "Father and Daughter" section "was autobiographical" and agreed to eliminate it, for "one should not put one's Father's sins into a tract. . . . I felt, when I read it after your letter, that it was splenetic and personal." She asserted that "someday I believe I shall write a treatise on step-mothers and second marriages, but *that* wasn't the place." Finally, she revealed that she "always felt that it was not the second marriage but the early Victorian *lies* that poisoned my life— nothing is poisonous except lies." She sensed how deeply her father's betrayal had hurt her, but she could never consciously admit it to herself. She did indeed excise this passage from the pamphlet version. But when "Homo Sum" appeared in *Alpha and Omega*, the passage had crept back into the text.[30]

Jane's anger at her father expressed itself in various ways. It surfaced most clearly in her attitude toward sexuality, both his and her own. The above passage indicts her father's, and indirectly all men's, sexuality. The hypothetical father's statements get closer and closer to the truth until at the end of the passage he scornfully rejects his daughter's pitiful offerings in favor of his new wife's "fire." The little girl can never fulfill her father's needs, and his rejection is (in her eyes) complete. Thus, sexuality must be avoided since it is the force that separates her from her father, the force that cast her out of his circle. As she wrote to Mary Murray, "I think [sex] *the* wonder and beauty of the world—only apt to go all wrong and ugly." To blame the father totally, however, is dangerous. She relies on him for love and approval, so despite his rejection of her, she cannot place the blame squarely on his shoulders. The only psychologically acceptable solution is to focus her anger on the stepmother who has exposed her inadequacies. Jane certainly deflected a great deal of her anger onto Miss Meredith. She never recovered from the trauma of the second marriage, and she revealed her sympathy with other stepdaughters in a letter dating from 1912. While on a holiday in Arundel with Alys Russell, Bertrand Russell's first wife, Jane noticed Alys's fondness for Julia Strachey. Julia also had a stepmother, and Jane felt a kinship with her, which prompted her to write, "how my heart goes out to a step-child however kind the step-mother."[31]

Jane's fear of sexuality offers a striking contrast to some of the current scholarship on Victorian sexuality. For example, Peter Gay has marshaled an impressive array of evidence suggesting that the Victorian bourgeoisie was much more enlightened about sex and love than twentieth-century scholars have believed. His work has provided a necessary counter to contemporary snobbishness toward the Victorians. In general, the nineteenth century may well have approached sex and love openly, but Jane's case offers compelling evidence that, for some Victorians at least, sexuality remained a frightening and unfathomable force. Her attitude was, of course, overdetermined, but the experiences that nurtured it were not so uncommon as to make her ambivalence unique. Whatever the upper levels of the bourgeoisie thought about sex, their influence did not reach the Harrison household.[32]

The passage from "Homo Sum" also demonstrates Jane's successful internalization of the Victorian obsession with self-control. Her own prevented her from directly attacking her father, and she veiled all her criticism of him, although often very poorly. Her self-control stemmed from both personal experience and cultural conditioning. Deborah Gorham, for example, after surveying Victorian prescriptive literature on child rearing, has concluded that conventional wisdom encouraged mothers to inculcate habits important to bourgeois culture. "Cleanliness, plenty of exposure to fresh air, and simplicity of diet" possessed both "health-giving properties" and "moral significance." Victorian child-rearing advice emphasized "the need for a strict routine in handling children, from the time of their birth, and . . . the need to teach habits of order, cleanliness and self-control." Experts generally agreed that "if children were treated in an orderly manner, they would come to expect and prefer it, and in this way they would be well on the way to becoming orderly, self-controlled adults."[33] These practices produced both family and social harmony, but they allowed no outlet for anger, especially in little girls. Another childhood incident from Jane's "Reminiscences" reveals how well she learned to "silence the reproach upon her lips."

I learnt to ride . . . on an adorable donkey with long furry ears and soft
kind eyes, and a small furry donkey slept in my bed every night for
years. One night the nurse took it away, saying it was time I learnt not
to be a baby. I said not a word, *I had long learnt to keep silence.* But I
was found at midnight with swollen eyes, staring wide awake. The
nurse, being a sensible woman, put back my donkey, and I slept soft and
warm. (RSL, 315; italics mine).

This passage and the longer excerpt from "Homo Sum," both emphasizing repression of anger and misery, clearly demonstrate how well Jane internalized the denial of all improper emotion. Instead of fussing over the removal of her donkey, she suffered in silence until the nurse took pity on her sleeplessness. Instead of reacting overtly angrily to her father's remarriage, she brooded silently over his betrayal and finally wrote about it sixty years later. The little girl who had "long learnt to keep silence" grew up to have, in Hope Mirrlees's words, "such splendid self-control."[34] But anger, an irrepressible emotion, will manifest itself in subtle ways, and Jane, as a young woman, expressed hers through rebellion.

Her discontent at home increased as the second family grew. Hope blamed Jane's unhappiness on the communal life necessarily led by such a large family. "Don't blame Jane for not getting on with her stepfamily," Hope admonished, for "it was quite natural to find that almost communal life trying—& is an evidence of the beautiful temper of Jane's own mother. Jane's equanimity & perfectly just mind were partly an inheritance from her mother & partly a lesson learned from the chaos produced by the opposite." After years of hearing Jane's stories, Hope had come to share her almost morbid reverence toward Elizabeth Harrison. They had the ideal mother at hand—a mother who died before she could disillusion her child. Hope would have been prey to this same delusion because of her problematic relationship with her own mother, who lived more than long enough to prove herself, unfortunately, only too human. At any rate, Jane's unhappiness more likely resulted from her being supplanted in her father's attention by his growing brood. She had no inherent predilection for solitude; she preferred a group so long as she shone at its center. But the large family eclipsed her by sheer strength of numbers. Faced with a stepmother of lower status and vastly different background who had nonetheless managed to alienate her from her father, Jane rebelled against her rule. But overt rebellion would antagonize her father, so she settled for looking disdainfully upon her half brothers and half sisters. Unable to be the center of the circle that revolved so stubbornly around the second family, Jane had to beat a retreat. Ever resourceful, though, she found many ways to show her displeasure. To ensure that she made herself clear, she chose two actions guaranteed to upset her Evangelical stepmother most thoroughly.[35]

Her first, relatively minor infraction was to start smoking. Jane named her brother-in-law, Elizabeth's husband William Lane, as the culprit who taught her to smoke "in her girlhood." "It always tickled her," Hope recalled, "to think that she had learned this sinful habit from an Evangelical clergyman." There is no evidence of a row over the smoking issue, so perhaps Jane's parents never learned of her habit.

A more serious escapade in 1867 resulted in Jane's literal expulsion from the family circle.[36] She and her stepmother finally came to figurative blows over Jane's adolescent romance with a Scalby curate named Houseman. Jane's humorous account of the incident in her "Reminiscences" revealed that the curate, "fresh from Oxford and not . . . averse to showing off" caught her attention by pointing out a mistranslation from the Greek Testament during one of his sermons. This revelation filled Jane "with excitement and alarm," as she could see "that the whole question of the 'verbal inspiration of the Bible' was at issue." She later "waylaid the hapless curate," whose knowledge of Greek turned out to be "more slender" than her own. She related that even "if embarrassed, he was friendly" and could not "confine his attentions to the Greek text" (RSL, 320). Jane could not understand how a purely intellectual interest, so innocently expressed, could evoke a romantic response.

Lucy Harrison, however, related a far different version of the episode, and comparing the two accounts reveals Jane's shameless editing of her memories. According to Lucy, "Jane fell madly in love with him [Mr. Houseman] & he within the limits of his nature . . . with her." They flirted during choir practice, at which Jane played the organ, and met surreptitiously between the Harrison house and the church. Unfortunately, Mrs. Fox, the gossipy wife of the curate in charge, revealed the truth to her good friend Mrs. Harrison. A "terrible scene" ensued, with Mr. Houseman "forbidden the house" (much forbidding of the house occurred in this family) and Jane sent off to visit an aunt and uncle in Normanton while her parents pondered her future. Her scandalous behavior prompted Mrs. Harrison to accuse her of "behaving 'like a kitchen-maid.'" But "considering the subject" of her discussion with the curate, Jane wrote maliciously, she failed "to see the analogy" (RSL, 320). Although Jane shrugged off the incident, Lucy recalled that she threw herself to the floor "in a paroxysm of grief" when she heard, a year after the incident occurred, that Mr. Houseman was engaged.[37]

If Jane wished to anger her stepmother, she certainly succeeded. But her father's reaction astonished her. As she put it, "my father, as usual, said nothing. He scarcely ever did say anything" (RSL, 320). These two terse sentences hide an enormous sense of anger and betrayal. Jane could not believe that he would side with her stepmother. Although she minimized the curate episode in her "Reminiscences," she also stressed her father's "great natural silence." She described hearing her stepmother once "passionately haranguing my father. From him not a sound. But when we met for dinner, we saw with some embarrassment that a portrait of my mother, long consigned to an attic, was hanging on the wall opposite my father's seat. Such was his dumb reprisal" (RSL, 320). Jane and her father shared two characteristics: an inability to articulate anger and a tendency to wield the image of Elizabeth Harrison, either figuratively or literally, as a weapon against the second Mrs. Harrison.

Jane's description of the whole curate incident is revealing, and remarkable both for the style in which it is told and the editing of its content. The event proved more significant than it might appear at first glance. Rather than fading away as a youthful indiscretion, it escalated into a battle of wills: Jane pitting her quiet, calm natural parents against her stepmother's "Celtic volubility" (RSL, 320). The ostensible Harrison calmness connected her to her father. She faced the terrible dilemma of watching her father, who by nature and blood should take her part, side with her stepmother, the Welsh intruder so strangely different in temperament, religion, and status. In light of the punishment she suffered as a result of her romance with Mr. Houseman, she considered herself betrayed once again. But this time she was not only excluded from the center of the circle; she was literally cast out of the circle altogether. Because of her indiscretion, Jane was "summarily dispatched in dire disgrace to Cheltenham [College]" (RSL, 320).

Both Jessie Stewart and Robert Ackerman insist that Charles Harrison recognized Jane's talent and that this recognition motivated him to send her to Cheltenham.[38] But given his views on woman's role, such clear vision seems unlikely. Morever, Jane knew better than anyone that the running battle for her father's affection could not be effectively fought from a hundred miles away. She blamed her father for banishing her to Cheltenham, thus making clear that her interests came second to Mrs.

Harrison's. But protest proved useless, and off she went. For a young girl with such a craving for attention, it was a bitter punishment. Despite this inauspicious beginning, though, Jane achieved great success at Cheltenham. She triumphed over her traditional and inadequate at-home education because of her natural ability and benefited from Cheltenham's more stimulating atmosphere.

Like most proper Victorian middle-class young ladies, Jane's education had begun at home under a series of governesses. Her stepmother engaged "a rather rapid succession of governesses," all of whom were "grossly ignorant," albeit "good women, steadily kind to me" (RSL, 317–18). Jane recalled that "they taught me deportment, how to come into a room, how to get into a carriage, also that 'little girls should be seen and not heard,' and that I was there (in the schoolroom) 'to learn, not to ask questions' " (RSL, 318). Although she perceived Victorian education as "ingeniously useless" and believed that she had "learnt certainly a great deal of miscellaneous rubbish," she conceded that "odd scraps of information are stimulating to a child's imagination" (RSL, 318). Her favorite governess was "a woman of real intelligence, ignorant but willing and eager to learn anything and everything I wanted." They attempted languages such as German and Latin, but "alas! my kind governess was shortly removed to a lunatic asylum" (RSL, 319–20). About Jane's contribution to her breakdown she "did not care to inquire" (RSL, 320).

Many women raised in the Victorian era shared Jane's unhappiness with their useless education. Mary Paley, one of the earliest students at Newnham College and later a lecturer in economics there, spent the years between the ages of nine and thirteen being taught by a series of governesses. Languages and literature were taken most seriously, but she had similar feelings about her experience. Ironically, the next step in her education appeared to be a step back. Mary and her sister went "once a week to a select school for young ladies in our nearest town, kept by two maiden ladies, where we were taught 'Magnall's Questions,' the 'use of globes' and deportment."[39] Two related factors contributed to the appalling quality of girls' education, both at home and in school: Victorian ideas of what women should learn and the incompetent governesses and teachers the system produced.

Recent scholarly attention to women's education has fostered great debate and achieved virtually no agreement on the relationship between education and the ideal of womanhood.[40] Few nineteenth-century educators, either male or female, viewed girls' education as a vehicle for making concrete changes in women's status. Elizabeth Sewell's *Principles of Education* (1865) represented the typical conservative view of women's education and their place in the world. She favored home instruction and thought "gregarious" education, as she called it, "injurious" to young girls and detrimental to preparing them for their roles. "Girls are to dwell in quiet homes, amongst a few friends; to exercise a noiseless influence; to be submissive and retiring. There is no connexion between the bustling mill-wheel life of a large school, and that for which they are supposed to be preparing." One reviewer of Sewell's book lashed out at the opening of local examinations for university entrance to girls, citing a statement by Miss F. Martin, head of the Bedford College School in London, that "the Local Examinations for girls and women 'foster vanity.' " Women had no power to choose their lot, Sewell believed, and education could at most prepare them to cope with whatever might befall them. Overtraining only threatened to make women discontented.[41]

Even the founders of the best girls' schools certainly believed that, although women were capable of different levels of learning, the provision only of some form of vocational training for women who might not marry justified education. They envisioned single life as a last resort. Ideally, women should marry, but education enabled a woman to earn her own living if her father could not support her or, given an unfavorable ratio of men to women, she never had the opportunity to marry. Women such as Dorothea Beale and Frances Mary Buss, headmistresses of two influential girls' schools, opted for a single life, but they stressed their commitment to a noble cause.[42] Whatever their unconscious motives for remaining unmarried, they did not believe that many women would share their dedication.

Nineteenth-century England produced many women educational theorists. Some addressed the questions of primary education, some those of secondary education; they also varied according to their interests in different social classes. A host of conservative writers opposed them out of fear of the inevitable changes that would occur if women were educated. All these theorists contributed to dominant attitudes toward women's education in this period, but Dorothea Beale, headmistress of Cheltenham College for nearly fifty years, played an even more direct role in Jane's life.[43]

Dorothea Beale based her convictions on a religious view of womanhood. She was born in 1831, the daughter of a London physician who dominated the Beale family. He also exerted "a strong and formative influence on her life."[44] Her family held firm religious beliefs, which echo in her writing and ideas about woman's education. She viewed religion as "an integral part of family life . . . not mere observance but a potent, vigorous element."[45] After a succession of daily governesses had provided her with a "disjointed and incomplete education," Beale attended a boarding school. Ill health forced her to return home at age thirteen, whereupon she began a course of self-education. "She was given every encouragement to study," sharing her brothers' lessons in the classics and having "access to two libraries, at the London Institution and Crosby Hall."

When she was sixteen, she and her sisters attended a "fashionable finishing-school in Paris." In 1848 Beale entered Queen's College, originally founded to improve teacher training. After completing her studies, she taught for seven years at the preparatory school attached to Queen's College. She resigned over a difference of opinion on the issues of the limited power given to women tutors and a lowering of admission standards.[46] She then taught for one year at the Clergy Daughters' School at Casterton (the model for Lowood School in *Jane Eyre*) before becoming principal at Cheltenham Ladies College in 1858.[47]

Founded in 1853, Cheltenham had already become a "favourite abode of the strictest sect of the Evangelicals,"[48] which explains why Jane's stepmother sent her there. The college had been designed as an institution for upper-middle-class daughters. In testimony before the Taunton Commission investigating the state of women's education in 1866, Beale stated that "none are admitted but the daughters of independent gentlemen or professional men."[49] Cheltenham's founders were concerned "primarily for the larger class of girls who were not likely to teach or to follow any particular calling, but whose influence as they grew to womanhood was wide and pervasive." For a fee ranging from six to twenty guineas per year, girls studied " 'Holy Scripture and the Liturgy of the Church of England' . . . 'the Principles of Grammar' and . . . 'the Elements of Latin;' . . . Arithmetic; and . . . Callisthenic Exercises." They also learned "Drawing, French, Geography, History, Music and Needlework." Initially, townspeople and parents applauded this curriculum. But in the 1850s, feelings turned against the college. Critics complained "of 'imperfect knowledge in serving and cutting out': that the children had not enough use of the garden: that there was not enough conversational French." In short, they complained of too much emphasis on real education and insufficient training in accomplishments.[50]

One of the most interesting aspects of college life, however, was its silence rule. Students were not allowed to speak to each other during school hours, except for a twenty-minute period in the morning. Beale enforced this rule, begun by Cheltenham's first vice-principal, Anne Proctor, to "inculcate habits of self-control," to avoid "the making of undesirable friendships," and to discourage "gossip and the betrayal of confidences." Furthermore, Beale asked parents' help at home in "carrying out the spirits of these regulations [in such a way as to prevent all] indiscriminate conversation." In the school's boardinghouses, where Jane lived during her student days, "talking was not allowed in the bedrooms," for Beale believed that silence was " 'a great boon to those who find the value of quiet at the beginning and end of the day.' " The same rule applied at Frances Buss's North London Collegiate School for Girls, and the Girls' Public Day School Trust adopted it for its own schools. In the late 1970s, the silence rule still held during the change of classes at Cheltenham, although it had disappeared from the North London Collegiate School. Josephine Kamm, biographer of Buss and Beale, states that at least at Cheltenham the girls did not mind the silence rule, but it is difficult to believe that they never resisted or even overtly rebelled against such a strict practice.[51]

Some parents and staff opposed Beale's appointment as principal, finding her "too intellectual, not genial enough in manner, too 'High Church.' " Nonetheless, her long reign over Cheltenham indicates that parents and colleagues eventually accepted her ability and personality. Certainly her view of education encouraged such acceptance. She defined an educator's job as provision of "an environment where light with its life-giving power could flow in freely and energize the whole personality: the special field of service was then decided by vocation."[52] She envisioned a community of women scholars, "an order of teachers, a dedicated sisterhood vowed to a life of austerity and self-denial."[53] This unmistakably religious image of educated women as a sort of cloistered sect reverberated in some of Jane's later writings, and she found herself cast into just such a milieu in 1868.

At this point, Jane's story and Cheltenham's converge, and her experiences there give some insight into a girl's life at school. Little material remains, but reminiscences from Jane's sister and from a school friend, Caroline Dutton Mitchell, offer a glimpse into those early days.

Charles Harrison agreed only reluctantly to send Jane away to school. Lucy Harrison told Hope that "Mr. Harrison had promised his first wife that none of her girls should ever go to school."[54] He must have found breaking his word on this important question painful, and that he did so at all testifies to the second Mrs. Harrison's power in the household. No wonder Jane felt betrayed by his refusal to take her part. But Cheltenham, a haven for Evangelicals, would certainly have appealed to Mrs. Harrison, and the gossipy Mrs. Fox sent her daughter there, so the Harrisons decided it was the place for Jane.

Some of the themes that recur in Jane's life originated, or at least first came to light, in this period, notably her ill health. Lucy Harrison told Hope that Jane had started to menstruate at age thirteen, but that she stopped for six months while at Cheltenham.[55] Hope blamed this cessation on the climate; Jane herself, although not mentioning this condition, told Hope that she "was missing Yorkshire." Hope also recorded that Jane suffered from severe headaches while a student at Cheltenham, and that "Mrs. M [Caroline Dutton Mitchell] used to soothe them by stroking her broad head & said that not only was it so beautiful to look at but the feel of it was so wonderful."[56] Jane also had a troublesome cough that she eased by wearing a respirator. She later saw Sir James Paget, a noted Cambridge physician, about the same problem, and "he diagnosed it as purely nervous."[57]

Although a physiological root to these problems cannot be dismissed out of hand, all of them could have been psychosomatically induced by stress, repressed anger, and unresolved conflict. The incidence of respiratory problems is particularly revealing. Difficulty in breathing may testify to the internalization of anger, the manifestation of stress that results from repressing emotion. A young girl caught between anger at her father for his actions and a need to retain what love he offers her will not allow herself to feel anger: it is too dangerous. Yet she must acknowledge its existence, if only unconsciously. Respiratory difficulties can offer both a symbol of the valiant attempt to keep emotions contained and a punishment for harboring such destructive feelings. Illness of any sort may be, paradoxically, a means of indirectly admitting defeat while reminding those around one that there is still something amiss. The Victorians, who valued order and self-control above all else, considered anger a terribly upsetting emotion. Jane had already learned to keep silent when in distress, but her body allowed expression of the emotions her mind would not admit.

Jane arrived at Cheltenham during a difficult period in her life, and the circumstances surrounding her arrival there hardly facilitated a peaceful transition from sheltered daughter to student. It is impossible to determine if Jane knew of her mother's wishes regarding her education, but if, as is likely, she had sensed her father's conflicting feelings, she must have been angry at him for reneging on his word.

Another theme that crystallized during this period concerns Jane's conduct in her friendships. F. Cecily Steadman, writing about Jane's arrival, stated that "her mind was far in advance of her companions, who were considerably in awe of her at first, though, as one of them says, she became much more human in her intercourse with them after a time."[58] The separateness of the highly intelligent girl figured prominently in Jane's life at Newnham, but even Hope admitted that "there is no doubt that a great many of Jane's old friends are rather bitter when they talk about her. There seems to be an almost universal sense of Jane's having been ruthless & fickle in her friendships." She remembered hearing D. S. MacColl say to Jane soon after World War I that "the reason why *you* keep young is that you are always making new friends & forgetting your old ones!"[59]

Jane's friendship with Dorothea Beale best illustrates her penchant for throwing people over during the Cheltenham period. Caroline Dutton Mitchell revealed that Jane had a passion for Beale that Beale reciprocated. Hope reported on Jane's reaction when her parents decided that she should return home for good at the end of her second year. Hope recalled "Jane's telling me herself that her G.P. [grand passion] was so violent that when Miss B. told her that her people wanted to take her away, Jane fainted dead away."[60] Since Beale viewed fainting as "a major crime, indicating a quite unnecessary and most reprehensible loss of concentration and control," one wonders how she reacted to Jane's fainting at the thought of leaving Cheltenham.[61] Nevertheless, fainting as a response to crisis became almost a habit with Jane, and fainting episodes figure at various points in her life. This is the first recorded one. In response to the threat of Jane's departure, Beale offered to keep her on as a student for free, as "she was such a credit to the school." Her fainting had worked, and the Harrisons allowed Jane to remain for one more year.[62]

Beale had good reason to want Jane to remain, if only to enhance her school's reputation in the long run. Hilda Lane, Jane's niece, recalled Beale's astonishment at Jane's intellectual abilities.

My grandmother once told me that when she wrote to Miss Beale sketching a course of the things she wished Aunt Jane to study (Aunt Jane was always interested in everything) she had a very severe snub as Miss Beale intimated no girl could manage such an extended course— But after Aunt Jane had been a little time at Cheltenham Granny had a letter saying she had no way exaggerated her abilities but even understated them.[63]

Beale's appreciation of Jane's intelligence is not surprising, but Mrs. Harrison's interest in Jane's course of study is.

Jane in the end rejected Dorothea Beale after experiencing a drastic change in religious belief. Until her early twenties, Jane seems to have held conventional beliefs, her later unorthodoxy notwithstanding. She kept up a secret correspondence with her old governess, Miss Cook (the unfortunate woman who was later consigned to an asylum), and included comments on Miss Beale's Scripture lessons. Miss Cook, who was apparently even more conventional in belief than Jane, "began to suspect Miss Beale's orthodoxy" because she was "tending toward Ritualism" and threatened to tell the Harrisons of the apostasy being taught at the college. Instead, she turned first to the Reverend William Lane, Jane's brother-in-law, who put her mind at ease.[64] But before leaving school, Jane's convictions wavered. She began to sympathize, through some very schoolgirlish poetry, with those German writers who claimed that "Nature . . . is God."[65] D. F. Strauss's *Life of Jesus*, which had appeared in English in the 1840s, apparently shook Jane's faith completely. His interpretation of Christ as a mythical representation did more than challenge her religious faith, however. Her interest in his theory also illustrates how early she turned to ritual and mythology.[66] Dorothea Beale, who tried to coax Jane back to the straight and narrow path, paid for her efforts by being rather brutally dropped. Hope stated emphatically that "Jane detested Miss Beale after she left school,"[67] and Jane's remembrances of Cheltenham in her "Reminiscences" support that assertion.

Jane "carried away from Cheltenham College a dislike for history which has lasted all my life," and criticized her lessons as nothing more than "moralisings on the doings and misdoings of kings and nobles." Besides finding the method unsatisfactory, the fact that "Miss Beale was Cromwellian and I, like all children, a passionate Royalist," kept her in a "constant state of irritation" as they studied the Stuart period "in tedious detail" (RSL, 323). She also claimed that "there was an odd rule throughout the College that no girl might buy a book," stemming from "Miss Beale's horror of what she called 'undigested knowledge.' " Of course, Jane triumphantly "broke the rule and bought a small life of Archbishop Laud" (RSL, 323). Interestingly, though, Steadman, in her biography of Dorothea Beale, found no evidence to corroborate the existence of this rule.[68] Nevertheless, while relating an incident centering on receipt of a postcard, Jane spoke most contemptuously of Beale. Peveril Turnbull, a childhood friend of Jane's, promised to send her a postcard just before she sat for the London matriculation exam. Her own words best describe the subsequent uproar.

No letter reached me, but one morning I was summoned before Miss Beale's throne where she sat in state before the Lower School came into prayers. She had in front of her a post-card (post-cards had only just been invented) written in a schoolboy scrawl and signed "Peveril." "That," she said, pointing a disgusted finger at the signature, "is a boy's name." "Yes," I said, "it's Peveril; he promised to write to me before the examination," and I put out my hand for the post-card. "No, this must go to your parents," and then came a long harangue. It ended with these words which intrigued me so that I remember them exactly: "You are too young, and I hope too innocent, to realize the gross vulgarity of such a letter or the terrible results to which it might lead." I was indeed, and still am, for what do you think was the offense? After his signature "Peveril" had written *"Give my love to the Examiners!"* The story may stand to mark the abyss of fatuous prudery in to which the girls' schools of the middle Victorian period—even the very best—had fallen. (RSL, 320–21)

Partly Jane's indignation reflected changes in standards over the years; partly, though, her words also constituted an attack on Beale herself. Beale's intrusiveness and her religious bias became intolerable to Jane the more both came to resemble those qualities in her stepmother, inevitably leading to a complete break.

In addition to their religious differences, however, Jane rejected Beale's power over her. Beale might have served as a good model because of her belief in women's right to an education, but her vision of an educated woman's future differed considerably from Jane's. Jane had not yet fully articulated or even formulated her own ambitions, but she did not plan to use her innate intelligence to fulfill Beale's vision. Ultimately, she found Beale's association of education with personal responsibility stifling. Whereas Beale viewed the life of the mind as a way of serving others, Jane explicitly rejected that model.

Another memory of Lucy Harrison's provides a final look at the state of stepmother-stepdaughter relations. Lucy described the rather dowdy fashion in which Mrs. Harrison dressed the girls and remarked that Jane traveled to Cheltenham with an unimaginative wardrobe and a piece of gray stuff to be made into a Sunday dress. Upon her arrival, Miss Caines, the boardinghouse mistress, took Jane to a dressmaker in Cheltenham's best shop and had the fabric made up into a stylish frock that cost two pounds. Mrs. Harrison, accustomed to paying the Hull seamstresses five shillings, created a scene when Jane presented her with the bill at the end of the term. "As Lucy says, it was a strange greeting for a girl who had so brilliantly distinguished herself. And not a word of praise did she ever get from her parents for all her triumphs at Cheltenham."[69]

Little evidence survives concerning events of the years between Jane's departure from Cheltenham and entry at Newnham. Charles Harrison offered to have her teach her younger siblings at home, and she spent a good part of her time between 1870 and 1874 at this task. Hope says this was also the period during which Jane read Strauss's *Life of Jesus*, which set her permanently at odds with Dorothea Beale. It was now, too, that Jane developed an overwhelming desire to see something of the world, and Hope says her family thought her very selfish for acting on her desire. No doubt the stifling provincial atmosphere and the fact of being closeted with so many younger siblings took their toll on her. Jane paid for her trips abroad with the money she had inherited from her mother, however, so there was little the family could do to stop her. She visited Holland in 1871, accompanied by a chaperone, and traveled in 1872 and 1873 with the Duttons. Her fortunes changed in 1874, when she took and passed the Cambridge University examination and received a scholarship to Newnham.[70]

Poised for flight to Cambridge, Jane presented the image of a frustrated and angry young woman. It is a sad portrait: an extraordinarily bright woman trapped in a provincial home and surrounded by a family unwilling and perhaps unable to recognize and cultivate her talents. Faced with opposition at every turn, it is no wonder that Jane found happiness and relief when she finally escaped to Newnham. Once arrived there, she created a new family—a new circle—and firmly established herself at its center.

# THE FIRST CIRCLE:
# NEWNHAM COLLEGE

*The one thing men do not like is the man-woman, and they will*
*never believe the College or University woman is not of that type.*
*Sensible men will always like sensible and cultivated women; but*
*they will always prefer that their good sense and cultivation*
*should have come through channels which they recognise as suit-*
*able for the womanly character.*
> —*"Female Education,"* Quarterly Review, *April 1869*

*I sometimes fancy I shall do great things, but will it not all come*
*to nothing! Yet I should like never to be forgotten, to do some-*
*thing great for my country which would make my name live for*
*ever. But I am only a woman.*
> —*Anne Clough's diary*

IN THE SECOND half of the nineteenth century, English women who
sought an education inevitably confronted doubt or hostility. Jane
Harrison's experience at Newnham illuminates several critical aspects
of the debate over women's education. On a personal level, her college
experience freed her from her stultifying provincial and Evangelical up-
bringing. On a broader level, it illustrates the quandary that confronted
women who aspired to an intellectual life rather than a traditional family life. Finally, the women's colleges generally reflected an emerging
social trend: the difficulties northern provincials faced in assimilating
into the English intelligentsia.

To date, scholars have primarily described and analyzed the campaign for reform in women's education. The opening of women's colleges, although unquestionably important, is perceived as having been
an end in itself. But, in addition, women students' experience at college
profoundly affected their lives. The opening of women's colleges, far
from closing the debate over women's social role, raised it to a new
level by creating both new problems and new opportunities for women.
Reformers and students viewed education differently, and they inevitably clashed over their differences. The reformers saw it as a political
issue, whereas the students saw it as a personal one.

Critics of women's education presented their arguments in both ideological and economic terms. Conservatives dreaded the inevitable

changes in gender relations. "We have to consider," a representative critic, the Oxford historian Montagu Burrows, wrote in the *Quarterly Review*, "the whole complex phenomena of life, the relations between the sexes, the formation of the *whole* character of woman, the difference between men and women." Occasionally, however, supporters of women's higher education advocated learning for learning's sake. Joshua Fitch, an examiner for the Taunton Commission, based his belief in women's right to higher education on the ideas "that human beings, whether male or female, come into the world not only to 'get a living' but to live; that the life they live depends largely on what they know and care about, upon the breadth of their intellectual sympathy, upon their love of truth, upon their power of influencing and inspiring other minds; and that for these reasons mental culture stands in just as close relation to the needs of a woman's career in the world as to that of a man." Both sides believed that women had a responsibility to fulfill social expectations but disagreed on how to define their duty and how best to prepare them for it. Some believed the status quo offered the best for society, whereas others pressed for substantive changes in gender relations.[1]

Women educational reformers, however, often believed even more firmly than men in the traditional ideal of womanhood, and their writings frequently invoked the educated motherhood argument. Aside from Emily Davies, founder of Girton College, few educational reformers favored education for self-improvement alone. Women reformers also utilized the economic arguments for women's education. Even critics of higher education approved of better teacher training in order to provide jobs for the increasing number of "redundant" women. In response to Emily Davies's plan for Girton College, Montagu Burrows advised her to abandon the idea of equal education in favor of a college that would simply train good women teachers. In pragmatic terms, he claimed that parents would not pay "for this University education which is to lead to nothing tangible, if it does not lead away from much that is tangible." Offering "a word of friendly advice," he exhorted Davies to make Girton "a *true College for women*. Let its promoters give up the ambitious notion of an institution on the same footing as a man's College." As a course of study, he suggested that "simplicity of living, the strictest economy, so as to suit governesses; training in housekeeping, regular needlework, and, if possible, actual schoolteaching should be parts of a system to which all should, with very slight exceptions, conform." He then invoked medical arguments against strenuous education, citing the dangers of "evening reading" and advocating strict rules. He posed this solution for women of the middle classes and above; for lower-class women, "there is nothing effectual on a large scale but emigration." His article advanced nearly all popular arguments against women's education.[2]

As much of the recent secondary literature on women's higher education points out, leaders of the movement generally supported traditional Victorian ideas of womanhood and did not initially challenge them.[3] Economic realities dictated some action to relieve the dire poverty even middle-class women could slip into if forced to support themselves with inadequate training. But the educated motherhood argument at least allowed that education did not necessarily have to be vocational training in order to gain acceptance. All these theories paid lip service to upper-class ideas of womanhood.

The women who founded or governed the earliest colleges, such as Emily Davies at Girton and Eleanor Balfour (later Sidgwick) and Anne Clough at Newnham, guarded their charges carefully to keep their behavior above reproach. Yet their students—only one generation younger—developed their own, different ideas about the purposes of education. Many students arrived at college fully convinced that they were preparing for educated motherhood or making themselves better companions for the educated men they anticipated marrying. Some of them wanted to break from these projected futures and found comfort in the colleges in which they no longer felt themselves anomalies. Still others arrived with traditional expectations but found that their needs and desires changed during the course of their stay. Regardless of their individual circumstances, finding themselves surrounded by other intelligent and often ambitious women encouraged them to create a female culture based on intellectual kinship. The women's schools, at both the secondary and the college levels, proved to be radical simply because they offered young women the chance to form strong extradomestic bonds. This different focus put students in conflict with society in general and their college guardians in particular. But escaping from an often dreary home life and associating with like-minded women eased the transition from traditional home life to the predominantly masculine world of academia.

Such a shift in focus, however, still left unresolved the question of women's role. The first two women's colleges at Cambridge themselves embodied this conflict, in which Emily Davies at Girton and Henry Sidgwick at Newnham took opposite positions. Davies used her plan for Girton's structure to make a point about women's equality, while Sidgwick tackled the larger question of university reform and seized the issue of women's education in order to strike a blow in this larger context.[4]

Davies's tactics in her passionate crusade for women's equality often provoked resentment among critics of women's education. She believed that women were capable of performing intellectually under the same conditions as men, and she founded her college (originally at Hitchin, a few miles from Girton) to prove this point. Critics reacted strongly to her single-mindedness. "They [the founders of Girton College] believed that it would be of great service to the cause of women's education generally if they could prove conclusively that women were capable of the same intellectual work as men, and it seemed to them that any difference in the conditions observed would weaken their case in the judgment both of the University and of the world outside."[5] To that end, women students had to complete their requirements for the degree (which they could not receive) in the same amount of time as men, with the same residency requirements, and with no special treatment when they took their exams. Girton paved the way for women students to take the tripos examination by having examiners first test them independently. Cambridge formally opened the tripos to women in 1881, although until 1948 they received only certificates, not degrees.[6]

Although Davies expected resentment from people outside the college, she probably did not expect it from her students. Louisa Lumsden, an early Girton student, pointed out a disadvantage of the Girton experiment that Newnham students escaped. Lumsden asserted that Davies's blind determination to prove her students' abilities closed her eyes to their needs. The student was "a mere cog in the wheel of her great scheme. There was a fine element in this, a total indifference to popularity, but . . . it was plain that we counted for little or nothing, except as we furthered her plans." In addition, despite Davies's ideological radicalism, she feared the potential harm from perceived irregularities in personal behavior. She coupled her zealousness to prove women's equality with a strong streak of conventionality. She aimed to show the world that her charges could remain true women. Barbara Stephen, Davies's biographer, states that she had "what seemed to some of the students an excessive regard for the proprieties which caused resentment against what they thought unnecessary restrictions."[7]

Louisa Lumsden again provided one example of the students' fomenting a small rebellion. In the dining hall during the first year at Hitchin, "it was expected that we should sit in a formal row down one side of our table, lest we be guilty of the discourtesy of turning our backs upon the 'High.' But this was too much, and we rebelled." The students eventually won the right to face each other at table so that they could talk. "So academically formal . . . was the order imposed from the first at Hitchin—we might have been fifty undergraduates instead of five harmless young women."[8]

Notwithstanding Davies's contradictory attitudes toward public opinion, she understood what female students needed to succeed. She recognized the importance of privacy to students who had generally spent their lives in a family setting and included provisions for solitude in her original outline drawn up in 1868.

Each student will have a small sitting room to herself, where she will be free to study undisturbed, and to enjoy at her discretion the compan-

ionship of friends of her own choice. Of all the attractions offered by
the College life, probably the opportunity for a certain amount of solitude, so necessary an agent in the formation of character, will be the
one most welcomed by the real student.[9]

Davies directed her efforts toward providing women with as rigorous and
rewarding an education as men received. She believed that women should
seek self-improvement, not vocational training, through education.

Newnham's founders followed different principles. Henry Sidgwick,
the noted Trinity College philosopher and the driving force behind the
plan for Newnham, first broached the subject of organizing lectures for
women at Cambridge in 1869. Since 1867, women had attended the
Cambridge local lectures given in other cities, but they followed no
structured program. Now Sidgwick enlisted the aid of Millicent Garrett
Fawcett and several Cambridge dons in forming a General Committee to
study this question. The lectures scheme began in 1870, and nearly
eighty women attended in the first term.[10]

Sigdwick married Eleanor Balfour in 1876, and together they built
Newnham into a strong women's college. But Sidgwick had other concerns in mind when he agitated for the admission of women to Cambridge. He envisioned a larger plan of university reform and saw the
women's college as a means of accomplishing his goal. Sidgwick especially castigated the traditional approach to classical education, which
required students to perform such tasks as composing poetry in Greek
and Latin. "An artificial education," he claimed, "is one which, in order
that a man may ultimately know one thing, teaches him another, which
gives the rudiments of some learning or accomplishment, that the man
in the maturity of his culture will be content to forget." He despised this
education for show and campaigned tirelessly for reform. In fact, he
opposed compulsory classical study for both men and women. He believed that "a liberal education has for its object to impart the highest
culture, to lead youths to the most full, rigorous, and harmonious exercise, according to the best ideal attainable, of their active, cognitive, and
aesthetic faculties." He believed this "natural" education far superior to
the "artificial" education Cambridge then offered. Part of the liberal
reform of higher education allowed—even required—the admission of
women to the universities. He envisioned Newnham as part of a more
all-encompassing plan for change. Thus, in a sense, Davies at Girton
forced women to strive for an ideal that other reformers considered
obsolete.[11]

Sidgwick's scheme permitted women to take different exams to reflect variations in their preparation. It also allowed them more time
before taking the exams to compensate for inadequate training. He believed that

while the more elementary lectures should prepare students for the Higher Local Examination, more advanced teaching, supplementing the professional lectures opened to women, should enable those who had passed through this preliminary trial, and wished to go further, to go through a complete course of academic education in one or other of the departments into which academic study is divided at Cambridge, and which form the subjects of the Honours Degree Examinations.

In her description of Sidgwick's efforts, Blanche Clough, niece of Newnham's first principal, Anne Clough, points out that few women desired to prepare for the honours degree. The group's size and the need to educate its members separately made their education particularly expensive. "The Lectures Association [governing Newnham College] . . . required all students who wished to enter for a Tripos Examination to give evidence of general education, and expected them, as a rule, to prove this by passing the Higher Local Examination; but it did not require or, indeed, encourage them to take the Previous Examination, and it did not insist upon exact adherence to the rules as to terms." Women received preferential treatment because they were often ill prepared for study. Moreover, Sidgwick and some of the other founders, "while they were anxious that the classical curriculum should be fully opened to women as any other of the Honours Courses," believed that "the education of girls would not be benefited by the imposition of Greek and Latin, required for passing the Little-go [Previous Examination], as a necessary preliminary to all higher branches of academic study."[12]

Sidgwick's experiment finally started when the lectures began in 1870. Sympathetic Cambridge professors helped by donating money or offering their services either free of charge or for a nominal payment. Several dons, including Cayley (algebra), Seeley (modern history), Jebb (history), and Sidgwick himself, taught women students in separate lectures. The women attended in small groups, always accompanied by chaperones even though they did not mix with the male undergraduates. Despite the inconvenience, the women students enjoyed the same high-quality education as the men. In 1873, twenty-two of thirty-four professors formally granted women permission to attend their lectures; within a few years, the number had increased to twenty-nine. Christ's College was the first men's college to admit women to lectures alongside men.[13]

Meanwhile, however, the earliest students in residence needed housing and proper guidance. Regardless of Davies's and Sidgwick's disagreement over the structure of women's education, both recognized the necessity of maintaining appearances. Therefore, both Girton and Newnham adhered to strict notions of propriety. Much depended on choosing the right woman to govern the young ladies who would be the first students. Sidgwick felt so strongly about his cause that he hand-picked his staff and even paid for the housing out of his own pocket. In the spring of 1871, Sidgwick took a house in Newnham for the use of students and asked Anne Clough, an educator from Liverpool with connections to such reformers as Emily Davies, Barbara Leigh-Smith Bodichon, and Frances Mary Buss, to preside over it.[14]

Anne Clough, the daughter of a Welsh cotton merchant, was a conservative Evangelical who became active in women's education reform after the death of her father in the 1840s and her mother and brother in the 1860s. Clough was one of the founders of the North of England Council for the Higher Education of Women in 1867, and through this organization she met such active reformers as Josephine Butler and Emily Davies. Blanche Clough rightly claims that Clough facilitated the women students' acceptance in the Cambridge community because "it was impossible to associate her with anything unfeminine, and her character gave an assurance to all who came in contact with her, that any movement with which she was concerned would be conducted with moderation and with scrupulous consideration for the feelings of others." Her impeccable character assuaged Sidgwick's fears but alienated her students.[15]

The term began in October 1871 with 5 students in residence. By the end of the academic year, 3 more had arrived. In its first ten years, Newnham served 215 students. Ironically, many of them were teachers who came for only a term or two in order to enhance their skills and improve their marketability. Only 20 of the first 215 students read for the tripos.[16] The founders extended opportunities for higher education to greater numbers of women by keeping costs low and encouraging those interested in teaching.[17] The teachers who attended Newnham only briefly paid less for their courses, however, and often received special treatment, but the most interesting aspect of their association with Newnham is their conspicuous absence from most descriptions of college life. They usually lived in lodgings, not in college, and remained only for a term or two. Although they composed the majority of the first 215 students, few accounts mention them. No doubt their experience of college life bore no resemblance to that of the residential students, but their story needs to be told elsewhere. For privileged upper-middle-class daughters, living communally among intellectual equals proved important to their intellectual development.

At both Newnham and Girton, the students resented their guardians' watchfulness. Sidgwick chose Anne Clough not only for her teaching background but also for her character; he thought her sufficiently upright and disciplined to keep the students in line. Despite assistance and support from many Cambridge dons, "many people in the University disapproved strongly of the presence of women students in Cambridge, and probably most people looked upon them with some suspicion. . . . There was, of course, also a widely diffused prejudice against all women who desired opportunities of obtaining higher learning." Sidgwick believed Anne Clough the perfect choice to allay these suspicions and fears. Clough felt that "education should be kept quite apart from other questions and causes, and she meant to show that a desire for education, and even the possession of it, did not involve any departure from recognised customs and conventions."[18] H. M. Kempthorne (Peile), a daughter of one of Newnham's founders, remembered Anne Clough's relating "with amusement how Professor Henry Sidgwick came to her lamenting the 'unfortunate personal appearance' of the first students," who "were all remarkably good-looking women" and whose attractiveness disturbed the founders.[19] The early reformers insisted on the compatibility of education and true womanhood, genuinely believing that education would not alter women's characters or aspirations. Some of the young women arrived at Newnham harboring the same conviction. Experience proved them all wrong.

Although the students had been raised as young ladies, their status allowed them a certain amount of freedom. They brought this past experience, along with intelligence and youthful spirit, with them to Newnham. Henry Sidgwick noted their independence of mind. "There is such a strong impulse towards liberty among the young women attracted by the movement," he wrote, "that they will not submit to maternal government." Blanche Clough described Anne Clough as "always nervous lest the students should attract attention and criticism by any eccentricity in dress or conduct, for her great desire was to be unnoticed, and to make it clear that this little colony of women was harmless and inoffensive."[20]

This insistence on the college woman's harmlessness demonstrates that both students and guardians recognized the experimental nature of their undertaking. At the outset, most did not want to appear unique and conformed to established norms of female behavior. Members of the college community believed that if they maintained outward appearances, education would not drastically affect women's perceptions of their roles. Many women students undoubtedly felt that they only desired to learn, but the guardians, in their almost pathological fear of public opinion, may have had a better understanding of what dangers lay ahead. In any case, despite the students' initial docility, clashes soon occurred. They resulted largely from the closeness of communal life, combined with the intellectual freedom that the college experience afforded.

In 1870, Emily Davies, writing to Anna Richardson, described Louisa Lumsden's experience as a young woman. Lumsden had told her that "before she came [to Girton], she used to feel fearfully solitary. She was always having said to her, 'Oh, but you're so exceptional.' Now, she feels herself belonging to a body and has lost the sense of loneliness." Mary

Kennedy and Mary Paley Marshall, two members of Newnham's first class, shared Lumsden's feelings. They recalled how deeply their intellectual aspirations and their attendance at college distressed their families. Mary Kennedy's "brother who was up at Corpus was so annoyed with my venture that he wouldn't speak to me!" Mary Paley's father, an Evangelical minister, although "proud and pleased" that she earned a scholarship, agreed to the "outrageous proceeding" of sending her to Cambridge only because "his admiration for Miss Clough overcame his objections." Public opinion militated against women's presence at Cambridge, and often the students faced family objections as well. Once they arrived, however, they no longer felt out of place. They finally belonged to a group.[21]

The most compelling evidence for an unacknowledged ambition lies in the women students' frequent identification with their fathers. Whereas the women often mention their fathers' support, mothers are curiously and conspicuously absent.[22] If women students accepted their future roles, they were reluctant to talk about it. Opposition from siblings and mothers counted for little. If a father supported his daughter's educational desires, she satisfied them. Furthermore, the students barely concealed their hostility toward their conventional female guardians. If women like Anne Clough symbolized their mothers, then the young women clearly had difficulties with them. Consciously or unconsciously, some women recognized that acquiescence to social expectations led to a dead end. Although many women married after college, their educational experience brought them irrevocably into the larger world. Helping an academic husband, which many of the women students eventually did, represented a vastly different way of life than presiding over teas and supervising children and servants. The earliest generation of women students therefore took a greater leap than has been previously recognized.

The early students suffered other discomforts. In October 1871, Anne Clough and the first Newnham class moved into a house at 74 Regent Street in Newnham. As Mary Paley described it,

We lived very much the life of a family; we studied together, we had
our meals at one table, and in the evening we usually sat with Miss
Clough in her sitting-room. . . . During that first year at Regent Street
there were certain discomforts to be put up with. We went twice a week
to the town gymnasium, but otherwise walks were our only form of
exercise . . . and no doubt we made up for want of outdoor exercise by
being rather noisy in the house, especially at meals.

Behind the fond memories, she conveyed a sense of the oppressive atmosphere. Constant isolation in such a small group without exercise or freedom would have been a difficult adjustment for young women accustomed to a certain degree of liberty. When the group moved in the fall term of 1872 to a larger residence in Merton Hall, the situation improved somewhat. Mary Paley stated that "everything went better. . . . [Anne Clough] had her own sitting room; when we were together, it was from choice, not from necessity." But Anne Clough's journal made clear that the new house also had its disadvantages: "The new house was old and picturesque, with a lovely garden, but the students' rooms were very poor. . . . The garden seemed to make up for all, and the quiet. We were shut in from Cambridge in a corner among trees and shrubs and creeping plants, which bowered us all round." Although this passage conveys a sense of claustrophobia, Clough clearly preferred the closed-in atmosphere, probably because it kept her charges out of the public eye. The real enclosure reflected a symbolic separation from the life of the university. All the same, "their life was a joy to them, but they did work." For the students, the greatest benefit lay in the distance their new residence allowed between them and Clough. The constant separation from the rest of the university and the enforced closeness among students offered an opportunity for the women to create their own culture that nurtured their newly discovered intellectual freedom.[23]

Newnham was still in its precarious infancy when Jane arrived there in October 1874 after her high score on that year's Cambridge higher local examination won her a scholarship. She spent her first year in one of the two houses in Bateman Street taken as an interim measure while the college constructed its first building. When Newnham Hall opened in 1875, Anne Clough and her students

had now a good dining-hall, a library and other sitting-rooms for the students, and the students' own rooms were nearly all of them pleasant and convenient. Each student had a room to herself, which was furnished so as to serve both as study and bedroom, and the common sitting-rooms were always available. They had fires in their rooms when they liked . . . and they could and did see one another and give tea-parties and cocoa-parties among themselves freely.

College life now began to resemble more closely that of the male undergraduate. Yet a brief comparison of their environments immediately makes clear the modesty of the aspirations of the women's colleges. The men's colleges clustered in the bustling center of Cambridge, very much engaged in the public world while simultaneously enclosing a haven of manicured lawns and immaculately kept gardens. Even today the lawns are off limits to all but fellows of the colleges and their guests to protect them from the hordes of tourists who flock to view the majestic Gothic and baroque buildings. Newnham Hall, far less imposing even now, despite its additions, is set in the middle of a pasture and boasts small patches of garden scattered around well-traveled lawns. Although the buildings are handsome enough, Newnham's founders expended neither money nor effort to create an imposing facade with which to face the world. No hordes of tourists here; yet here Jane flourished.[24]

Jane settled on Newnham after a visit with her old acquaintance, Mary Paley, in Yorkshire. Mary "admired her exceedingly" and recalled that "she was graceful and her figure reminded me of one of the Sistine Sybils, and her eyes were most beautiful." She had "known her as a girl and even then she was called 'the cleverest woman in England.' " Jane undoubtedly felt even more keenly the sense of being exceptional that troubled Louisa Lumsden. Like Lumsden, she discovered a place for herself in the college setting. She quickly became one of the central figures among the Newnham students and the scourge of Miss Clough's days as principal.[25]

Some remarks Jane's friends made about her conduct at Newnham echoed sentiments voiced by her Cheltenham schoolmates. Elinor Ritchie, a contemporary Newnham student and friend of Jane's recalled that Jane would be alternately friendly and nasty to the younger students—"rabbits" as they were called—and could reduce them to tears simply by her "way of flickering her eyelids." Margaret Merrifield first mentioned Jane in a letter of October 1876. "Miss Harrison," she stated, "is much more amiable generally, this term; I do not think the new girls have any reason to complain of her, for though she does not go out of her way to be friendly, she has none of that very stand-offish manner." Apparently Jane grew more congenial after she had been at Newnham for a time. Students certainly sought her out. Alice Dew-Smith reminisced about Jane's flamboyance at the dining-hall table.

I can see her now, her tall willowy figure clad in a tight-fitting olive-green serge such as used to be supplied to Newnham students by Messrs. Boyd Burnett in the days of the aesthetic craze; her long neck and well-set head, with brown hair in a Greek coil at the back; her fine, deeply fringed eyes—all made an ineffaceable picture. . . . I can think of no one else who could pour forth such a continuous stream of delightful nonsense as Jane entertained us with evening after evening.

Jane's wit and intellect drew people to her even then, but her friends generally agreed that she was, as Hope wrote, "fickle in her passions, but very faithful in her loves." Perhaps her behavior is not so very hard to understand. Having been cast out of her family circle and hurt by her father's second marriage, Jane had difficulties maintaining close relationships with others. She needed to be the center of the circle, and at Newnham she found a group willing to revolve around her. The young women, drawn together by the common bond of a desire to learn, recognized Jane's fine intellect and offered her a chance to shine.[26]

Yet if Jane could be fickle and superficial in her attachments, she could also be passionate and irresistibly drawn to some people. She told

Jane Ellen Harrison as Alcestis, Oxford University Dramatic Society, Oxford 1877.
Reproduced by permission of the Principal and Fellows of Newnham College,
Cambridge.

Hope Mirrlees that as soon as she saw Ellen Crofts, a fellow Newnhamite, she wanted to be her friend. She came to admire Ellen's "extreme delicacy & sensitiveness of her moral sense." For her part, Ellen immediately noticed that Jane had "the most extraordinary eyes I ever saw." Jane's immediate and lasting fondness for Ellen Crofts confirms that she could as easily be attracted to some people as she shrank from others. And she could drop acquaintances abruptly. Alice Dew-Smith remembered that "Jane never chucked people for conduct; but invariably chucked them if they grew boring." She continued, "and she was so easily bored: people bored her if they talked too much, or if they had a vivacious manner; or if they were egoists. And if they put their faces too close to hers they completely alienated her." In other words, Jane "chucked" people if they threatened her supremacy. She was actually more easily threatened than "bored." A person who talked too much threatened a young woman who relied on her delightful conversation for popularity and acceptance. A vivacious manner threatened to eclipse her own. An egoist threatened her position at the center of the circle, for such a person might break off some of Jane's circle and induce it to revolve around her. Jane invested much more than a desire for education in her Newnham career. No longer encumbered by a provincial family and an antagonistic stepmother, she set out to prove that she belonged in this cultured world that represented the pinnacle of the English intelligentsia. Jane had found a surrogate family, and she feared losing her privileged place in it.[27]

Martha Vicinus points out the importance of class distinctions among college women and the pervasiveness of "patronizing condescension."[28] Although economic status and intellect largely defined cliques, place of origin quickly became an even more insidious criterion. Jane could hold her own on the first two counts, but she faced a serious struggle to overcome the handicap of her Yorkshire background. To the sophisticated southerners who filled Newnham, Yorkshire represented the depth of provincialism.

Vicinus cites a story written by "An Old Newnham Student" for a girls' magazine in 1903. The story conveys the cultural differences between North and South and southern perceptions of northern gaucherie. The author encountered a "North Country 'fresher' " at breakfast one day, and described their exchange.

At first I am rather stiff and bored with her (Miss Brown is not quite, quite—you understand), and we converse very stupidly about the weather and the thickness of the bacon; but by-and-by, I let myself go, and become quite witty and brilliant on the subject of Miss Hill's new blouse. The next stage is that Miss Brown becomes confiding and asks me how it is some people get invitations to parties in the town. I say I presume that most of us have had a cousin or brother or friend at Cambridge, and through them we have one or two introductions to dons.

Miss Brown says she supposed it was that way, but just wondered if it would be any good putting your name down anywhere!

I shake my head emphatically at this.[29]

The glaring contrast between the two women and the author's perverse delight in cutting down the other woman illustrate the difficulties that northerners faced in trying to assimilate. Presumably the author represented a common southern perception of northerners, since the article appeared in a popular magazine; she obviously expected sympathy from her readers. She unwittingly conveyed the loneliness northerners experienced at Newnham since they were so far removed from their own element. With their fewer contacts and less sophistication, northerners found it difficult to mesh with their southern classmates. The presence of many northerners in Jane's Newnham days indicates that they were beginning to filter down to the South, but they faced a very difficult journey. Vicinus's story makes Jane's behavior toward the younger students more comprehensible. Despite her intellect, she felt ashamed of her provincial background and reacted defensively. She renounced her provincial roots and identified wholly with the dominant culture, and could assure her own status only by repeatedly proving to herself that she had left her past behind. Her incessant battle to suppress her heritage indicates that it continually threatened to intrude on the present.

Both northerners and southerners, however, shared impatience with many aspects of college life. During the early years, the women students chafed at the regulations that governed their conduct. So ingrained were the rules that Mary Agnes Hamilton, a Newnham student forty years later, remembered the same restrictive atmosphere from her tenure there. Public opinion still dictated "total separation from the masculine undergraduate population" and "timid restrictions that irked and offended students." A "certain limitation in the variety of the student body" proved even more stifling; "too many were going, and knew they were going, to be teachers." But in Jane's day, contact with the future teachers remained, rightly or wrongly, limited. Her contemporaries in the college experienced a new freedom that often led to the formation of strong extradomestic bonds and a varying degree of alienation from their families. The students could not thank their guardians, however, for consciously fostering these changes. The measures designed to protect them from the public eye only inadvertently encouraged a sense of community that proved a boon to serious students.[30]

Jane herself did not mention any details of her Newnham days beyond listing the notables who journeyed to Cambridge for a look at the college, but others remembered her from their own experiences and can provide a brief description of both college life in general and Jane's antics in particular. Mary Paley recalled that during the early 1870s, just before Jane arrived at Newnham, all teaching was done "by weekly or fortnightly papers, without coaching or supervision." Among the faculty, Henry Sidgwick and Alfred Marshall had most to do with the women students. Professors Birks and Fawcett also played a significant role. Mary Paley remembered Sidgwick's reducing some of his students to tears by reading them the scene in *The Mill on the Floss* that portrays Maggie Tulliver's reunion with her brother, Tom. The most interesting recorded conflict over policy occurred in 1877, when the students clamored to stage Euripides' *Electra*. Anne Clough naturally vetoed the idea, fearing the reaction of "the Cambridge ladies." Although the students' desire to stage a play about matricide raises intriguing questions, they chose Euripides partly to defy convention, for Victorian classicists associated Euripides with chaos and irrationality. Yet the students may also have been tempted to revolt against their surrogate mother, Anne Clough, when they still could not rebel against their own mothers. After all, Clough was not such an essential figure, and her compulsive propriety infuriated the young women. She represented traditional womanhood, despite her position as principal. The male teachers both served as surrogate fathers and represented the life of the mind. Women students thus reconstituted family relations in a complex manner: the male teachers represented good fathers, and the female administrators bad mothers. This split infused college life with conflicting emotions. The women found communal support invaluable, but tensions permeated their relations with male faculty and female guardians.[31]

On the positive side, seclusion from the Cambridge community offered an idyllic existence. After completing work in moral sciences and lecturing near her home in Stamford, Mary Paley returned to Newnham to become resident lecturer in Newnham Hall. The hall opened in 1875 with twenty students. "Among these early students were Katherine Bradley ... Alice Gardner, Mary Martin ... Ellen Crofts, Miss Merrifield ..., and Jane Harrison." She described the atmosphere in the hall:

This was the Pre-Raphaelite period, and we papered our rooms with Morris, bought Burne Jones photographs and dressed accordingly. We played lawn tennis and JH designed the embroidery for our tennis dresses. Hers was of pomegranates and mine of virginia creeper and we sat together in the evenings and worked at them and talked.

Mary claimed that Alfred Marshall, her future husband, almost persuaded Jane to read for the moral science tripos rather than classics. Jane "always afterwards called him 'the camel' for she said that she trembled at the sight of him as a horse does at the sight of a camel." Perhaps Marshall, who later become a steadfast opponent of degrees for women, already showed evidence of his prejudice. Jane also took credit for bringing about the engagement, said Mary, by "stitching clean, white ruffles into my dress on that day," which must have made Mary look more attractive to him.[32]

Mary Paley mentioned Sunday evening parties for students and their teachers in the hall as a favorite entertainment. Elinor Ritchie described these to Hope Mirrlees as "very innocent and provincial affairs," with refreshments and music.[33] Jane often sang at these gatherings, her repertoire ranging from German songs to favorites such as "Adelaide" and "In the Gloaming." Such Cambridge figures as Henry and Eleanor Sidgwick and Professors Seeley, Cayley, R. C. Jebb, Alfred Marshall, and R. D. Archer-Hind attended.[34] Before her marriage, Eleanor Sidgwick hosted "sittings" for the Cambridge group interested in psychic research.[35] Students, however, most fondly remembered the cocoa party. They would finish their daily studies late in the evening and take turns inviting each other for cocoa and treats. Oddly enough, the cocoa party tradition originated in a grant from a benefactor. Originally, the donor had intended to provide a lady's maid for every five students, a provision that clearly reflected the benefactor's mind-set. The students claimed that they did not know what they would do with a maid, so Newnham's administrators altered the terms of the grant to provide half a pint of milk for each student when she had finished studying.[36]

Cambridge men viewed the Newnham students with "curiosity mingled with hostility." Hope Mirrlees mentioned "a particularly brilliant group of young M.A.'s either actually in residence, or often in Cambridge on visits, who used to come and play tennis with the Newnham students. This group included F. W. Maitland, A. W. Verrall, H. S. Butcher . . . Harry Cust, and the present Lord Balfour [Eleanor Sidgwick's brother, Arthur Balfour]." Clough's regimen, then, allowed for some carefully supervised mingling with the men.[37]

The novel experiment attracted many other visitors as well, both male and female. Turgenev came, and Jane was "sent off to show him round," only to be disappointed to find that "he spoke fluent English," depriving her of a chance to hear him speak Russian (RSL, 327). Ruskin visited, and Jane showed him the college's library. He gravely informed her that "each book . . . that a young girl touches should be bound in white vellum" (RSL, 327). Jane, a "rigid Tory," refused to "join the mob of students in cheering and clapping" for Gladstone's visit, and when her "friendly enemy" and fellow student, Gladstone's daughter, Helen, playfully brought him to Jane's room, she shocked him by citing Euripides as her favorite Greek playwright (RSL, 327). Jane may have been a Tory because of her northern roots, but it is interesting to note that she remained one while repudiating her background in so many other ways. She never completely rejected Yorkshire, and her politics were as much a subtle rebellion as a genuine conviction. She might don the trappings of Cambridge culture, but her anger at being forced to deny her past found other ways to emerge. Helen Gladstone represented everything Jane aspired to, but Jane felt ambivalent about those aspirations. Apparently she used Helen as a scapegoat and projected her mixed emotions onto both Helen and her father. She could rebel safely on political grounds, since politics never interested her. Disagreement on such issues posed no serious threat.

Among the visitors, "last, but oh, so utterly first, came George Eliot," who visited Jane's room, making her "almost senseless with excitement. I had just repapered my room with the newest thing in dolorous Morris papers. Some one must have called her attention to it, for I remember that she said in her shy, impressive way, 'Your paper makes a beautiful background for your face.' The ecstasy was too much, and I knew no more" (RSL, 327).

Contact with such distinguished visitors and the aura of Cambridge seemed heavenly to Jane. She had "quickly become the centre of a very select little coterie that included all the most sophisticated of the Newnham students."[38] This group accepted her partly because of her intellect and character, but primarily because of the persona she had created. She was able to preserve the Yorkshire elements she admired and look disdainfully at her companions while simultaneously embracing the ideal of a higher status. Cambridge signified a great step up for Jane, since she gained admission to a circle of upper-class families and exposure to important literary and scholarly figures. But the past proved inescapable. After outwardly casting off the taints of business, of provincialism, and of her stepmother's strict Evangelicalism, she now confronted the power of yet another stern Welsh woman, Anne Clough.

Hope Mirrlees perceptively pointed out that Jane disliked Clough because she shared Mrs. Harrison's Welsh background. The two older women differed greatly in temperament, but they also shared two characteristics: a pathological concern for public opinion and a certain power over Jane's behavior. Once again, Jane defied the attempt to curb her independence. Clough's "main work was . . . the management of the hall of residence, and it was in the internal life there that her influence was chiefly felt." That life entailed virtually constant interaction, in which Jane and Clough regularly clashed. Blanche Athena Clough, writing about the tension between Anne Clough and her students, might have had Jane specifically in mind when she described it. She wrote that although most early Newnham students accepted Clough's leadership,

they were most of them old enough to have already tasted some amount
of liberty, and there were some among them who, not unnaturally,
thought that they could judge for themselves what it was or was not

well for them to do, and who consequently saw no necessity for Miss Clough's supervision of their doings, and were not disposed to submit to her authority. Nor was Miss Clough possessed of precisely those qualities which were likely to make an immediate impression on girls in this stage of development. She was not learned, and her way of talking was rather confused, and she seemed to them to be fussy and nervous and inclined to interfere unnecessarily with what they chose to do.

Jane, whose career at Newnham spanned her twenty-fourth to twenty-ninth years, had successfully escaped her home only to fall under the supervision of another version of her stepmother.[39]

Elinor Ritchie and Alice Dew-Smith remembered Jane's clashes with Clough over her appearance. All accounts concur that Jane's unique style made her a striking woman, but Ritchie claimed that many, Jane included, considered Jane's face very plain, despite her aesthetic dress.[40] Violet Hunt, who met Jane after she had turned thirty, "says that her mouth & chin were always those of an elderly man. She herself [Jane] used to say that whenever artists painted her the portrait was sure to turn into that of a very distinguished gentleman." But Hunt also admitted that Jane had "the most beautiful figure she [Hunt] has ever seen." Jane's height and her often garish clothing particularly disturbed Anne Clough, and Ritchie recalled her pleading plaintively with her and Jane, " 'my dears, don't you think you could try to look a little less *tall*!' " Jane's ulster, "a frightful object, very loud yellow checques," offended Clough, who once offered to loan Jane a shawl to wear in its place.[41] She offered a shawl on another occasion "when she considered Jane's dress too *outré*," observing that "you can go in something, then you can take it off."[42] These offers infuriated Jane, who balked at the idea of pandering to convention. Clough also objected to the women's tennis clothes, "narrow flannel skirts and white shirts." Elinor Ritchie believed that Clough did not like the closeness that developed between her and Jane, and that she was "terrified" of Jane.[43]

Some of the few accounts of these years that survive indicate that her behavior as a student resembled her behavior as a young woman at home. She continued to rebel, and she attempted to set her own stamp on her life by wearing outrageous clothing and smoking. Had she been faced with another principal her response might have been less extreme. But Miss Clough, with her religious beliefs, Welsh heritage, and fear of public opinion which so closely resembled the same traits in Jane's stepmother, stirred her anger. Clough's role turned out to be that of a standard against which Jane rebelled.

Ostensibly, Jane rejected Clough's control because she felt that the movement for women's education needed no special protection or fostering.[44] In Jane's eyes, woman's desire for education did not directly challenge her place in society. In fact, the students generally went out of their way to assert their harmlessness. In many ways, they remained genuinely unselfconscious about their role. Although they perceived the portentousness of their experience, they were not politically minded enough to foresee its ramifications. Being on their own and enjoying the company of equals was a heady experience, but at first they were satisfied to study and were thankful for the opportunity. Their joy at having rooms of their own, sharing ideas over hot cocoa, and being away from home seemed harmless enough. Newnham students, at the start, did not aim to change the world; they merely wanted to fulfill their female roles as best they could. Their families, who had recognized their talents, allowed them an education, but they too expected no radical changes in behavior or ethos. Some of the students did indeed pass through the college relatively unscathed, but others, like Jane, sought something much more revolutionary than access to the public sphere. They discovered the power and attraction of the life of the mind and determined to use it to carve out a new place for themselves. Yet to a woman like Jane, becoming a part of the public world soon took second place to the other advantages of education: it became a means to regain lost status, to reject her provincialism once and for all, and to find a circle of which she could be the center.

College life, then, often alienated women students from their families by exposing them to new ideas. In her autobiography, Mary Paley offered a poignant glimpse of the breakdown of family ties. Her father, an Evangelical minister, "cared little for the outward forms of religion and had a horror of all tendencies towards laying stress on those rather than on its spirit." This was the religious atmosphere Paley grew up in, but her experience at Newnham confirmed society's fears about women's education. "Mill's Inductive Logic and *Ecce Homo* and Herbert Spencer and the general tone of thought gradually undermined my old beliefs. I never talked on these subjects with my father but we both knew that the old harmony between us had melted away." Jane described her alienation even more dramatically. Rather than to Mill or Spencer, she attributed her revelation to Aristotle. "It happened," she recorded,

that the *Ethics* was among the set books for my year at Cambridge. To realise the release that Aristotle brought, you must have been reared as I was in a narrow school of Evangelicalism—reared with sin always present, with death and judgment before you, Hell and Heaven to either hand. It was like coming out of a madhouse into a quiet college quadrangle where all was liberty and sanity, and you became a law to yourself. The doctrine of virtue as the Mean—What an uplift and revelation to one born in sin! The notion of the *summum bonum* as an 'energy,' as an exercise of personal faculty, to one who had been taught that God claimed all, and the notion of the "perfect life" that was to include as a matter of course friendship. I remember walking up and down in the College garden, thinking could it possibly be true, were the chains really broken and the prison doors open. (RSL, 342)

This passage made clear the stifling provincial atmosphere in which she had grown up. Aristotle's work alone could not account for the sense of liberation she experienced. Exposure to new ideas in general freed her from old constraints. No wonder that Janet Hogarth Courtney, daughter of a Lincolnshire Anglican clergyman, was sent to Oxford's Anglican Lady Margaret Hall in the 1880s rather than to one of Cambridge's women's colleges, which were thought to be centers of " 'advanced,' and therefore 'dangerous' notions."[45]

Carol Dyhouse points out that many women reconciled their ambitions with ideals of womanhood ingrained since childhood by marrying men far above them in ability and public stature.[46] Many Newnham students followed this path: Mary Paley married the Cambridge economist Alfred Marshall; Margaret Merrifield married the Cambridge classicist and subsequent colleague of Jane's, A. W. Verrall; Ellen Crofts, Jane's closest friend, married the Cambridge botanist Sir Francis Darwin. Having come to terms with their places in society, these women could marry and, in some cases, still teach (as did Mary Paley) without feeling deprived. They both internalized Victorian ideals of womanhood and utilized their knowledge in the new lives they led as members—if only by marriage—of the academic community. They rejected many values inherited from their families, but retained much of the old ideology of women's place and function in society. Jane, however, chose a different path. She could never reconcile that ideology with her own ambitions and spent most of her life using her intellectual work to make sense of her personal experience. The perpetuation of this tension, which her close contemporaries resolved fairly easily, accounts in large part for her extraordinary creativity and intellectual achievements.

Since education brought alienation from the family, it threw the women into even greater reliance upon each other for encouragement and companionship. College life as well as study fostered such intimacy. Thus the cocoa parties, tennis playing, and amateur theatricals assumed an even greater meaning. For the family was the center of Victorian life, especially among the upper classes. To reject it, if only to a small degree, meant leaving oneself unprotected from the rest of the world. The college provided a surrogate family based on common goals, and the intimacy fostered by shared living space and interests brought the women closer together.[47] Tension between students and principal further strengthened the relationships among students. For the first time, these women possessed power; power of the intellect and power to govern their own thoughts. Even if they never entered political life (Jane barely noticed the suffrage movement), their experience and contribution differed radically from their mothers'. These women took a giant step away from the security of traditional family life and began, albeit tentatively, to form a sort of female intellectual elite.

This intelligentsia became much more than a group of educated women, however. Besides absorbing new ideas, the students used their newfound intellectual freedom and mutual support to redefine their place in the world. Once they arrived at college and discovered mutual interests with other bright young women, they created a community in which they fit. At first fragile and tentative, their community grew and flourished as it reinforced their needs and desires. Having loosened the bonds that tied them to traditional ideas of womanhood, the women students set about filtering their acquired knowledge through their own experience and questioning old interpretations of women's role.[48]

Despite taking the radical step of forming their own fledgling intelligentsia, the women students remained conservative in motivation. They had not yet developed the self-consciousness to formulate a distinctly feminist ethos. Instead, they acted out of a desire to appropriate male experience. They identified with the concept of an intelligentsia because they wanted what their brothers—literal or figurative—had. Common intellectual experience seemed to set men apart and confer advantages that women lacked. Unconsciously, women students strove to create a separate but equal institution for themselves. They had no female models to follow. If they wanted to achieve, they could look only to their fathers or brothers for guidance. Nevertheless, identifying with males brought them firmly into the public world. Once they established themselves in academia, however, they used their knowledge to reflect on their own experience.

Jane turned her attention to the past by studying classics, and she offers a fine example of the influence of female experience on scholarship. She brought her own past to bear on the ancient past. By studying ancient Greece, she wrestled indirectly with the problems that troubled her. In turn, studying the ancient world helped her come to grips with her own world. Her gender influenced her work, and her years in the female community at Newnham helped reinforce this influence. The female community helped cushion the landing when she leaped from the stifling security of family life.

Like Dorothea Beale, Jane recognized the importance of communal life to the scholar. "If I had been rich," she wrote in her "Reminiscences," "I should have founded a learned community for women, with vows of consecration and a beautiful rule and habit; as it is, I am content to have lived many years of my life in a college. I think, as civilisation advances, family life will become, if not extinct, at least much modified and curtailed" (RSL, 345). The college thus took on the air of a convent, for it excluded men. College life could not completely eliminate hierarchy or personal responsibility, but it could free women from their most burdensome duties: their obligations to families and, especially, to men. In the traditional family, women's needs were subordinated to men's, whether they played the role of wife, mother, or daughter. Jane recognized, as had Christine de Pisan and Mary Astell, that so long as society tied women primarily to family interests, they could not carve out an independent existence.[49] The college offered intimacy and companionship without the necessity of family obligations. It vanquished, by replacing, the family, that center of conflict and barrier to independence. Jane sought not so much public participation as an end in itself as intellectual freedom and the chance eventually to understand her own experience through authorship. The act of writing conferred power—power to interpret and therefore control her own experience.[50]

Although college life may have seemed idyllic to those women who succeeded in forming new bonds, it could not protect them from all unhappiness or totally erase family ties. Two events shadowed Jane's years at Newnham: the death of her favorite half sister, Jessie, and a mysterious unhappy love affair, both of which occurred in 1876.

Jane rarely mentioned any of her stepfamily in either her correspondence or her memoirs, but Hope Mirrlees asserted that Jane thought Jessie very bright and urged her to come to Newnham. But in 1876, Jessie died of complications from appendicitis, a subsequent abcess, and scarlet fever. Jane so loved Jessie that she had missed a term at Newnham to nurse her at home.[51] But a subsequent event eclipsed even the tragedy of Jessie's death.

The event was an unhappy love affair with a Trinity College lecturer that Jane's friends, especially Hope Mirrlees, tried—even decades later—to cover up. When Hope referred to it in her papers, she wrote in the man's name and then scribbled over it, as she did with the name of the woman he eventually married. But she referred to him as Jane's "coach," which indicates that it was Henry Butcher. He came from Trinity to tutor Jane in Latin and Greek and often played tennis with the Newnham women. Two of his sisters, Augusta and especially Eleanor, became close friends of Jane's. All accounts describe him as a brilliant scholar, even as a young man, and his work in classics won him many honors throughout his career. He became a lecturer in classics in Trinity in the fall of 1874 and during the next year became engaged to Rose Trench. Since he could not marry and remain at Cambridge, he accepted a tutorship at Oxford in 1876. He was "the centre of a brilliant group of friends" as an undergraduate at Trinity and sounds the ideal match for Jane; but for his engagement to Rose Trench, he might have been.[52]

Hope gathered some of her information by writing down questions asked of and answers received from her correspondents, and she asked Elinor Ritchie if Jane knew of the man's engagement. Elinor replied, "We knew vaguely that there was a sort of engagement but I don't know why we didn't think it was final & it certainly came as a terrible shock when he told her it was irreparable—he broke it to her." Jane and her friends hoped he would change his mind about marrying Rose Trench, but he did not. Elinor wrote years later that "the tragedy of the wedding day is still as poignant with me as if it had been yesterday—but in spite of all she suffered I believe she would rather have gone through it than not." In her outline of Jane's life, Hope wrote melodramatically that "the great overshadowing event of her Newnham years was her tragic passion for [Henry Butcher]. He was her coach, & his beauty & charm were that of some Fairy Prince. He was already engaged to Miss [Trench] to whom he was devoted. This, however, did not prevent his falling in love (I gather) also with Jane. He seems to have been in love simultaneously with both young ladies. Everything else during her student years shrink into significance [sic]. The passion lasted for a good many years." Hope's description certainly made the affair appear tragic. But her caveat, the "(I gather)," gives reason to pause and examine this incident further. The estimable Mr. Butcher may well have been a cad, but Jane may also have misinterpreted his intentions. Proper Victorians took engagements seriously. The evidence suggests that Jane loved Henry Butcher, but that he did not love her.[53]

Jane herself connected the fate of her love affair and Jessie's death. Hope recorded that "Jane told me (but without a trace of bitterness) that it was partly owing to [Jessie's illness and death] that she only got a Second in her Tripos [in 1879]. It meant also leaving the man she was in love with at a very critical moment. And Lucy told me that she ascribed the calamity to her absence."[54] Hope makes yet another revealing parenthetical statement here. If she felt compelled to emphasize Jane's lack of bitterness over the tripos standing and the failed romance, odds are that Jane actually felt very bitter about them. Hope tended to protest too much when she feared Jane might appear human.

It is also interesting that Jane attributed her second to events that had occurred three years earlier. Either the affair truly devastated her or she needed a scapegoat on which to cast the blame for her academic performance and the unhappy love affair. Jessie, safely dead, could be held responsible for these failings. By playing a truly female nurturing role with her, Jane had fulfilled her responsibility and could not be held accountable for subsequent events. Above all, although references to Jane's love for Henry Butcher exist, no concrete proof that he ever made advances toward her survives. He broke the news of his engagement and presented it as final, but he may have done so only to discourage Jane from becoming interested in him. His engagement preceded his meeting

Jane, and that fact effectively made him unavailable. Hope commented acerbically in her notes, "mercy they didn't marry, as his mind remained stationary." In any case, he married Rose Trench in June 1876 and moved to Oxford, leaving Jane to pick up the pieces and continue her study of classics.[55]

In March 1879 Jane sat for the classical tripos. While waiting for the list to come out, a fellow student, Mabel Malleson, remembered, "Miss Harrison stayed in bed to hide her excitement." When the list appeared, she discovered she had received a second. She scored the highest of anyone in philosophy and the examiners were divided over giving her a first or second, but finally agreed on the latter. Jane mentioned the second only once, to Jessie Stewart. Her standing upset her, but it never stood in her way.[56]

No record remains to tell where Jane spent the remainder of 1879 or early 1880, but she probably returned home for a rest. In 1880, she took a job teaching Latin at Notting Hill High School, an Oxford girls' school, for one term. Notting Hill, only the second girls' public day school, had opened in 1874. Hope corresponded with a certain Mrs. Hogg, who had been a student of Jane's that term and remembered her as an uninspiring teacher. In a rare fit of generosity, Hope declined to blame this perception on Mrs. Hogg's inadequacies as a student. Instead, she attributed Jane's ineffectiveness to the belief that "both her heart & her brain were too full that year" for her to be a good teacher. No wonder: she had ended up right in the town where Henry Butcher was living, presumably in wedded bliss. Her students liked her, though, despite her distracted air. Hope wrote that they would "rush up after her lesson & ask if they might engage her for walking round the playground during the recess—'Miss Harrison, will you walk with me next Thursday?' 'With me next Friday?' etc.," to which she would reply " 'by all means, as long as you don't expect me to remember.' "[57]

Teaching did not satisfy Jane, however, and she remained in Oxford for only one term. Certainly, proximity to the man who aroused such painful memories must have made her uncomfortable. Still determined to escape her provincial background, Jane decided to go to London. She had heard Sir Sidney Colvin lecture in 1878 on his archaeological excavations at the Temple of Zeus at Olympia, and this lecture had stimulated her interest in archaeology. She left Oxford for London in 1880 to study Greek art and archaeology at the British Museum under Sir Charles Newton, keeper of Greek and Roman antiquities and a distinguished scholar who had excavated the Olympia site with Colvin in 1875. Jane felt she was leaving her past behind her and gazed hopefully toward the future, arriving in London on the heels of the aesthetic movement and embarking on a new plan of study.[58]

# 3

# FROM ART TO MYTHOLOGY: LONDON, 1880–1897

*"Comparatively few people care for art at all, and most of them*
*care for it because they mistake it for something else," which in a*
*way is true, but not necessarily unwise on the part of the major-*
*ity, for art, as the Nineties were beginning to learn, was less im-*
*portant than life.*
                              —Holbrook Jackson, The Eighteen-Nineties

*Happily . . . bit by bit, art and archaeology led to mythology, my-*
*thology merged in religion; there I was at home.*
       —Jane Ellen Harrison, "Reminiscences of a Student's Life"

FIN-DE-SIÈCLE London's artistic and literary culture formed the
backdrop for the eighteen-year sojourn between Jane Harrison's departure from and return to Cambridge. In addition to studying art and
archaeology with Sir Charles Newton, she began to lecture and lead
tours at the British Museum. Her published works dating from this
period reflect the influence of her training at the museum: these years
saw the appearance of her *Myths of the Odyssey in Art and Literature*
(1882), her *Introductory Studies in Greek Art* (1885), and her collabora-
tive effort with the art historian, D. S. MacColl, *Greek Vase Paintings*
(1896). But although she finally attained the status she desired through
education and a life in the city, her success left her dissatisfied. Her
struggle to reconcile autonomy and dependence, love and work, ex-
hausted her. Nevertheless, a new intellectual direction emerged from
her experience and set a different course for both her intellectual and her
personal lives.

Of all the swirling ideas and images of London in this period, Jane
embraced aestheticism most enthusiastically. Besides drawing new attention to art, aestheticism also challenged conventional Victorian notions of propriety, gender relations, and sexual stereotypes. The debate
over whether aestheticism's popularity justified its being referred to as a
"movement" or an "ism" or whether it even existed at all matters less
than its appeal to Jane. She embraced aesthetic tenets warmly enough to
hope that readers of her *Introductory Studies in Greek Art* could "nur-
ture their souls on the fair sights and pure visions of Ideal art."[1] Moreover, her enthusiasm for ideality in art led directly to a personal and

intellectual crisis that steered her away from the study of art and down the road to mythology and, eventually, religion. She needed the Cambridge experience to find her home in the study of religion, but the London period marked the transition from art to mythology.

London life heightened the tension between Jane's background and her aspirations. Success in the city freed her from the stigma of provincial philistinism but challenged some of her most deeply rooted illusions about the superiority of high culture. She tried to leave her Yorkshire past behind, but she could not easily disregard the fundamental characteristics and beliefs formed by her Yorkshire childhood. Her presence in London, to say nothing of her conduct there or the people with whom she associated, itself constituted a repudiation of her past. Yet Jane rebelled more against the way in which her family imposed its Yorkshire ethos on her than against the ethos itself. Her excursion into high culture assumed an intensity of purpose because it freed her from the narrow vision of her family as well as providing scope for her many and genuine talents.

Judging by much of the company she kept in London, Jane was only one participant in a sizable migration of provincials to London. Sir Charles Newton, Jane's mentor at the British Museum, grew up in the county of Shropshire on the Welsh border, and D. S. MacColl came from a Scottish family. Jane gravitated toward fellow provincials who shared her cultural background. Ultimately, however, they assimilated far more successfully than she did. A man's university career provided him with contacts in the city that could be easily exploited. In addition, the desire to reject one's past and aim for a higher status seemed more appropriate in men than in women. Many of her acquaintances shared another important advantage. They came from clerical, rather than merchant, families. Jane knew many fellow northerners, but few of them faced similar class barriers. Finally, some obstacles remained insurmountable to women, as Jane learned during her London years. Despite her fine education and obvious capabilities, not all doors opened for her.

These London years also highlighted the larger social issue of the increasing number of women who chose to remain single. This trend created social upheaval, especially in London. For one thing, the presence of several thousand unmarried bourgeois women in London raised the issue of appropriate housing. Working-class women had obviously faced this dilemma for decades, but the influx of middle-class professional women brought a heightened awareness of the need for adequate housing. In addition, the growing number of single women created a demand for women's clubs. Initially, the clubs answered a need for good meals and companionship for busy women, but increasingly they created intellectually satisfying surroundings as well. Most important, though, the trend toward the single life (always assumed, in the public mind, to be celibate) made social critics and the general public reconsider its meaning. Most saw it as an alarming trend, but some looked beyond the immediate issue to examine why women might choose not to marry. At bottom, the debate centered upon the issue of choice. Did women consciously choose to remain single, or were they simply not asked to marry? The most perceptive writers on the question recognized that bright, educated women had to choose between an interesting career and a traditional marriage. All these issues played a part in Jane's London experience.

In later life, Jane looked back on this period as "mentally demoralising and very exhausting," and admitted, "I regret those lecturing years" (RSL, 335). She felt then, as at Cambridge later, nervous in front of audiences. Although "almost fatally fluent," she "could never face a big audience without a sinking in the pit of what is now called the solar plexus" (RSL, 335). Because she was a member of a large family, her "fortune was slender," while "social life [was] costly" (RSL, 335). Nonetheless, she still traveled extensively, making three journeys to Greece and then lecturing to varied audiences in London and the provinces. Her circle widened at this time, and she formed some of her lasting, if not most intimate, relationships. And, in spite of the difficulties of the period, she achieved great success.

Hope Mirrlees described Jane in her London days as a "passionate excited creature always in love & always emballée with someone fresh, rushing down to Cambridge to pour it all out to Mrs. V. [Margaret Merrifield Verrall]—who evidently took it all with a certain cool cynicism." Hope stated that "Jane suffered very much by what were purely Platonic attachments on her side not being understood & their object suddenly flinging his arms round her neck."[2] Jane's suffering, like the number of such attachments gone awry, should be taken with a grain of salt, although clearly she experienced intense emotions during this period. She worked hard in the mornings but was "socially at the disposition of her friends in the afternoon and evening" in her "rather austere sitting-room . . . which was furnished chiefly with books, a large writing-table, and a few comfortable armchairs."[3]

In 1880, Jane began studying at the British Museum, started on her *Myths of the Odyssey in Art and Literature,* and successfully applied to the Albemarle Club. She met Sir Charles Newton through a Newnham friend, Mabel Malleson. Jane was the "country cousin" in London, and the Mallesons' introduction to Newton "enabled her to get her foot upon the first rung of the ladder." Jane told Hope that Newton tried to "teach her worldly wisdom & the art of cultivating people who would be useful," but gave it up as a "hopeless task" because she was "too North-country." Jane cast off as many provincial traits as possible, but she never lost her contempt for mere social climbers. Eugenie Sellers, an acquaintance who later became an expert on Roman art, angered Jane by the "unscrupulous way she used people just to get on."[4] In that regard, then, Jane never fully assimilated into London circles. Newton helped Jane gain entrée to London cultural circles despite her social shortcomings. Although Elinor Ritchie characterized him as "very cold & inhuman," Jane enshrined him as "the original of one of her favourite comic characters, 'the old gent'—a dealer in what she called 'polished jests,' & quotations from Horace." As a fellow provincial, she probably better understood his character. Her own fear of appearing provincial may have accounted for her "very formal manner" with strangers, but Newton's exasperation with her, finally, proves that she never completely overcame her background.[5]

The Malleson family played a central role in Jane's early London career. Besides introducing her to Newton, Mrs. Malleson served as a personal confidante. Jane felt closer to her than to the daughter, Mabel, with whom she had been up at Newnham. Alice Dew-Smith described Hope Malleson paradoxically as "a chronic invalid with amazing vitality & an eager humorous delightful mind." Jane once "pleased her very much by telling her that her crest should be 'an express train rampant,' " which seems a decidedly odd insignia for an invalid. Late in 1881, Jane and Mabel Malleson set out on a trip to the Continent. They traveled to Hamburg, Berlin, and Munich, where they met the archaeologist Heinrich Brunn. They also visited Rome, Naples, and Athens, which they toured with Jane's old friend Henry Butcher and his wife, Rose Trench. Jane wrote to Mrs. Malleson that, with Jane's "Oxford friends" (the Butchers) for company, "Mabel's theology is likely to be well seen to," as "the husband is the son of a bishop and the wife the daughter of an archbishop." Not a hint of the old unhappiness over Henry Butcher's marriage appeared in the letter.[6]

*Myths of the Odyssey* was published while Jane was away on this trip. She wrote to Mrs. Malleson expressing pleasure over its publication. "I was delighted to see that my poor little book is not to perish unprinted," she wrote. "I began to tremble for it—but I am very cross with Mr. Rivington for exposing the fact that I belong to the frail gender. I specially desired to stand or fall irrespective of that." She had good reason to wish her sex kept secret. First, men dominated classical scholarship and would undoubtedly deride a woman's attempt to enter their field, which had long been an integral part of upper-middle-class male identity. Men who aspired to gentlemanly status built their self-image around a classical education.[7]

Even more important, *Myths of the Odyssey* constituted Jane's first scholarly endeavor. Both insecurity about the strength of her claim to a place in the world of classical scholarship and fear of what the initial reaction could mean for subsequent works fed her anger. So much was at stake, and she feared that disparaging critics would sabotage her first venture. Moreover, she recognized male society's devaluation of women's abilities. If she had used only initials instead of her full name, readers and critics would have assumed her to be a man, an assumption that would have made them more favorably disposed toward what she had to say.

The great contradiction of Jane's life, however, was that she combined an intense desire to succeed in a male field with an insistence on using a distinctly female voice. Such a voice remained tremulous in her first book, for she lacked conviction and faith in its validity. Writing about art under the influence of the aesthetic movement did not allow her to speak freely. She was, after all, still an outsider in London, and in *Myths of the Odyssey*, she tried to mimic the voices around her rather than train her own. Perhaps unconsciously she sensed this dissonance and worried that it marred the book. By the time of her great works on Greek religion two and three decades later, Jane had discovered her own voice and was no longer concerned about her gender. She later challenged traditional scholarly perceptions of Greek culture partly because she had learned from the new trends in anthropology and archaeology, but mostly because she refused to accept the preeminent theories of male scholars. During the London period, she was still internalizing a sense of control over her own experience and rejecting male society's attempts to interpret it for her. This rebellion against male authority joined forces with her rebellion against her family's authority, enabling her finally to control the interpretation of her experience and the creation of her sense of self.

Through her connections with the Mallesons and Charles Newton, Jane had the opportunity to lecture at the British Museum and at schools in the provinces. Although she found her life exhausting, her memoirs indicate she also benefited from her experience. If nothing else, she learned to look more realistically at the haute bourgeoisie to whose ranks she aspired. She observed women of London's upper class firsthand and criticized the emptiness and futility of their lives. In an 1891 interview in the *Pall Mall Gazette*, Jane came closest to addressing women's issues directly until her publication of two essays on women's questions between 1912 and 1914. Commenting on the popular revival of interest in Greece, Jane asserted that "what people want who attend lectures on Greek subjects is not a deep insight into these subjects," but rather "something, not very much, of the life and manners of a highly-cultured and intellectual race of older times." She accused her audiences of being driven by "curiosity rather than a desire for thorough knowledge." Women constituted a majority of her audience, and she divided them into two camps. The "mothers of young children are the most eager attendants" because they "want to share the interests of their children" and "to be able to talk to their boys . . . about these things, or they want to assist them in their studies." A few attend "so that they themselves may teach their children at home." But

> another large section of the audience is formed by the well-to-do women who have a good deal of leisure. They have nothing to do in the afternoon; their lives are somewhat dull and empty; they want some outside interest, and have not the energy to create one. To them the lectures come as a new amusement. They do not require very much, and the lecturer has to make the subject as light and varied as possible. Also he or she must be prepared to generalize a good deal, which is apt to result in much personal demoralization—the hunger for generaliza-tion in half-educated women is a fact that I have observed without quite understanding.

This passage contains a mixture of contempt and envy: contempt for the perceived frivolity of these women's lives, yet envy of their leisure. Throughout her London years, Jane had to worry about money and clearly resented her audiences which, with all their privileges, lacked the self-discipline to pursue a strenuous course of study and exhibited a high degree of philistinism. Moreover, had it not been for her stepmoth-er's intervention, Jane might have aspired to the status of leisured lady herself. Instead, economic hardship had forced her to support herself by working.[8]

Aside from the economic motive, Jane also projected her own drive for intellectual growth and achievement onto her audiences. She realized that, as attractive as it might appear on the surface, the life of the leisured lady could also be stultifying. Her lectures drew the ladies out of themselves.

> I believe the great good is that lectures on Greek art create for these ladies an interest that is *non-personal*. You want to be a woman to know what the rest of that is. People talk of the good that lectures do by bringing people and classes together. I should like to talk of the good they do—for women, at least—by sending them away from each other into a decent place, to think where you only can think—alone; and the more remote the subject, the more averse from modern association—as Greek art is—the better.[9]

She recognized that conflicting demands on women created a frag-mented life and prohibited female achievement. Even more significant, she emphasized education as discipline of the mind rather than voca-tional training. She accorded the greatest value to individual thought. Tellingly, she also believed that the ancient world made better food for thought than the modern. Its romance captured students' attention, but its paramount virtue for Jane lay in its potential for deflecting attention from the muddled present.

In her "Reminiscences," Jane spoke more maliciously about her London audiences. She referred to them as "British Lions and Lionesses" (RSL, 330). The Lionesses made an indelible impression on her. They were

all spinsters, well-born, well-bred, well-educated, and well off. They attended my lectures on Greek Art. Greek Art was at that time booming and was eminently respectable. At home they gardened a great deal; they, most of them, had country houses. Their gardens were a terror to me, for I never could remember the names of the plants with slips attached to them, and to blunder over a plant's name was as bad to a Lioness as a false quantity. They kept diaries in which they entered accurately the state of the weather on each day. If they lived in London they promoted Friendly Girls and Workhouse Nursing. Above all, they kept a vigilant eye on the shortcomings of local officials. . . . In the spring and early summer they went to Italy, accompanied by a "young relative," whose expenses they paid; they voyaged mainly to Rome and Florence, but the more adventurous went to Assisi. Attired in mushroom hats, veils, and dust cloaks, they sketched a great deal. . . . The ordinary man was to them negligible, but they spoke of their own male relatives with respect and frequently quoted the opinions of "my uncle, the Dean," or "my cousin, the Archdeacon." They were a fine upstanding breed, and I miss them. They had no unsatisfied longings, had never heard of "suppressed complexes," and lived happily their vigorous, if somewhat angular, lives. (RSL, 330)

Jane sketched only a brief description of the Lions, noting that she had to watch them "from afar" as "real intimacy between the two genders was not in those days usual" (RSL, 330). From her experience with them at prize-givings during her tenure on the Girls' Public Day School Company, she observed that no Lion could give an address on such occasions "without telling you that it was the writing of Latin Prose that had made him what he was!" (RSL, 330). She concluded with an anecdote from a yachting trip she took with an unnamed British Lion: "He was oldish and had a deck-cabin. I happened to look in in passing. On the table lay a Bible, on the Bible a toothbrush. Cleanliness was 'next to Godliness' " (RSL, 331). These are mischievous portraits—loving, yet with an edge of contempt.

In addition to her work at the British Museum, Jane also lectured on Greek art at prestigious boys' schools. Both her style and her sex created a stir in these schools, which epitomized male privilege. Clifton's Archbishop Wilson, who arranged for Jane's visit there, later admitted that "he had not dared to tell his Council that the lecturer was a woman till all was over." In her audience, she later learned, had been Roger Fry and J. M. McTaggart, who "had deigned to discuss my lecture" (RSL, 331). She spoke at Eton and Winchester as well. At the latter, "one of the masters asked a very small Winchester 'man' if he had liked the lecture. 'Not the lecture,' he said candidly, 'but I liked the lady; she was like a beautiful green beetle.' In those days one's evening gowns were apt to be covered with spangles, and mine of blue-green satin had caught the light of the magic-lantern" (RSL, 331). Needless to say, neither blue-green satin nor the magic-lantern were standard equipment for most lecturers, and Jane undoubtedly appeared very dramatic. Her youngest half brother attended Harrow at this time and "wrote to say he had heard I was lecturing at Eton. It didn't matter, apparently, what I did at that be-nighted place, but he 'did hope I wasn't coming lecturing at Harrow as it would make it very awkward for him with the other fellows.'" Jane "saw his position and respected it" (RSL, 331). She had good reasons for avoid-ing professional contact with her family. At a Hull lecture she gave on Greek funereal monuments, her uncle Edward whispered, after viewing a slide depicting a mourning dog, "I don't think much of the Greek breed of dog!"[10] Spoken like a true Yorkshireman.

Jane succeeded as a lecturer not only because of her fluency but also because of her distinctive style. Besides her aesthetic dress, she used the technique (never quite abandoned) of incorporating dramatic bursts of light and sound in order to stir up her audience. Alice Dew-Smith re-called that she "lectured in a high strained voice, quite different to the voice her friends were accustomed to in her less formal moments, and had numerous affectations of speech about which we, her none the less devoted and admiring pupils, did not fail to chaff her afterwards." Alice also told Hope Mirrlees that one of Jane's favorite phrases was " 'this beautiful figure which I will now place before you,' " after which "would appear some very archaic figure . . . with arms pinned to its sides."[11] Frederick Myres, a Cambridge don but a prefect at Winchester when Jane lectured there, described her as a "splendid creature . . . with her splendid head of hair & bright eyes." Hope wrote that at the Winches-ter lecture, Jane spoke and showed her slides, and then finally, "throw-ing back her head, she burst into a chorus of Euripides in Greek. . . . The school jumped onto the chairs & cheered themselves hoarse—& for a week she was the talk of the school."[12] No wonder the Winchester man preferred the lady to her lecture.

Jane's work brought her into contact with some of the period's leading artistic and literary figures, and she described some of them briefly in her "Reminiscences." Robert Browning was "a cheerful, amusing gos-sip"; Tennyson, a "vain old thing" who was "very kind . . . according to his fierce lights. . . . He was intensely English and therefore not at his best as a conscious thinker; but he felt soundly, and his mastery of language was superb." Walter Pater and his sisters "opened their home" to her; she characterized Pater as "a soft, kind cat" who "purred so persuasively that I lost the sense of what he was saying." Henry James was an "ingenious spider" whom she liked to watch "weaving his webs," but to her "he had no appeal." Edward Burne-Jones "used often to come and sit with me, turning over drawings of Greek vases with eager, delighted fingers." She sometimes "sat with him as he drew strange visions" and regretted destroying the "many letters with whimsical illustrative drawings" that he sent her. She became close friends with Walter Raleigh and his sisters, especially Katherine (Kate). But the two figures she "most longed after, Christina Rossetti and Swinburne, were not diners-out," so she never met them (RSL, 328–39).

Other friends shared their memories of this period with Hope Mirrlees. Alice Dew-Smith and Henry Butcher's sister, Augusta, made slides for her lectures.[13] Elinore Ritchie Paul acted with Jane in a series of Homeric theatricals and tableaux staged in the 1880s. Jane appeared in some performances to benefit the London University Fund. These performances boasted "everybody of note—except Bernard Shaw" as participants, according to one source.[14] A professor of Greek at London University staged other theatrical performances at a Mrs. Peke's house. Hope Mirrlees dismissed the artistic Mrs. Peke as "a very rich vulgar woman." In one performance of The Tale of Troy, Jane appeared as Penelope, Elinor Ritchie Paul as Andromache, and Lionel Tennyson (the poet's son) as Odysseus. Jane's performance "caused quite a sensation. Everything about her performance—Mrs. Paul told me—her appearance, movements, voice, diction—was exquisite. And her performance received special praise from two of the most distinguished members of the audience, Gladstone and Tennyson."[15] Apparently, Gladstone had forgiven Jane her cool reception of him at Newnham several years earlier. Looking back, Elinor regarded The Tale of Troy of 1883 as "rather an absurd affair," but recalled that she and Jane enjoyed searching the British Museum's collection of Greek vases for inspiration. It was all "a very amateur affair & rather laughed at as giving society ladies an opportunity for dressing up & displaying their beauty as they did in the groups. It was all so unusual then. But Jane's acting was beautiful."[16] Moreover, Jane undoubtedly reveled in being perceived as a society lady.

Despite her wide circle of friends, Jane once told Hope that she "never felt really in sympathy with any of the generations whose *florait* was in the nineteenth century. It was F. M. Cornford's generation she first began to feel in sympathy with."[17] When she returned to Cambridge, she gravitated toward the Bloomsbury-Cambridge group, composed of people at least a generation her junior. Jane's outlook clearly situated her between her own generation and the next. Shackled by convention that both limited her sphere because of her sex and marked her as solidly middle class because of her family background, Jane felt more at ease with the younger people who supposedly did not pay such close attention to these factors. A part of her, however, desperately craved acceptance into London's cultural establishment. After all, much more than two hundred miles separated London from Yorkshire, and Jane's conflicting feelings toward her background intensified her desire for a place in London culture.

By all accounts, Jane reached the height of her attractiveness during her thirties. She also seemed within striking distance of attaining the status to which she had aspired for so long. She made many friends among London's haute bourgeoisie. Her work captured her imagination while leaving her time to socialize in artistic and literary circles. But if in her "Reminiscences" she skipped lightly over her difficulties in this period, her acquaintances did not. One of her difficulties was a long and complex friendship with a woman referred to as "Get" Wilson, and Jane's friends provided the few sketchy details that survive. Get and Jane shared a series of living quarters for many of Jane's seventeen years in London. When Get moved to the city in 1882, she met Jane through Mabel Malleson, according to Hope Mirrlees, and the two women took a maisonette in Notting Hill Gate. Get worked at "procuring trained nurses for the workhouse infirmaries," and Hope Mirrlees asserted that they "had nothing whatever in common." Jane's later snide reference to the British Lionesses who "promoted Friendly Girls and Workhouse Nurses" conveys resentment that may have lingered from her London years with Get. Hope Malleson, who knew both of them, believed that Get's "great sense of humour" was "their only bond." Get grew ill and finally became an invalid, and Jane later told Hope Mirrlees that the London years had been a "great strain on [Jane's] constitution" because of the "continual train journeys, the very great strain of lecturing, continual dining out & people," as well as ultimately having to nurse Get. Jane obviously felt torn by her London experience, for although she reached dizzy heights in her work, she felt keenly the pressure of keeping up appearances in society. As Charles Newton perceived, she may well have been "too North-country" to maintain the pace.[18]

Jane and Get's living arrangement presents another curious aspect of this story. Generally, middle-class women who did not live at home sought the comfort and protection of women's communities such as clubs or other housing specifically designed for them, both of which blossomed in the late nineteenth century. Often, these women worked within institutions that provided them with alternative living places, such as colleges or settlement houses.[19] Late in the century, however, the educated, middle-class woman living on her own became an increasingly familiar phenomenon. This new style of living created a demand for new kinds of housing. For her sixteen years in London, Jane was not connected with an institution that provided her with a place to live or a network of support. Her need to live on her own in London reflected her attempted entry into the male world of classical study and the British Museum. Jane belonged for many years to London's Sesame Club, which opened in 1895 and catered to bourgeois working women.[20] Her frequent travels alone during these years rounded out a striking picture. The "continual train journeys" to lectures in the provinces would have been novel experiences for a typical provincial middle-class woman. The professional woman sharing an apartment with a friend and commuting to her work presents an interestingly modern picture.

This aspect of Jane's experience also raises the issue referred to earlier, that of the increasing number of women who remained unmarried in the late nineteenth century. They created two problems for society: first, understanding why they did not marry, and second, trying to decide what to do with them. Education played a critical role in women's choosing to remain single. Freed from economic dependence on men and increasingly aware of opportunities in the public sphere, bourgeois educated women shrank from relinquishing their chances at an interesting life by marrying. They lived in a time when the ideology of marriage had not kept pace with broadening opportunities for women. For the most part, they faced a clear-cut choice between an interesting and fulfilling career or a traditional role as wife and mother. As was shown in chapter 2, some of the academic women Jane had known at Newnham could combine the two since life in Cambridge made it easier to maintain an active part in the academic world while also being married. But usually women could not find a way to "have it all," in modern parlance.

Some observers argued vehemently that women did not choose single life. Moreover, many of them could be particularly nasty in their attacks:

Be patient, fair and gentle readers . . . we are well aware that you, and
you, and you, might, had you chosen it, have been married. . . . And
why are you still single? We do not know; nor would you yourself, perhaps, find it easy to account for the fact with historical distinctness.
One thing only can you and we alike predicate negatively, yet surely:
whatever may have been the causes which induced or compelled you to
remain unmarried, we can name one which found no place among
them. It was not love for single life itself; it was not deliberate prefer-
ence for an estate alien to the whole constitution of women's nature.
You did not *intend* to be an Old Maid.[21]

If women responded defensively to discussion of their marital status, no wonder; this author's attitude could provoke no other reaction. Observers linked marriage to ideal womanhood and perceived the very real threat that education posed to the continued viability of bourgeois marriage. For the most part, the women did not deliberately set out to revolutionize gender relations, but their actions and society's hysterical reaction no doubt made some of them recognize the radical nature of their ambitions.

Other writers worried over how middle-class women would live on their own. Their distinctive needs prompted some writers to address the housing question. In an article in the *Contemporary Review*, Alice Zimmern pointed out that lodgings modeled on establishments for men would not suit women's needs.[22] They needed a more psychologically stable environment to call their own. Men could live comfortably in lodgings that required them to leave their belongings in lockers during the day, but women needed to have a place that resembled home. The Ladies' Residential Chambers at Chenies and York streets and Sloane Gardens House met this need, but demand far outpaced supply. Usually, the units consisted of small separate bedrooms and sitting rooms with larger areas available for communal use. Zimmern applauded these efforts but raised a revealing point. She urged future planners to arrange for housekeeping service, claiming that professional women had no time to perform the work necessary to maintain their middle-class standards. Her concern for this aspect of single life reflected the great disparity in tone between discussion of middle-class and working-class needs.

More conservative critics suggested that young ladies in London lodge in private homes.[23] Such arrangements would both protect the young women from the dangers of city life and reassure their parents at home, presumably, many of them in the provinces. No doubt parents would have felt more comfortable if they could persuade their daughters to take this route not only to assure their physical safety but also to keep them within a traditional family setting.

Seeking support in the face of a world that did not understand their ambitions, bourgeois women began to congregate around the ladies' clubs that sprang up in the 1880s. Initially, these clubs provided a safe, comfortable, inexpensive place for bourgeois working women to have their meals. The planned housing did not provide kitchen facilities, and although they usually had some sort of dining room, many women preferred the sense of community fostered by shared interests in the clubs.[24] For most of Jane's years in London, she followed the alternative housing route of taking unfurnished rooms. She had brought a long-time family servant named Joanna from Yorkshire, who presumably provided meals, housekeeping, and a suitable bourgeois standard of living.[25]

The mystery of Jane and Get's relationship deepens as a result of a curious letter Jane wrote to Hope Malleson on April 30, 1882. The letter is marked "Private," and the absence of any other surviving correspondence discussing the issue only makes this fragment more incomprehensible. Jane and Get had "talked over plans a great deal," the letter states, and "she has given up the idea of Richmond"; apparently they had contemplated a move. Jane pointed out that if Hope

had been in town as in the old plan she [Get] would so have liked the amalgamated scheme but she feels what I have been growing to feel more strongly day by day that without you it would be too complicated and difficult—we should be 4 sets of people in the house and no one there to be an oiler of intricate wheels—we both have the feeling that it is just the presence of some one like you that would make all the difference. As to my own personal difficulty I took counsel with my friends and they think that the malicious (not the merely conventional) and it is only the malicious I fear would at once if they found out you were not always in town think that the chaperonage I pretended to was merely specious and would be more inclined to gossip afresh than if I faced them independently—I feel the justice of this knowing as I do the sort of tongues I have to dread but I do not expect you will understand it for you are so far removed from these villainies.

At present then Get and I think of looking about for unfurnished quarters of a very modest kind and as she is obliged to be very oeconomical I shall be so too and try to get a good deal of time abroad for a few years at least so that my constant presence in London living alone may not keep me too much before the public eye. I feel as if I had given you a great deal of trouble and worry for no purpose but I think it is Fate who has altered plans not I.[26]

It is impossible to tell what sort of indiscretions she hinted at, but her concern for chaperonage and public perceptions of female behavior indicate that she probably meant sex. At the very least, the letter implies that some people reproached Jane for some aspects of her behavior. The letter throws a different light on her passion for travel during her London years. She went on trips as much to escape from wagging tongues as to fulfill her desire to explore new worlds. Nothing in Jane's papers sheds light on who would have shared the house with her, but whatever the circumstances she could not face the inevitable criticism. A resurgence of Yorkshire conventionality may also have fueled her reluctance. Certainly her parents would have disapproved of any arrangement that appeared improper, but Jane herself retained a strong streak of conservatism. Above all, this letter offers an instance of a potentially revealing incident's being obscured by Jane's destruction of her letters, leaving behind only the mystery and no clues with which to unravel it.

Get's decline into invalidism coincided with yet another personal crisis in Jane's life: her failed romance with the art historian and critic D. S. MacColl. Jane attracted other admirers in the London period, but none to her liking and none very serious. Hope Mirrlees stated that "there had been a man in her life, whose name she would never divulge, who had an agonising passion for her." According to Hope, Jane "admired & liked him tremendously & did everything in her power to make it easier for him." She referred to the man only as "T.," but Bella Napier, a good friend of Jane's during these years, mentioned a Mr. Tatton, a suitor of Jane's of whom Bella used to say, " 'my dear, of *course* you can't marry a man with a face like a penny bun!' "[27] R. G. Tatton administered the Oxford University Extension Lectures in London. He thought Jane "perverse" because she disliked Bernard Bosanquet, who "was certainly one of the cleverest men she had ever met in her life." He attributed her dislike of Bosanquet to the fact that "she liked people to be warmhearted" and "felt something cold about Bosanquet." He also quoted Jane's description of her attempt to give up smoking: she felt " 'not so much a craving, but a *terrible* loneliness.' " But poor Mr. Tatton paled into insignificance beside the brooding Scot, Dugald Sutherland MacColl, who influenced both Jane's personal life and the future direction of her scholarly work.[28]

Sutherland, nine years Jane's junior, was the son of a Scottish Presbyterian minister. He was born in Glasgow, but the family moved to London's Kensington borough in 1873. He went up to Lincoln College at Oxford in 1881, placing in the second class in 1884. After inheriting a small income from his mother, he spent much of his time traveling, lecturing, and painting. When he and Jane met, he was traveling extensively. From 1890 to 1896 he was art critic for the *Spectator* and then until 1906 for the *Saturday Review*. He wrote on art and architecture, and in 1906 became keeper of the Tate Gallery. From 1911 to 1924 he served as keeper of the Wallace Collection, and then devoted the rest of his life to writing and painting.[29] Augustus John, whose first exhibit Sutherland reviewed favorably, characterized him as "pawky and didactic," an "accomplished writer" with "somewhat limited" perceptions.[30] He exhibited his didactic nature in his behavior toward Jane by denouncing her lecturing style as too aesthetic.

Although scholars have referred to the affair with Sutherland, none has fully explored its implications.[31] Consequently, the true nature of their relationship has remained shrouded in mystery. In her notes, Hope Mirrlees offered a skewed version of it. She warned that "one must not take the *crise* [of Sutherland's attack on Jane's style] too seriously. Without doubt it was very serious for one of the personages; but I am sure Jane bore it with the greatest equanimity. Jane's *ironeia* prevented her, & would prevent her taking any *crise* too seriously." Elsewhere, Hope admitted that it was "by means of this *crise* that [Jane] became a mythologist." In all fairness, even many of Jane's closest friends also denied or underestimated Sutherland's importance in her life. Helen Salter recalled that her mother, Margaret Merrifield Verrall, "at first considered

D. S. M. purely a passing fancy."[32] Alice Dew-Smith, who should have known better, told Hope Mirrlees that Sutherland "was a dear comic character to Jane," who "used to call him 'the old post' in the tone of voice she used when speaking about old dogs." Perhaps out of loyalty, Jane's friends refused to acknowledge how much the failed romance devastated her.[33]

The main facts of the case are that Sutherland accused Jane of being too aesthetic in her work; that he later asked her to marry him; that she refused; and that she fell into a deep depression when he married Andrée Zabé in 1897.[34] It appears that the damage caused by Sutherland's criticism of her work continued to affect her long after the immediate crisis had passed: she refused to marry him precisely because she could not reconcile herself to his intellectual and personal power over her.

Jane first met Sutherland at a luncheon in the winter of 1886 at Ashbourne, the home of her old friend Peveril Turnbull and his wife, Phyllis. Sutherland must have heard Jane lecture soon after they met, for the apparently scathing letter arrived sometime in late January or early February 1887. It no longer survives; Jane "tore it up in the fury of first reading," but responded in a letter dated February 6, 1887. She said in passing that his visit the previous night would not have been unwelcome "a month ago," for then he "had not written that—to me—fatal letter."[35] It is disappointing that the letter no longer exists, but the story seems to be as follows. Jane's lecturing technique attracted audiences, but Sutherland believed that her lectures were "performances of an overheated, sensationalistic and superficial kind and related them to her desire to live as intensely and beautifully as possible."[36] Certainly she adopted an aesthetic style. Aestheticism appealed greatly to a young woman raised in a strict Evangelical household, who rebelled throughout her life against the drabness and formlessness of her stepmother's religion. Her behavior, however, greatly displeased Sutherland, and his criticism so devastated her that she actually changed her style. This response alone seems ample evidence of how deeply she cared for him.

Her surviving letters to Sutherland from this time, though, reveal more. It is not clear exactly when he proposed to her, but even these early letters, written when they had been acquainted only a few months, indicate a growing intimacy. Some are charming, probably dating from the early days of their friendship, and others reveal Jane's growing trust in him. She frequently lets the mask slip and tells him things about herself that she does not want made public. Tracing their deepening relationship through the letters proves two things: that it was an intimacy of equals, despite Jane's surrender to Sutherland's criticism, and that it was a much deeper, more intuitive attachment than any that followed. Sutherland's background and temperament closely resembled

Jane's, and the surviving letters attest to a shared sympathy unequaled in any of her other relationships.

A sample of some early playful notes demonstrates how charming Jane could be, especially to those closest to her. Inviting Sutherland to the theater, she wrote, "God wills that I and three others of his chosen ones should go and see 'Partners' (Haymarket—Mr. Tree) Thursday or Friday. Will you be one of us? . . . The piece is, I believe, bad, and only Mr. Tree is much good—but the leading seems so plain I feel I must go and chance disgust. It is the last theatre I shall enter till I sit with Dionysos himself beneath the 'hill-top'—so please come." In a "left-hand invitation," she said, "should you not be too bored to try 'gringoire' Friday, Nov. 4, I am almost sure I have a spare ticket. I had asked another man, but have had no answer for 5 days so I conclude he is out of town." She asked forgiveness for her tactless wording by explaining that she thought he was "not available Friday." Just before the great aesthetic crisis, she invited him to tea at the Albemarle Club, to which she had once belonged. "I cannot play hostess to you, for I was turned out of that select club years ago, but I have suborned one selecter than myself to provide tea and muffins, and my Kensington Square playfellow [Lionel Robinson] is coming here to chaperone us and to meet a mere heiress—not a beauty, so no fasting is enjoined—you can come in your worst mood." The letters exhibit great charm and vivacity; unfortunately, soon after the last one, the great crisis occurred and they took on a new tone. They also began to illuminate the dark side of Jane's London experience.[37]

The letters are worth quoting at length, for they fully reveal the complexity of Jane's relationship with Sutherland. On February 6, 1887, right after receiving his criticism, she apologized for treating him rudely during his last visit.

I think I had better tell you the real reason that your presence was so unwelcome last night, as I do not want you to credit it with any form of personal rudeness.

A month ago I should simply have been a good deal gratified by your coming but then you had not written that—to me—fatal letter. I daresay you have forgotten its—rather strongly worded—contents, which have been rankling in my mind ever since—I tore it up in the fury of first reading but unfortunately that only made me remember every word of it. I knew from the first that my rage against you was caused by the simple fact that you were right & I was wrong—but it was not till I began my work again that it was borne in upon me *how* wrong—how much more wrong than you could possibly divine—The worst is that all the success I have had has been based on wrongness, I could always hold an audience—any fanatic can—not by the proper & legitimate virtue of my subject or its treatment but by the harmful force of an in-

tense personal conviction—I had grown into a sort of Salvationist for
Greek art—probably a sort of educated decency withheld me from the
constant obtrusion of my gospel or someone would before now have
told me less politely—not more pointedly—that I was a fool—but none
the less the faith in my gospel was the secret of my strength.

The practical proof of this is that I feel now that all virtue is gone out
of me; lecturing this term has been nothing but a dreary mechanical
struggle & if my hearers have not found it out as they soon will it is
only that something of the manner of conviction clings.

Last night to this depression your coming added a hitherto unknown
sensation, that of absolutely paralysing nervousness—I can only recall
that I went on for an hour doggedly determined to make audible
sounds—however the failure more or less matters very little & the
term's work has to be got through somehow—

It will seem to you—with your sane mind—as absurd that the shattering of a theory should depress as that the building of one should
inspire—& indeed it is not the shattering of any particular theory but
the giving up of the habit of mind that demands a creed—I know by
experience that one gets on much better in practice without a religious
creed than with one, but it was none the less desolate at first to live
without God in the world—art has to me taken & more than taken
the place of religion & my work for it was I see only another form of
an old & I thought long dead personal fanaticism—which is, it seems,
hydra-headed.

I have added to this personal misery the depressing reflection that I
have done a great deal of harm tho'—as you pleasantly point out—'not
as much harm as I might.' . . .

At the present moment I feel that I shall never teach & certainly not
preach any more after this term—, I tried indeed a wild plunge from
theory into practice but with no relief. . . .

A right-minded person would be grateful to you & perhaps I should
have been but that some of your arrows were dipped in a peculiarly
irritating poison.[38]

Such an extraordinary outpouring deserves a closer look.

As Jessie Stewart and Robert Ackerman noted, this crisis resembled a
religious conversion, a revolution in ethos on the purely intellectual
level. In true Evangelical style, Jane overstated the error of her old ways
and berated herself for indulging in such egotism. The conversion interpretation is sound, as far as it goes. The letters that follow chronicle a
change from deep depression to a final acceptance of the new order. But
Jane's self-awareness may be the most impressive aspect of this letter. In
the middle of the crisis, she clearly recognizes her motives for studying
and lecturing and struggles with her most terrifying demon: the need to

believe ardently in something, to fulfill the religious impulse without resorting to theology.

The subtle but highly significant undertones of the series of letters are remarkable. Sutherland's influence and Jane's wholehearted acceptance of it are equally important. For one thing, they had been acquainted for only a few months, at most, half a year. Second, Jane had achieved enormous success with her extravagant style, which Sutherland found so objectionable, over a period of nearly five years, and she had reached many of her goals. It seems curious that one man's opinion so radically disrupted and altered her work. It appears that Jane was not only in love with Sutherland but so completely and uncharacteristically taken with him that his power over her threatened her autonomy. Sutherland shared Jane's North-country background and temperament, although he seemed more at ease in their London world. His Scottish Presbyterianism and taciturnity may well have reminded Jane of her father, thereby increasing her attraction to him. He played the role of mentor and therefore established an intellectual connection with her. The intellectual crisis, Sutherland's marriage proposal, and Jane's refusal are intimately connected. If the crisis over aestheticism had not occurred, Jane may well have married him and never produced her great works.

Ever resourceful, however, she threw up smoke screens to cover both the intellectual conversion and the refusal to marry. In her "Reminiscences," she indirectly excused her surrender to Sutherland's criticism by claiming that art was "a subject for which I had no natural gifts," and that since her reactions to art were "always second-hand," she was "docile and open to persuasion." She felt more confident about literature, where she was "absolutely sure" of her own tastes (RSL, 335). Judging by the ease with which she deflected the barbs of her later critics and the ferocity with which she defended herself and her colleagues, it is difficult to imagine her being persuaded by anyone.

In personal terms, she justified her refusal to marry Sutherland by citing an unnamed condition that prevented her from bearing children. Hope Mirrlees referred only vaguely to "fibrous tumors." In her early thirties, Jane learned "that she could never have children at risk of almost certain death" and "immediately decided that she could never marry." With characteristic denial of her emotions, she later told Hope Mirrlees that "it was not a really great tragedy." After Sutherland married, she said, "so far as was possible I kept clear of passion & threw all of myself into close friendship based on work. I starved the physical side of my nature & as sometimes happens with ascetics grew into a certain distaste for it." This extraordinary admission at least acknowledges her abhorrence of sexuality, but altogether ignores the enormous effort required to suppress the anger that led to it. After her passion for Sutherland nearly betrayed her self-control, Jane reined in her emotions and clamped the lid on all feeling. She sensed the value of the emotional life in her observations on ancient society, but only because of the price she paid of keeping her own emotions rigidly controlled.[39]

Her letters to Sutherland also reveal a depression much deeper than hitherto recognized. The next letter is undated, but its contents indicate that Sutherland responded to her outburst of emotion and tried to calm her fears. She wrote in return:

Thank you more than I can say—you give me a sort of hope not that I have not been intensely wrong but that I may work right again—& not give everything up—my work is so absolutely my life that the horror of feeling it go as I felt on Saturday utterly unnerved me—

The sting of your first letter was that you understood me & the help-fulness of your last is the same. I am generally so well supplied with *autarkeia* that I must own in self defence that I cannot sleep now ex-cept under drugs; but commit this secret to the grave as I would not have it known for worlds—I know in this state one cannot—if one ever can—distinguish between the moral & mental & the physical so I shall commit myself to nothing desperate till I can sleep—I wish I could think that all the remorse I feel would be resolved with sleeplessness but I cannot—probably your letter only lighted a long laid train of dis-content, but it seemed to cast a sudden flash of light on every foolish thing I had said or written. I am horribly ashamed of the trouble I have given you—thank you again.

It seems remarkable that Jane confided her dependence on drugs for sleep—however harmless a habit it may have been—to someone she barely knew and who had just upset her whole world. Sutherland's criti-cism alone probably did not reduce her to this state. Clearly, the London period had not gone as smoothly as she would have had the world be-lieve. Hope Mirrlees remembered hearing that Jane once became vio-lently ill upon witnessing a torture scene in a play during these years and had to be helped from the theater. Such sensitivity to staged vio-lence indicates a great deal of fear, anxiety, and repressed anger and provides more evidence that she suffered from depression in those days. She was unhappy, despite her triumphs, and Sutherland delivered the crushing blow.[40]

For all his audacity, Sutherland helped nurse Jane out of her despair. In response to a letter in which he must have suggested a new direction for her work, Jane wrote:

I am not quite sure what I ought to say. I have decided . . . to give up entirely next year all lecturing that is purely lecturing, because I see only too clearly that it is the Epideiktikos Logos that has been my undoing—but I am not sure whether I need exclude Extension work in

my Self-Denying Ordinance—&, if I can persuade myself I need not,
new work for it would be a god-send as I shall have a good deal of spare
time & energy on my hands—

    You would not so readily stand sponsor for me if you knew how
badly—just because I lacked the sensational element—I have done my
Wimbledon extension work—however, I do honestly think I can put all
that behind me—

    The pay question happily does not matter to me next year—it is only
when I have to be abroad a great deal that I am constrained to avarice.

The subtle jab at Sutherland connecting the lack of the "sensational
element" with her inadequacy as a lecturer shows a resurgence of spirit.
She envied Sutherland his ease before audiences and wrote after hearing
him lecture that he had "found for lecturing the 'more excellent way' as
remote from dulness on the one side as from sensationalism on the
other." She thanked him for "forgoing sleep or smoke to 'exchange
ideas' " with her.[41]

By November, Jane could write a more encouraging letter describing
her return to lecturing.

    Don't write me down a confirmed egoist if I tell you that your good
wishes *did* bring me good luck—I had a superstition they might that is
why I asked for them.

    I was wretched & almost desperate about the Eton lecture & all the
demons of last spring were camping about my bed but I was resolved,
come what might to try your plan & trust the subject to its own value
& rid myself of my hateful habit of trying to force upon it meretricious
effects—& you were absolutely right. I felt directly I began to speak it
all went ever so much better. . . .

    I wonder why you so often say just the right thing to me—I acquit
you of all intention you must be an instrument of the gods—I certainly
won't call you anymore a 'messenger of Satan'—happily I don't now
mind the least being your debtor. . . . I have begun lately—only quite
lately & perhaps too soon—to think of you as friend not foe—I think
you must promise (as the candid friend)—if you see me falling into the
old or any new form of lunacy to write me a thoroughly unpleasant
letter. . . .

    Of course I feel all the more keenly what a knave or a fool (I am not
sure which) I was last year & what dishonour I did to a peculiarly self
sufficing subject but no remorse can mar the holy calm that has set in—
a peace better even than that born of whiskey & soda.
P.S. Do not answer this & do not laugh immoderately—you may laugh
a little—but at yourself—cast for the double role of Paraclete as
Convincer of Sin & Consoler in my miracle play—

    Is it that ministerial ancestry of yours that will out?

The crisis past, Jane and Sutherland settled into a friendship that lasted nearly ten years and led to the publication of a joint work, *Greek Vase Paintings*, in 1896. Jane's conversion was complete. For his part, Sutherland claimed merely to have "turned her attention to the folk lore & ritual side of Greek mythology." Hope Mirrlees credited him with introducing Jane to the mythological studies of Wilhelm Mannhardt and Theodore Best. Clearly, to Jane the experience held far more significance. There is a feeling of total collapse in the letters—a radical break with a very successful past. It is not clear when Sutherland proposed to her, but it is not so hard to understand why she refused him. He held tremendous power over her, and she gave up an integral part of her style to appease him. It seems as if the intellectual conversion frightened her; it was one thing to relinquish her style, but quite another to face losing her meticulously crafted self to another person.[42]

Sutherland's criticism touched other aspects of Jane's work, also. Her *Introductory Studies in Greek Art* (1885), which expressed her aesthetic infatuation with Greece, contains ideas that disappeared from her work after her "conversion." She remained passionate about Greece and the Greeks, but drastically changed her focus. Before 1886, the glory of Greece meant the Parthenon frieze and the Olympian gods; everything prior to the fifth century B.C. existed only to contribute to the greatness of Athenian art. After Sutherland's devastating letter, Jane abandoned ideality and kind words for the Olympians. Ironically, Sutherland himself sounded the aesthetic note in his preface to their *Greek Vase Paintings* in 1896. He cited the book's great virtue of making high culture accessible to a mass audience.[43] But he apparently failed to notice that Jane's first work, *Myths of the Odyssey in Art and Literature* (1881), contained hints of her later fascination with religion and ritual.[44] In this work, Jane took her first tentative steps toward religion. She immediately backed away from many of the issues she raised, but nevertheless lifted the veil that hid the archaic past from the classical age.

In the preface to *Myths of the Odyssey*, Jane justified examination of artistic works on Homeric themes by claiming that they shed light on the larger context of the myths and helped in tracing their origins. The search for origins became her primary quest after her conversion to the study of ritual, but her first book prefigures it. Commenting on the relationship between literary and artistic representations of Homeric myths, Jane wrote, "frequently we have plain evidence that it is not the artist who is borrowing from Homer, but that both Homer and the artist drew their inspiration from one common source, local and national tradition. Nothing perhaps makes us realise so vividly that the epics of Homer are embodiments, not creations, of national Sagas, as this free and variant treatment of his mythology by the artist."[45]

She later transformed the assertion that a group experience precedes literary or artistic representations into the belief that ritual emerges from group projection and precedes both mythology and religion. The difference lies in emphasis: she still followed principles of aestheticism and therefore focused on the artistic rather than the social or ritualistic. But she was already growing impatient with the traditional literary and rational approach to the ancient Greeks, dating back to the Greeks themselves; the "writings of scholiast and grammarian" lead to "much verbal intelligence of our poet, but perhaps attain to but little additional sympathy" (vii–viii). Early in her career Jane understood intuition's part in creating a picture of ancient Greece. Most telling, however, is her reason for not "dealing, except quite incidentally, in the questions of comparative mythology." Aside from her view that "the express object" of the study "forbade my treating of the several myths in their purely *literary* form," she believed "the materials for such treatment to be at present incomplete" (xii). She did not close the door on comparative mythology; she merely recognized that it remained in its infancy.

The aesthetic influence reared its head throughout the book. She stated her aim succinctly in the preface:

> I believe the educational value of a study of archaeology to consist far more in the discipline of taste and feeling it affords, than in the gain of definite information it has to offer. . . . the best gifts of archaeology,— the trained eye, quick instinct, pure taste, well-balanced emotion,— these we may be thankful if we gain in a lifetime; and each man must strive to attain them for himself. (xii–xiii)

She remained under the spell of the perceived rationalism of ancient Greece although the very source of her study, the Homeric epic, dated from the disorderly archaic period. Jane extricated herself from this paradox by examining later classical and Hellenistic representations of the myths.

Mainly in her comparison of classical Greek with Roman artists Jane gave full reign to her aesthetic prejudices. *Myths of the Odyssey* contains analyses of such myths as those of the Cyclopes, the descent into Hades, the Sirens, and Scylla and Charybdis. All offered horrifying tales warranting graphic depiction, but Jane consistently preferred the classical interpretations, which tended to soften their terror. In her discussion of a bas-relief portraying Odysseus' offering of wine to the Cyclope, Polyphemus, before he gouged out the giant's eye with a log, Jane attributed its popularity with classical artists not to its dramatic content but to its "scope for skilful grouping and posture," which "needed only some hint of horrors past and to come to make the picture dramatic and yet not disgusting." Late Roman artists portrayed the incident more graphically, but "Greek vase and Etruscan sarcophagus are alike free from this revolting realism" (5). Furthermore, in a footnote to this section, Jane praised Greek and Etruscan artists for portraying Polyphemus with two eyes, as opposed to the reprehensible Roman artist who insisted on giving him only one. Such "shameless realism" showed, in her opinion, a "most morbid craving after sensationalism" (8).

Her analysis of the Cyclopes also prefigured her dislike of the family, which reached its pinnacle thirty years later in *Themis*. First, she discussed their ambiguity as neither mortals nor gods and their association with nature deities:

These wild nature-forces, whether of water or of fire, were in themselves, so to speak, neutral; they might be tamed to the service of the
gods and of men; then we have Cyclopes for giving thunderbolts and
uprearing masonry; they might expend themselves in lawless violence;
then we have the giant-robber of many lands. (29)

But it is not their ambiguous status or natural power that made them so distasteful to the Greeks:

The special characteristic of the Greek giant-robber is, as was likely,
that he lacks *social* virtue; no more dismal, more barbarian picture
could be presented to the mind of the city-loving Greek than that of a
"froward, lawless folk, who have neither gatherings for council nor ora-
cles of law." Thus the Cyclopes became for Greek political writers the
type of primitive barbarism, *when the family was the only social unit.*
(29; italics mine)

In Jane's view, archaic Greece denounced the family as the sole basis of society. Families only encouraged competition among members for limited attention and resources and worked against the interests of society at large. Ironically, the classical Greeks attached grave importance to the family unit, so much so, in fact, that they based social organization on family membership. Jane projected her loathing of her own family onto the ancient past and attributed to archaic Greece her own disdain for the family as the basis of society.

Etruscan artists' failure to maintain their distance from the horrors of Odysseus' descent into hell and its graphic portrayal in art prompted Jane to muse that "perhaps it was only for a few happy centuries, when beauty reigned supreme, that even the Greeks could resist the strong doctrinal impulse which besets mankind to people hell with horrors" (144). Ever mindful of her stepmother's rigid Evangelicalism, Jane knew firsthand of this irresistible impulse. Comparing the grotesque style of Etrurian to the earlier Greek depictions of hell, Jane mourned the loss of "that Hellenic euphemis, that quick instinct for beauty and limit, which prompts the true Greek artist to conceal deformity and soften terror" (141).

When she turned to the final chapters on the powerful female figures in the *Odyssey*, the treacherous Sirens and the grotesque Scylla, she changed her tune slightly. She switched rather abruptly from dogmatic aestheticism to a more subtle understanding of these portrayals, and the change can be explained only by a concomitant shift from purely artistic to more mythological-religious analysis. In the process, Jane exhibited the germ of familiarity with anthropological data and fascination with nature deities that became the hallmark of her later work. Her analysis retained the aesthetic belief in the moral uses of art, but also showed a glimmer of comprehension of the power that these symbols exerted.

The classical interpretation of the Sirens disgusted Jane, for it marked the failure of her beloved Greeks to live up to her expectations. One believed that, since the Sirens have a beautiful song, they must be lovely in form as well. But even the classical Greek artists, for all their love of serene beauty, knew that these temptresses could be simultaneously alluring and dangerous. Moderns like Jane might

turn, perhaps with something akin to disgust, from these hybrid bird-women creatures with heavy wings and awkward flight, and ask almost indignantly, Why care to investigate an art whose sole purpose seems to be degradation? But a closer inquiry, here as elsewhere, will modify our views; we shall learn to see that our conception even of Homer's Sirens loses nothing, and by antithesis gains much; we shall feel that these quaint forms which at first so vex our imagination have a strange beauty, a deep moral and religious significance of their own, which the conditions of Homer's art and time alike forbade. (146)

Despite her ultimate need to fall back on the Sirens' "deep moral and religious significance," she implicitly accepted their mystifying natural force. The archaic literary vision and its classical representation agreed when it came to the power of these female figures who were so intricately connected to the natural world.

In discussing the artistic representations of Scylla, Jane appears to retreat from her temporary infatuation with the terrible Sirens and initially offers the reader a celebration of the classical triumph of artistic beauty over literary evidence. Quoting Butcher and Lang's translation of the *Odyssey*, she gives her readers a portrait of the fierce Scylla:

Her voice is indeed no greater than the voice of a new-born whelp, but a dreadful monster is she; nor would any look on her gladly, not if it were a god that met her. Verily she hath twelve feet all dangling down, and six necks, exceeding long, and on each a hideous head, and therein three rows of teeth set thick and close, full of black death. (183–84)

She further asserts that such a grotesque figure would never find its way into Greek art.

one to poor Mr. Murray—No doubt he made light of my weight but I am deeply & painfully conscious of a good nine stone—it was a hateful fate that just when I wanted to "crown him with many crowns" I should set him so hateful an *athlon*—My stern stepmother used to say "No one faints but the kitchen-maid." I am not in a position to share her social prejudices but I *do* feel that people who reel into ditches should be left to lie there—by the by please tell my kind preserver that I would rather have been left lying in a ditch than have to be told next morning that I was "an over-worked failure." That hurt badly & rankles still, but I was too weak & meek . . . to resent it at the moment—my better self would have hurled the bad books on the hall table at the admonisher's head.

I wonder what happened on Monday & oh—dare I ask? Would you be very kind once more & send just a post-card to say how Andromache goes on the 24th [the staged version of Gilbert's translation]. I meant to ask Mr. Murray but I shall never dare to ask him anything again.

She recovered from this crisis, but plainly the stress of visiting Barford and meeting the Murray family proved too much for her.[15]

Two years later, Jane expounded on her theory about fainting and inadvertently shed light on the 1901 incident. In response to a fainting spell that Mary described, Jane wrote, "I believe in fainting as a blessed dispensation of providence to break the threads of consciousness, just for a moment when they are spun too fine & taut—& all your threads moral & physical are spun many degrees too fine, as is patent to the nearest observer!" She expected that Mary's were "moral faints," while her own were "grossly physical." Jane probably misinterpreted her own tendency to faint, but understood that anxiety and nervousness could underlie it. During Jane's first visit to Barford, Mary may have exhibited some jealousy toward her for receiving so much of Gilbert's attention and thereby unsettled her. If so, Jane was neither the first nor the last woman to arouse Mary's jealousy. According to Murray's biographer, Francis West, Mary feared Gilbert's interest in any woman who shared his extrafamilial interests such as classical study or the theater. Hope Mirrlees believed that Jane invariably overcame any doubts that jealous wives might have and developed lasting friendships with many of them, but Jane could be exceedingly flirtatious.[16]

She carried on much of her correspondence through Mary, but despite the cordial tone they were not, at least initially, the best of friends. Perhaps Mary resented such intrusions as a letter Jane wrote from Naples in 1903 while she and Gilbert were studying Orphic tablets. It would be an unusually patient and understanding woman who could bear the implied criticism and Jane's wifelike concern for Gilbert's health without reacting angrily.

I have a theory about his health in general which, at the risk of being called an ignoramus & a nuisance I will impart—I think what he wants is a long, quiet stay in a *warm* climate—it seems to me half his rather small stock of vitality goes in keeping warm. he reminds me in so many ways of Mr. Maitland, who has nothing in the world the matter with him but that he just shrivels up at the touch of cold—& the warmth they both need is not artificial heat but shaded sunlight. It is quite pathetic to see how he thaws & brightens when his feet are in a spot of sun!

I wish oh I wish so much—that next winter you would let Barford & take him to Sicily or Tangiers—or somewhere where there is no struggle with cold—I feel he is quite able to work moderately & in good conditions—& indeed that he is all the better for doing things, if they can be done with no strain—I think the little time he has been away will have done him good as a break & a change—he says travelling about with me is a "worry-cure" not a rest-cure! but I feel sure what is really wanted is a *long* quiet stay, a whole winter in real warmth. . . . You would have to pack up the children & root yourself up—for he would never settle unless you were there, he is restless now to be back. . . .

Here I am yarning on—but I *do* so want him to get well.

Part of Jane's concern grew from her morbid fascination with the state of her own and other people's health, but her proprietary feeling about Gilbert is highly significant. Since Gilbert lived to be over ninety, he clearly had no life-threatening health problems, but Jane delighted in sharing her health woes with others and playing up their illnesses. Mary Murray probably resented her interference, especially since Jane ended her letter by admitting rather condescendingly that "I feel by sympathy other peoples aches & emptinesses [presumably Gilbert's for his family] & have some human longings of my own after you—& yesterday, when we went to the Aquarium, I even longed for the children!" Jane bowed to the supremacy of family life but asserted her own superiority in the intellectual realm.[17]

Although complicated by Jane's and Mary's mutual jealousy, Jane's love for the Murrays ran deep. Even her cynicism and distrust of most people could not blind her to their essential goodness and decency, and she spoke of them in a manner reserved for very few of her friends. Moreover, she often expressed her fondness openly and directly. They had many differences of opinion, chiefly regarding religious and social questions, but Jane accepted their views with more tolerance than she usually displayed. As she wrote to Gilbert,

Quite seriously you are both bad for me—Lady Mary I think worst because she is best but you are both so hypermoralized & super-spiritual-

ized that you force me to think of "righteousness—Temperance, &
judgment-to-come" &, in the words of my own Baptismal Service I have
by a healthy instinct of self-preservation "renounced them all." Everything is a danger to me that cannot be instantly translated into hard
thinking. . . . As I said to Lady Mary I say to you that you have done me
good in one way, I will never set my influence as I have done in the
past, against good things because I see in you two how beautiful it all
is—but I will not think about these things or try to practice them, because for me that way madness lies and in my family we are already
liberally supplied with lunatics! It is all right for you because you were
made like that & can preserve thro it all a holy calm that makes me
sometimes want to send books . . . at your head.

She showed even more uneasiness in a letter to Mary at approximately
the same time. Jane apologized for some incident that remains unknown, but went on to vent feelings about the Murrays in general and
Mary in particular.

It is on my mind that I teazed you with questions when you were
tired last night & ought to have read Clarissa—but I did so want to
know what you thought at first hand. I can't tell you how upsetting &
bewildering it is to me to find all these things that I have labelled
"fads" held steadily as principles by you two—who—much against my
will—I am forced to feel are far away above & before me. I have never
known anyone before you held these views—I mean anyone I took
seriously—people like my dear Alys Russell & the Marquessons I can't
take quite seriously. I don't know the least whether you are right or
wrong, but if you are wrong your wrong is something that makes me
more ashamed than any right. . . . But the worst is that I know with a
horrid certainty that you have let me get to know you on false pretences. I never shall be like that—it isn't in me—all I can say is that
some things will be different ever after, I mean I shall never again sneer
or laugh at the things that are sacred to you.
Well it is no use repenting on paper & I am glad I did get to know
you even on false pretences! I never felt so happy & at home in
anyone's house before—how do you do it? perhaps after all as the hymn
says "Heaven is my Home"—I doubt it tho!

Presumably this letter refers to their political differences. The Murrays
were liberals, while Jane, despite a half-hearted attempt at liberalism,
remained a Tory virtually all her life. Initially, political differences
caused friction, and Jane later disagreed with Gilbert when he enthusiastically supported England's participation in World War I. These were
still early days, though, and the series of letters stretching out over the
next twenty-five years demonstrates that Jane and the Murrays settled

into a friendship that remained remarkably tranquil—especially considering the smoldering rivalries—until the end of Jane's life.[18]

Jane relied on Gilbert for scholarly help, and they often discussed their work at Barford. After a January 1902 visit, Jane wrote Gilbert asking him to inform another guest that "I hate him for he is sitting at this moment in *my* seat smoking *my* cigarettes in your study." She thanked him for his kindness and explained, "I was too dumb to say any polite things, besides I inwardly felt all the time that you were longing to tear up my untidy mind & put it neatly into its proper place—the waste-paper-basket." In 1904, she sent the following list of grievances "To the Complaints Committee, The Study, Barford":

re—*Waste paper basket*—
   Housing conditions for poor-translations cramped. Ventilation fairly adequate but system out of date.
re—*Rack on Writing-Table*
   Class distinctions between half-sheets of paper too rigidly enforced.
re—*Stamp-box*
   . . . empty
re—*Ink-Pot*—jarring note in otherwise harmonious & elegant environment.
re—*Chimney piece*—Poison exposed unlabelled—result: total moral collapse of—Temporarily Resident Ker
Remedies suggested—Flight.

Other visitors shared amazement at the "harmonious & elegant environment." Pernel Strachey, Jane's Newnham colleague, visited Barford in 1911 with some of her family members, and Jane wrote that "they are all quite hysterical (a rare thing in Stracheys) about the spring-freshness of the house & your arch-angelic goodness in heavy books unlocked up, & the symmetry & rhythm with which the clean towels are arranged each in its own house."[19]

When Jane left Barford after her last visit before the Murrays moved to Oxford, she "felt . . . like a dove leaving a nice kind ark. You do make your home very like an ark for all sorts of strange weary beasts and birds." She vowed she would "always keep the two white feathers [a gift from Rosalind Murray] in their silver casket for a charm to bring me back" and predicted that "wherever you set up that Ark it will be a blessed Tabernacle."[20]

To one seeking order as Jane was, Barford and later the Murray's Oxford home seemed an oasis of calm and serenity. The Murrays extended their kindness so far as to allow Jane, over her protests, to sleep in their bedroom during at least one visit. She viewed this "turning out" as "disgraceful," and insisted that "if I had had a spark of spirit I should have set to & had an internecine pillow-fight with you & driven you back dead or alive to your own place." But she gave in easily as "a poor backboneless woman with no Free Will & what is worse no Proper Pride."[21]

Gilbert's visits to Newnham did not always go as smoothly as Jane's to Barford. After they began to collaborate, Gilbert often planned visits either to lecture or to discuss scholarship with Jane and usually stayed with his old acquaintances, the Verralls. Jane's letters, however, indicate that his plans frequently changed at the last minute and, furthermore, that she could become quite incensed at his cancelations. She shared her nervousness with him, writing before one planned lecture to discuss the most suitable sort of desk for him to use when he spoke.

As usual I have left out the only important thing—what sort of a desk do you like? I have a great big thing against which I can bear up in moments of emotion, but a lecturer the other day swore at it & had it removed before he began—also is it high enough? I am 5 ft 6½ (the perfect height for a woman) but it can be built up higher if you like—a wrong sort of desk paralyzes me with nervousness—but if you are above these details of course don't bother to write.[22]

Gilbert's response, if any, has not survived, but it is unlikely that he was quite as compulsive about lecturing arrangements as she.

Planning for the same visit, Jane wrote to tell Gilbert, "as a 'confirmed habitual' philanthropist you will remember—won't you? that if you fail me [by not coming to visit] you will just spoil the day I most look forward to in the whole year." He did let her down by falling ill just before the lecture, which was scheduled for February 14. Jane responded to the news in the most charitable manner Gilbert would ever see, urging him to cancel because of his illness. "I am going to be a real Xian—for the first & I sincerely hope the last time—& suggest that you give it all up & not come at all. But I shall arrange this with your lawful *despoina* & you will not be consulted at all so don't write & argue but just lie still in bed & get well." She continued, saying, "I knew for certain yesterday morning some disaster was impending for I had a fearful fit of the blues about nothing," but unable to diagnose the problem, she had "resolved to cheer up & go to Girton. . . . I came back to find the fallen bolt your telegram."[23]

On some visits, Jane had to defer to Gilbert's interest in politics. She resented a scheduled discussion on political issues because "I shall have to sit meekly in a corner listening while you & Mrs. Sidney Webb reconstruct the Liberal Party in your loud dogmatic way—I shan't like it, but 'I know my station.'" Immersed in the *Prolegomena*, Jane knew that she would "be seething with Orphic eggs & Wild Bulls & really important things." She was not above jealousy in other ways as well. Before a November 1902 visit, she tried to cover a very real irritation with a playful tone. When Gilbert arrived he would "be met by a Shut Door," for he was "in deep & dire disgrace: you have been & gone & read at least 2000 lines of your dull epic to Bertie [Bertrand Russell] & never a line to me—The blood of many (& wild) Bulls will stain this river—& in vain—in vain." She signed "yours more in anger than in sorrow—*much more.*" Jane thought he had neglected her and fiercely resented it.[24]

Before long, she stopped being charitable when Gilbert canceled. Her responses varied. On one occasion, she joked, "I am going to assassinate all your relations."[25] On another, she claimed, "I knew you couldn't come, all the time—but I toiled away finishing my lecture prematurely to be free for a little converse about Moons & Milky Ways—& now alack—alack." She sympathized with him over this particular bout of ill health, asserting that "the only thing that matters is your resting as much as you can & saving your strength & giving the lie to that ominous Hell-hound [her name for his doctor]." She urged, "don't be depressed—you have a thousand beautiful things to do in the world yet."[26] She brightened at the prospect of an impending visit by all the Murrays, "tho of course I never expect to really see any one bearing your holy name until I *do* see them—I am therefore armed for the reception of telegrams all day with a fresh disease in each which you will have carefully caught to annoy me." They were to meet at Jane's favorite retreat, the Suffolk coast town of Aldeburgh, and Jane promised Gilbert that "there is a balcony sheltered from every North & East wind waiting for you, it was built for you from the beginning of time."[27]

Her close friendship with Gilbert and Mary allowed her free rein in speaking on some of her favorite topics: ill health and the problem of children. All three seemed to be chronically ill, although the seriousness or legitimacy of some of their complaints is dubious. Nevertheless, the letters provide evidence of how Jane worried over her health and discussed it endlessly with a true hypochondriac's enthusiasm. She suffered real symptoms, but they were probably brought on in part by her inability to confront her feelings of anger and anxiety. Discussion of illness provided one avenue of interaction with Mary, who was not particularly interested in scholarship, as did Jane's thinly veiled mixed feelings toward the Murray children.

At times, Jane could be positively gushy toward Mary. When Mary could not accompany Gilbert to a lecture at Newnham in 1902, Jane wrote to her proclaiming, "I was so bitterly disappointed, I wanted it all to be quite perfect—& it just wasn't because you weren't there. . . . Also I want you so badly this morning to talk over the lecture with & tell all the things that people have said to me, which would be simply indecent to repeat to the lecturer." The lecture was "a brilliant & beautiful success," although Jane "raged inwardly thro the first half which was solid politics [on the Boer War]—exquisitely done, but still politics." Ten years later, she expressed gratitude for all the occasions on which Mary "allowed incursions on Mr. Murray's time & strength which your wifely & guardian angel self must have disapproved."[28]

Jane could also grow lyrical over Mary's appearance and demeanor. Writing from Chinon during a visit to France, Jane advised Gilbert "for the sake of educating your family you ought to take a chateau in Tourraine." She had "seen several that would just do, one especially with a wonderful door-way, coming out of which Mary would look simply perfect—Mary ought always to be standing in a beautiful door-way welcoming guests." After Mary suffered a spell of illness, Jane speculated, "perhaps it was partly your beautiful white gown that made you look more like a tired angel than a sick mortal," and asked that she "never wear a scrap of colour when I am in sight—it spoils the . . . effect: but I think I can remember it, even without that photograph *which has never been sent.*"[29]

When speaking to others, however, Jane could be less kind in her appraisal of Mary. When Mary arrived for a visit in Aldeburgh, Jane wrote to Jessie Stewart that "Lady Mary has been and after the usual drains-v[ersus]-milk Sturm and Drang period she has actually taken a small house for her babies and nurse." On another occasion, when Mary came to join Jane, Gilbert, and Frank Darwin at Aldeburgh, Jane mourned the end of a perfectly good vacation. "Tomorrow Lady Mary comes & we shall all have to sit up—till then we are very slack." Gilbert and Frank were such good company to her and to each other that she wished "it could go on much longer."[30]

Whatever Jane's private opinion of Mary, she wisely never expressed it to Gilbert. She always referred lovingly to his family in her letters and showed interest in their lives. She lived largely a family life through the Murrays, and her mixed feelings about families emerged in her relationship with them. She tempered her desire to belong with a need to maintain distance. The Murrays served several functions for her. Gilbert was her intellectual companion; Mary a friend whose abilities and personality did not threaten Jane; the children, especially the daughters, young people with whom Jane could identify. They opened their home to her, and she enjoyed the warmth of their family circle. She had no desire, however, to play any of their roles or to carve a larger niche for herself in their lives. She had rejected family life as too stifling and appreciated the freedom that choice had given her. Jane would not trade her intellectual companionship with Gilbert for Mary's position as his wife. Their friendship flourished largely because of the geographical distance they maintained, which mirrored their emotional distance. The Murrays lived far enough away for Jane's visits to be special occasions. Any closer contact might have changed the nature and course of their friendship.

Jane was at her playful best showing concern for the Murray's health.

She thanked Gilbert for helping her with work when he was ill with "that large sore throat too." She blamed his illness on "Jahweh" who was "a beast I always knew it." She wanted to see him, but knew that "if Jahweh caught you starting he would make you all one long throat. . . . The Lord bless you & keep you—but he's never any use."[31] When Gilbert had to be admitted to what Jane referred to as "that accursed 'Home,' " she wrote, "it is monstrous of whoever arranges these things to send this curse upon you—The only good thing that can come out of it is that you will be quite quiet in bed for a few days—but then what is the use when you will be sick with ether & chloroform & things—Will it make you really much better & do you mind it horribly? please answer all these questions." But Jane added an affectionate postscript, insisting that he "tell the fiend of a doctor that you are of more value than many humans."[32] She herself eventually concluded that Mary was "a heart case" and that Gilbert's "extreme weakness" was "an almost certain sign that your *chiffre* (blood pressure) wants raising."[33]

Jane enjoyed discussing her own illnesses at length as well. She advised Mary to try a drug called Kola, which "pulls one together astonishingly & even takes away the sick horror of nervousness. I believe it is *non* alcoholic," which would be important to the teetotaling Murrays. Her often light tone covered up concern for a chronic and rather serious nervousness. A letter to Gilbert soon after one of his visits to Newnham revealed its extent. During that visit, he must have helped her fight off an anxiety attack.

I was brutal to ask you, but you were very kind to come that night. I get so frightened when I cannot sleep—& now these three nights oh how I have slept! a great well of sleep at the bottom of a green sea—so I must send my blessing tho I laugh aloud at my absurd self—& to think that this magical thing whatever it is (Mrs. Verrall has been in to explain that it is super-auto hyper aesthetic, subliminal-something, which is of course illuminating & convincing) roused in me such a "sourde antagonisme" that I almost decided to drop the acquaintance—it was only sleep after all! as gracious & harmless a gift as the small white paper knife—But I did so hate the idea that I was sub-dominant! I thought it was unwholesome but it can't be for I wake up feeling like a new-born lion (no mere kid).

Her insomnia dated at least from the 1880s in London, and clearly the anxiety that provoked it ran like a current throughout her life.[34]

The pressure of writing infused Jane's academic career with bouts of anxiety. This pressure was not external but internal and surely derived from the displacement of her anger at family and society that she did not confront directly. She herself required that writing be painful and stressful, and her most energetic scholarly exertions produced her worst peri-

ods of ill health. Jane's association of creative work and stress was overdetermined by her use of writing as a response to personal crises. The
complex bonds between her personal and intellectual lives guaranteed
that she would live in frantic vacillation between despair and calm. In
her "Reminiscences" Jane described the psychological state that produced her works and stressed the unconscious but irrepressible need to
release energy through work.

One reads round a subject, soaks oneself in it, and then one's personal
responsibility is over; something stirs and ferments, swims up into your
consciousness, and you know you have to write a book. That may not
be "hard work," but just let me tell Professor Murray it is painfully and
pleasantly like it in its results; it leaves you spent, washed out, a rag,
but an exultant rag. (RSL, 335)

Jane relied heavily on her scholarship to defuse her anger over her mother's death, her father's betrayal, her failed romances, and her inability to
reconcile love and work, all of which contributed to her rejection of the
structure of Victorian society. And "once her theories had turned into a
book she ceased to be interested in them." Having dealt with a particular crisis by channeling her anger or frustration into a book, she could
become indifferent to it. Each work evoked painful, if unconscious,
memories that she preferred to forget. Although Jane herself believed
that she "had never written anything that was quite literature," Gilbert
Murray unknowingly put his finger on the appeal of her scholarship. He
"used to tell her that he could never read anything by her without being
seized with happy laughter—it was always so exactly like herself." He
correctly identified its appeal—it was "like herself" because she threw
her essence into every page. In her own way, she lived intensely and
fully experienced her life. Her writing helped her make sense of all that
had happened to her, and therefore she infused it with great passion.[35]

After Jane completed her *Prolegomena*, she had more to say about her
health. A month after finishing it, she was "a deeply dejected Ker" with
what her doctors diagnosed as a thyroid condition. She often referred to
herself as "Ker," a Greek term akin to "ghost" or "spirit" but with a
rather more sinister aspect as Keres were believed to bring disease and
other evils. She hoped that her "local Vet" would "say he need not
excavate my throat," preferring him to "those London swells . . . always
so ready & handy with their knives." The doctors believed her "thyroid
gland accounted for everything, short breath, nervousness, fainting, &
that, but for it, a great strong cow like me would have no nerves at all—
for my heart is as the heart of a wild bull." In addition to the thyroid
condition, her symptoms may also have been related to the stress of
working and her grief over the death of R. A. Neil, which occurred
during the period in which she wrote the *Prolegomena*. She cheered up

at the thought of her doctor's wanting her " 'on no account to be worried' " and admonished Gilbert to "remember this & accept all my theories & emendations unquestioned henceforth."[36]

Only a few days later, however, Jane wrote to Mary about her heart
problems and a new treatment. "I expect I am making a fearful & unnecessary fuss & probably you have borne heart-symptoms twice as bad
without saying a word," but she wanted to tell Mary about a new treatment with a drug called strophanthus, which was "the drug they are
experimenting on with 'confirmed dipsomaniacs.' " On Jane's next visit,
Mary would have to "have a big bottle of strophanthus on the table &
withdraw that hospitable & much too superior whiskey of yours." Another of the drug's miraculous powers was that it would "help one to
bear not smoking." Apparently her doctor, "who luckily is a smoker
himself," had urged her to quit. She felt better, but remained worried.

It is a wonderfully soothing drug & has eased my "beating heart" not a
little already—he says there is no disease in the heart at present but the
thyroid mischief would easily set it up if not checked—& at present my
poor old heart is doing all its work twice over.

I am so relieved that he doesn't want to operate—I am a horrid coward & I have seen so much of the resulting shock from operations.

It is such a blessing I am allowed to do my normal work here, in fact
allowed to do anything that doesn't make me nervous.

Part of her anxiety about facing an operation may have arisen from the
memory of her good friend Eleanor Butcher's death after a successful
operation in 1894, for Eleanor's death had hit her hard. It is ironic that
Jane's doctors allowed her to work—that made her more nervous than
anything else.[37]

The appearance of the *Prolegomena* (the "Fat One") in November
1903 should have cheered her, but instead she grew more despondent.

I will tell you at last about doctors I have been too sullen to write about
them. Macalister says the abatement in the heart's action from one fortnight's akaprica & strophanthus is little short of incredible—he gives up
all thought of operation & I ought to be . . . relieved. I *am* in a way for I
am a contemptible coward about physical pain, but yet I feel I would
screw myself up to any operation rather than face this dreariness—it is
a daily hourly misery that one cannot even dignify by the name of
pain—just to be told to get over a bad habit—ugh—If giving up drink is
like the wrench from a lover—who all the time you half-despise—giving
up smoke is like parting from the best friend who always comforts &
never torments—Also I hate asceticism & am compelled to practice it.
All my life I have meant to behave handsomely to my body & it has
done the like to me & now it goes & plays me a low trick—& I have to

paint my throat a bright orange & take vile drugs—& I have no work to
interest me & the Fat One at last sits on my table & grins at me & I
don't care enough for him even to turn over his horrid pages.[38]

Clearly, curtailing her smoking and drinking bothered Jane. And as
frightening as the prospect of surgery had been, she felt better when she
could attribute her illness to a physical cause. Without that excuse for
her misery, and with the *Prolegomena* finished and no new projects in
the wings, she felt depressed and at loose ends.

Jane derived some pleasure from experimenting with different remedies of dubious value. In 1904, she was "rather seriously ill" with "a
germ," but she fought it off with "a new medicine given me by Mrs.
Sidgwick 'as supplied to her by the Prime Minister [Eleanor Sidgwick's
brother, Arthur Balfour]' " and imagined the Murrays "would rather die
than take it." Two years later, she advocated a new "germ bread" as
medicine. "All mortals' ills are cured by eating the new germ bread. . . .
some one has discovered that anemia & all other sins are owing to
machinery that grinds out the germ—The Mills of God grind slowly—
for vegetarians—which I am almost one—it really is important & it is so
nice." She directed the last comment to the Murrays, who were vegetarians. The "cholera germ" attacked Gilbert, which was "hybristic of it—it
is the same germ I expect that nearly slew AWV [Verrall]. . . . it attacked
all sound scholars—it tried even me but was routed immediately—when
Ker meets Ker." But her greatest joy was meeting other people who were
willing to discuss their problems or, better yet, listen to hers:

> I also met at the Vice-Chancellor's a gentleman called Marcus
> Aurelius has he been to Oxford? his other name is Dr. Stein—I loved
> him—he had lost several toes in a snow-storm in central Asia & he was
> very sympathetic about my great toes being excavated—it is so seldom
> one can pour out about one's toe joints at dinner. I am sure you would
> like him.

Sir Mark Aurel Stein, the Hungarian-born explorer, had other traits to
recommend him to Jane. In addition to his health woes, his archaeological expeditions in Asia and his interest in Buddhism would have intrigued her. She must have felt an immediate kinship with him on many
levels.[39]

In addition to her own illness, Jane frequently alluded to Mary's several pregnancies and displayed her old conflicting emotions about children and childbirth. In 1901, on hearing of Mary's latest pregnancy, Jane
wrote anxiously: "Your news has completely taken my breath away. . . .
I am glad for one thing that it explains your not being well & that will
only be for a time, only it is a long & worrisome time I am afraid—I can't
think how you can think of anything or anyone except yourself." She

then added her own perceptions of what pregnancy must be like: "I always feel when it happens to anyone one knows that it must put everything & all the world out of focus or rather into a new focus—I should feel like God when he made the world." Unfortunately, her experience of watching sisters and friends undergo childbirth had opened her eyes to its pain and discomfort, and "from being much with many sisters who suffer untold miseries I know too well there is another side—it is part of the horrible tangle of things that it should be so & always makes me want to curse." The real specter looming over the issue of children, of course, was her own mother's death as a result of childbirth.[40]

Once the Murray children were born, Jane showed interest in them despite her professed disdain for babies. She wished that Basil "could have been a 'horned thing' but perhaps his mother likes him best as he is—mothers are so scareful." She offered to take him "out for a ride in my bicycle bag," claiming that she "did take a baby once & he has never given his mother a moment's anxiety since." Once she saw "that great big Basil smiling I think I feel he was worth while." A year later, Mary resumed her study of Greek, a step Jane applauded. "I am glad you have gone back to Greek, which you never should have let lapse—It is worth all the mere children in the world. Such is the mind of this spinster." The birth of another son, Stephen, led Jane to predict that "the new Baby will be as great a joy to you as Basil has been and is." Stephen also prompted her to say, "you know I don't love babies as babies—but he is himself." Stephen took to Jane as well, giving her "for my very own a white rabbit & a sheep" during a visit to the Norfolk coast, leading her to assume that she "must be in favour."[41]

Rosalind, the eldest daughter, seems to have had pride of place in Jane's heart. On hearing of her engagement to Arnold Toynbee in 1913, Jane responded joyously to Gilbert.

Oh what a letter of excitements—I went quite dizzy when I got it. . . .
Your own Rosalind engaged—she who has been more & *so* sometimes
less than any daughter—& it all coming so swiftly & strongly—my goodness he sounds something like a man to hold himself like that & run
such an awful risk he clearly thinks of something more than developing
his own individuality all over the place. He sounds just the right tower
of strength.

And you & Mary believe in him I am *so* glad—It almost makes me
believe in God almighty—it is so like a deus ex machina—saving the
whole situation—I have ached with longing to save Rosalind from the
pain of living & now—at least for a time—it is all done.

Privately, however, Jane had her doubts. In a rare burst of concern expressed directly to Gilbert, she commented on her own impressions of Toynbee gleaned from his writings.

Oh but reading his stuff gives one furiously to think about the
marriage—it will be one of the [illegible] contraries type—which I never
understand—but I am learning to know they are possible. There is no
literary touch in him—it is all science & good thinking—& R. has literature in every bone—in a way I can't help being glad because there will
always be great spaces when she will need you—but won't she find
empty spaces in him—well who knows—it *may* be all right—he has the
scientific imagination which is precious near art—I don't yet know
where the dividing line is.

It is impossible to know if Jane sensed what would eventually lead to the
breakup of the Murray-Toynbee marriage, since there is no way to determine conclusively what makes any marriage fail. The fact that Jane
feared the marriage would not last is less important than her recognition
of the strength of the father-daughter bond. She believed that Toynbee's
inadequacies would ensure a strong tie between Gilbert and Rosalind
and keep him from supplanting Gilbert in Rosalind's affection. Jane
rarely admitted the significance of the father-daughter tie, but in this
letter she implied equal concern for both parties.[42]

Jane's devotion to Rosalind ran deep enough for her to show concern for
Rosalind's health when she had her first child. After Arnold Toynbee
wrote to give her the news, Jane admitted to Gilbert that "I am quite
inhuman & take no manner of interest in the newly born—but till I got
his letter I scarcely knew how I had trembled for Rosalind." She remained
troubled over Rosalind's health, for a month later Ruth Darwin told her
that "she had come across Rosalind in a bathchair 'looking deliriously
happy but not at all well.' " Jane did not typically display this kind of
concern, and it demonstrates the depth of her feeling for Rosalind.[43]

Another way in which Jane displayed her great affection for Gilbert
was to bestow various names on him. In most of her letters after their
first year of correspondence, she addressed him as "Cheiron" or "Ther."
Cheiron was the centaur who tutored the heroes Achilles and Jason, and
the use of that name reflected Jane's perception of her indebtedness to
Gilbert as teacher. "Ther" is a trickier but perhaps more fitting term. It
is derived from "therion," or "beast." A theriomorph signifies an animal
or creature identified with an individual. Jane's theriomorph, obviously,
was a bear, and Gilbert's, because of his Australian origin, was a kangaroo. Perhaps more important, it denoted an intimate connection with
the natural world. Finding the perfect name for her friends meant a great
deal to Jane, and both of Gilbert's names suited him well. When illness
forced her, on her doctor's advice, to take a rest in sunny Algiers early in
1904, Jane wrote to Gilbert, "how absurd it is for this Polar Bear to be
sent sun-wards & a thin Kangaroo to be leaping about in the snow." In
one of her birthday letters, a long-standing tradition, Jane, who "never

understood before why [Gilbert was] born at the beginning of the Year," finally recognized that it was because his "theriomorph is a kangaroo" and he "came leaping into the world," thereby making him the spirit of the new year.[44]

As their collaboration progressed, Jane increasingly depended on Gilbert for help in her work. She often expressed her wish that they lived nearer to one another so that they could work together more easily. She showed great diffidence in her letters, generally deferring to Gilbert's judgments and always proclaiming, either directly or indirectly, his superior scholarship. Jane's work clearly shows the livelier imagination and breadth of vision, but insecurity about her position in the academic world prompted such self-deprecating remarks as "I should soon be such an elegant scholar if you lived here." Perhaps it was better all around that they lived apart; Jane complained that "whenever Mr. Murray looks over a paper of mine he always says at the end, 'This is quite admirable, every word of it,' then sits down & softly re-writes it all!" She joked that "that is how I should like my life to be—to sit reading & writing stuffage all day & every morning you to walk in for about half an hour & say it was all wrong!" Her joking probably hid some resentment, but his criticism, although sometimes making her feel unhappy, did not affect her train of thought. Gilbert offered his criticism constructively and in an egalitarian manner. Jane was much less likely to change her ways at the age of fifty or sixty than she had been at the age of thirty, when she reacted so angrily to Sutherland MacColl's criticism of her style.[45]

Jane's and Gilbert's collaboration was mutually enriching and marked by deep respect and genuine affection on both sides. Remarking on an upcoming social engagement, Jane wrote, "I am going to meet Mr. Mackail [classicist J. W. Mackail] at AWV's Sunday—I wish I soon met you anywhere at anything." After just missing him somewhere, she admitted that "sometimes when ages & ages go by & I don't see you I am tempted to—well—doubt the goodness of God. I know I should work just twice as well if you were here to do all the real thinking for me—or rather the imagining—I was so sick that evening [of a lecture] with nervousness that when the light went out I felt like going out too & then I said to myself—The only creature in the room that I am really afraid of has read it what do the rest matter—& they didn't really matter any more." The Ritualist circle was a small and exclusive one, and Jane derived her self-image from her participation in it. In a way, her deference to Gilbert testifies as much to her gratitude for his support as to her insecurity.[46]

This gratitude stemmed in part from his encouragement when she moved tentatively in new intellectual directions. His interest in classical literature and drama opened new doors by giving Jane fresh fields to examine for the connections among ritual, drama and literature. Gilbert's translations of Euripides struck her with their beauty and revealed new insights into the ancient world's relation to its gods. "When you first say those lovely verse-things to me I feel dazed & a little frightened—you see I am moving about in worlds half-realized—hence the obstinate questionings!" She felt unsatisfied with her work, as if somehow she never managed to capture exactly what she wanted to express. After praising his translation of Euripides' *The Bacchae*, she confided to him,

> You will laugh I know & well you may but I think the reason why your
> verses give me such intense & almost immeasurable delight is that they
> are just what I would have given my soul to do myself—As a quite
> young girl I had a dream of being first a poet & next a scholar & tho
> both dreams faded swiftly & completely they have always left a sort of
> empty ache of something never found. . . . I think at first I half-jealously
> resented it, but now I don't the least mind it being you not me—It is
> more resting so!

She went so far as to comment, when Gilbert's translation of Sophocles' *Oedipus Tyrannus* seemed stiff and unnatural, that "I am sure it is the fault of Sophocles if you can't translate him save with a sense of labour."[47]

Jane admitted that she felt her mind moved "at snail's pace" by comparison with other scholars. Gilbert, however, found her a great source of inspiration. In one of the few letters to her that survive, he wrote,

> You make me feel rather intoxicated, which is not good for Beasts, only
> for grown up men. But the inspiration really comes from yourself, as
> anyone who knows you at all knows. You only need a dry stick or two,
> to make a fire, & naturally the barking of the Theres round about you
> adds to the excitement of the blaze.

For her part, Jane recognized that Gilbert's calm detachment and serenity spilled over into his scholarship.

> You *are* strange—you sit like some great creating Spider & let all of us
> second rate flies buzz about & then when the tangle is hot & furious
> enough you begin weaving your web & it straightens out to your pat-
> tern & you chuck out our corpses—Just now I am thanking God that I
> happen to like you & so can learn from you, it's the merest chance—if
> you had had auburn whiskers like Menelaus I should have listened to
> nothing you said.

She cared deeply for Gilbert, but could express herself only humorously and indirectly.[48]

Jane may well have confused her feelings for Gilbert's work with her personal attachment to him. Although her work was far more imagina-

tive than his, she often praised his writing for its intuitive understanding of the past. She seems to have ignored his pronouncements when
they ran contrary to hers, as any true friend would, and focused solely on
the part of his work that complemented her own. She advised him to
read J. A. Stewart's *Plato's Doctrine of Ideas*, which she believed "explains why thinking is no good at all unless one feels & is excited—it
gives one the psychology of ecstasy—& of beauty the same thing." Its
greatest value consisted in its explanation for "the difference between
[Gilbert] & almost every other scholar & why everything you write
excites one all over & everything your pet lambs Percy [Gardner] & Mr.
[Lewis] Farnell write is so much dead lumber."49 Gilbert's main value,
however, lay in his "insulated" mind. Jane knew that "when I have shot
a rubbish heap down at your door you will build me a shining palace out
of it."50 She welcomed his advice but often felt a "cold fear" that he
would not approve of her work and credited him with the ability to
"subdue the natural vulgarity within me."51 His painstaking research
served as a counterweight to her impatient intuitive method. She "never
understood till I knew you what taking the right sort of fruitful pains
meant—one sees so much barren classical effort that I had let myself
grow to despise minute work—& take a sort of stupid pride in splashing
round inaccurately & superficially, & now you show me the beauty of
all that burrowing."52 Jane's research entailed more discipline than she
admitted, but the structure of her relationship with Gilbert required a
certain amount of diffidence.

Although she could be "the usual Doormat," Jane was capable of
pouncing on Gilbert's scholarship. Early on, she chided him for his translation of "Skirophoria," a Greek festival name.

Oh dear, dear! How can you expect an S. S. [Sound Scholar] like me to
"visit with" a person who thinks that Skirophoria means carrying "para-
sols"! Just look into your heart as I looked into mine & see if you cannot find some other meaning more "consonant with the Greek spirit."

Jane insisted that the *skira* referred to sacred objects made of gypsum,
perhaps combined with flour paste, which women carried in processions
during both the Thesmophoria and the Skiraphoria. Scholars generally
accepted the translation of *skira* as "umbrella" or "parasol," but Jane
adhered to her theory of the importance of ritual objects invested with an
aura of sanctity, remarking that "a white umbrella is a slender foundation
for a festival." Later she threatened Gilbert that their "acquaintance must
cease" if he insisted on using another particular translation.53

Gilbert's criticism could send her into a despondency similar in kind,
although not in degree, to her reaction to the earlier criticisms from
Sutherland MacColl. Now, too, she voiced doubts about the validity and
originality of her work. While writing the *Prolegomena*, she sent chap-

ters off to Gilbert for evaluation. When he approved, she was "relieved" because she "had begun to feel it might be all inflated nonsense & would disgust" him. Knowing that he believed "the main issues are worth stating," she could find "faith & courage to pull it more into shape & to look at details—drunkenness & things." In a less confident moment, Jane wrote sadly that she was "so deeply conscious that like S. Paul I know nothing 'by' myself. I always owe what the prefaces call 'the inception of my work' to someone else & it gives me cold misgivings as to whether such second-hand stuff is worth doing at all."[54]

Gilbert's criticism could make her feel "second rate & cheap all over" and as if she were behaving "like the thing I most despise in the world, a half-educated scholiast—piling up odds & ends of information & not taking the time or the trouble to see what they are really worth & how things really were." She asked why she could not

behave with dignity, recognize my limitations of mind & training & keep my second rateness to myself? Something that I have struggled against all my life compels me to write books but at least I needn't inflict my proofs on you. . . . I should like to begin everything all over from the beginning & pray to the Lord for a new mind—My heart is all right—it's my head damn it, & that's the only thing that really matters.

The *Prolegomena*, the cause of this anguish, would be finished "somehow because I am caught in the Wheel of Things," but she had reached the nadir of her confidence in it.[55]

Predictably, her unhappiness touched Gilbert and he responded quickly with encouragement. Jane thanked him for the "kind & most comforting letter" and admitted she may have been "rather morbid" as the result of a "sleepless night" which made things look "black." A. W. Verrall's criticism on another point in the work had hurt as well: "tho he was, as always, angelically kind, I could see that he thought [her discussion of the Erinyes] was all a much ado about scarcely anything, & was puzzled as to why a sane or fairly sane person should write such stuff." She regretted making Gilbert set her "right where I never ought to have gone wrong" and promised not to impose on his time in the future.[56] The next day, however, having "thought about proofs—or rather—which is more to the point . . . slept about them," she sent another batch. "The simple fact," she wrote, "is that your help is too valuable to be given up for conscience sake." She blamed him playfully for the fact that "the whole centre of gravity of the book has shifted"; having begun "as a treatise on Keres with a supplementary notice of Dionysos—it is ending as a screed on Dionysos with an introductory talk about Keres."[57] Furthermore, she feared he would force her to "rewrite most of Dionysos tho' I have watered him down till Semele herself wouldn't know him." Although Jane appreciated Gilbert's aid, unsolicited advice from Frank Darwin led her to remark sulkily that "my book it would seem is being written by everyone except me."[58]

Jane's doubts about her scholarship stemmed from an only vaguely recognized tendency to project her personal conflicts onto her sources. She knew half-consciously that her view of the past and her intuitive understanding of ancient religion and ritual often resulted in less than objective scholarship, which accounted for her doubts about the work. She failed to see, however, that this quality of imaginativeness made her the most interesting and foremost scholar of the group. Because of her empathy for earlier peoples living in an age filled with vague terrors, she evoked more skillfully than the others the liveliness and intensity of the religious experience. Moreover, she synthesized contemporary scholarship, giving her work more depth and breadth than Gilbert Murray's and Francis Cornford's. But scholarship infused with intuitive perception, a quality that her critics associated with women, offended many other scholars and caused Jane a great deal of nagging doubt. Her refusal to recognize how much her own experience shaped her view of the past made her work utterly unselfconscious and therefore both fascinating and relatively easy to interpret, but it also made her uncomfortable during its writing by filling her with nebulous, paralyzing doubts about its validity.

One observer has praised Gilbert Murray as "both [Jane's] master and her pupil" and for his "authority to curb some of her more fantastic flights of fancy." Gilbert himself recognized that she was "a woman of genius." Their mutual respect and admiration made their relationship rewarding both personally and professionally. But another figure cast an even greater shadow over Jane's life and work: the Trinity philosopher and fellow Ritualist Francis Cornford.[59]

# 6

# THE SECOND CIRCLE.
# THE CAMBRIDGE RITUALISTS:
# FRANCIS CORNFORD

*It is [Phaedra's] tragedy that she knows spiritually that the only*
*salvation is the utter blank of the shut door, just the thing intol-*
*erable to her passionate temperament. I suppose that was why she*
*fell in love with Hippolytus whose strength was to shut doors.*
 —*Jane Ellen Harrison to Gilbert Murray, December 1900*

FRANCIS CORNFORD was nearly twenty-five years Jane Harrison's
junior when they met in the late 1890s. He wrote asking her a question about a point made in one of her public lectures, and their
friendship—begun so auspiciously on an intellectual plane—grew from
that exchange. Jane appreciated his interest in her work and their shared
background in the classics, but such attention from a much younger,
attractive man probably pleased her as well. Francis was twenty-six
years old when they met, a tall young man with curly dark hair and
strong features, just exotic enough in appearance that he could not fail to
attract Jane's attention. Gilbert Murray, who met Francis through Jane,
remembered seeing him in her rooms, "listening intently to the lively
discussions, meditative, admiring, & critical, seldom arguing but always—so one felt—taking ideas away with him to think over and consider, & re-examine." Francis's main scholarly interest turned out to be
philosophy, but at an early stage he studied the origins of drama. Since
he and Jane both lived in Cambridge, they were able to work together
easily. They also spent much of their free time together, either taking
the long bicycle rides that became almost legendary events or traveling
together through Britain or on the Continent.[1]

Frances Darwin recalled images of those bicycle rides:

How well I remember the sight of them passing up the Madingley Road
in great leisure (for Jane's health was already not what fifty years of
trading on a magnificent constitution had led her to expect) on their
high old-fashioned bicycles: Francis very upright, with his usual rather
Spanish dignity, she with her sibyl-head (which yet always had an inde-
finable look of a sailor about it) thrown back and a long sea-green or

H. F. Stewart, Gilbert Murray, Francis Cornford (l. to r.), and Jane Harrison in Malting House Garden, Cambridge. Photo by Jessie Stewart. Courtesy of Jean Stewart Pace. Reproduced by Michael Manni Photographic, Cambridge.

silvery scarf blown about her, that somehow managed never actually to
be caught in the mudguard.

Although Cambridge folk thought these outings amusing, Jane treasured
them. Francis entered her life at a critical time: their friendship deep-
ened after R. A. Neil's death. Margaret Verrall considered Jane "rather
silly over FMC—sentimental & undignified," but he filled the void left
by Neil's sudden death.[2]

Jane and Francis traveled extensively together in the early years of
their friendship. Letters to Gilbert Murray and Jessie Stewart from the
coastal towns that Jane so enjoyed or from various European cities indicate that they spent a good deal of time roaming and exploring favorite
places and working on their respective subjects. Jane spent July 1904 in
Surrey, having found "a clean little lodging" with "just room for me &
Mr. Cornford." They traveled to Teckenham for part of the long vacation in 1905 and worked on some of Jane's Orphic studies. She joked
with Gilbert Murray that "I taught Mr. Cornford Hebrew & Phenician
that he might keep *me* straight—& now he is ten times madder than I
am—sometime I must have a long talk with a sane person." That spring,
she and Francis had traveled to Athens, and "the voyage from Marseilles
was like a beautiful dream." On that trip, Francis was "a great comfort—
as much as anyone merely human could be."[3]

In 1906, they visited Chartres and Chinon, where Jane found striking
scenes to describe to Gilbert Murray. He was translating *Medea* then,
and Jane found its violent passion disturbing. She hoped her visit to
medieval sites in Chinon would help her "feel better about Medea"
when she returned.

I expect it is mere physical weakness that gives me such a horror of any
sort of thing involving physical cruelty—I have felt it badly here—you
are shown an exquisite oratory which is all peace & loveliness & before
you know where you are, the guide is showing you instruments of torture & subterranean dungeons & you feel sick for the rest of the day—I
should like to have every monument of a cruel deed razed to the
ground.

Once again Jane's own tangled emotions, simmering beneath her outward calm, made her unusually susceptible to the presence of evil and
cruelty, even when buried in centuries of history. But she also rhapso-
dized over "the portal of the collegiate church of the Holy Bear—who is
Saint-Ours" and praised the Roman Catholic church for being "catholic
in her canonizations."[4]

This idyllic existence began to disintegrate in 1907, when both Jane
and Francis suffered periods of illness. In February, Margaret Verrall
informed Mary Murray of Jane's becoming ill and speculated that it

resulted from a general sense of overwork and unhappiness. Jane was about to leave for the Continent and did not want her condition to interfere with her plans.

Miss Harrison was much better by Monday afternoon & after a good night went off on Tuesday with a friend. She swore by all her gods—and she has more than most of us!—that if she were the least ill on the way she would stop at Dover. Sea air always sets her up. But as no post card has yet reached me, I take it that she was not ill & has gone on to Lucerne at least or perhaps Milan. She has a large & competent companion [probably Francis] & I expect all has gone well. The friend will stay with her till she joins the others, so I feel quite happy. I believe the change is what she really wants; Cambridge does not suit her for long & she had been working very hard to get things finished.[5]

Most interesting is her mention of Jane's unhappiness in Cambridge. After a decade, she still had not resigned herself to her exile from London and spent months on end away from Cambridge. Although her research interests generally justified these lengthy absences, she also used them to protect herself against the threat of stultifying provincialism and the often scurrilous attacks on her scholarship and personal style.

A letter to the Murrays during their visit to the United States in the spring of 1907 chronicled what must have been even more terrifying bouts with illness, although Jane described them good-naturedly enough. "I have been beset by evil Keres since you went," she wrote; "first they brought blindness to my eyes—just like them & the doctor has cut me clean off from Hebrew & hieroglyphics & Sanskrit & forbids me to read by artificial light." Even a temporary deprivation of work disrupted her life. What is more, this mysterious ailment recurred in June 1907 during a visit to Southwold with Francis. He recorded the memory of "coming in one summer afternoon at Southwold, when she had been lying in a long chair looking out at the sea. She told me she had been totally blind for perhaps an hour and she was wrought up by a visionary experience which she described." These eerie incidents are the more fascinating because, although they were probably hysterical in nature, there is no immediate connection to a specific event by which to explain them. This year should have been a relatively peaceful one for Jane. Her only major scholarly work consisted of preparing the second edition of the *Prolegomena*, and the Ritualists were working steadily at important books: Murray on *The Rise of the Greek Epic* (1908) and Francis on *Thucydides Mythistoricus* (1907). At age fifty-seven, Jane may have been suffering the effects of menopause, which could account for some of her symptoms. The other serious illness of this period, though, may also have provoked such a dramatic response.[6]

This, in its way, more sinister occurrence was Francis's sudden attack of appendicitis in May. Jane thoroughly depended on him by now for intellectual and personal companionship, and his illness undoubtedly raised the specter of R. A. Neil's death from the same ailment six years previously. Jane reported Francis's illness lightheartedly after the fact, but she must have been terrified at the thought of his dying. She jokingly rebuked men in general for being "so melodramatic in their illness—they go a long bicycle ride with you one day & the next you find them in bed with doctors & a trained nurse," but concluded thankfully, "he is out of danger now." The Southwold trip in June was designed partly to allow Francis to regain his strength, and Jane altered her plans for a visit with the Murrays in order to accompany him. "It *was* a wrench tho; changing my Oxford date—but it had to be done for you might as well send a cave-bear into lodgings by himself as this poor Mythistorical Man—he is picking up now with this air." Her cheerfulness notwithstanding, Francis described her as "alarmingly nervous sometimes."[7]

Despite Francis's illness and Jane's bout with temporary blindness, the trip did provide some amusement, primarily in the form of a visit from Jane Bury, wife of the classical scholar and King's College fellow J. B. Bury. Francis described her intrusion and gloated over his ability to escape her clutches while Jane bore the brunt of her incessant complaining. They had arrived at Southwold safely, only to find

that Fortune has raised up an evil spirit to torment us in form and voice—especially the voice, ceaseless, unmerciful—like unto Mrs. Bury, who arrived last night with a "migraine" just at dinner time & went to bed. Thereby Jane sits, fast held by the creature's claw, & listens, as a passive bucket, to a whole Iliad of woes, past & present, pumped into her by the remorseless voice which the "migraine" has no way enfeebled. Today the monster has descended to our lower sitting room; and thence Jane emerges from time to time, like a jaded & hunted fish coming up to breathe a mouthful of silence. . . . I am understood to be too weak to bear human society & so have escaped—so far.

It is difficult to imagine Jane so completely at the mercy of another human being: clearly Mrs. Bury's was a personality to be reckoned with. September 1907 found Jane and Francis back at Southwold again, but after that, their travels together not only became more infrequent but also took on a new character.[8]

Jane's relationship to Frances Darwin, who married Francis Cornford in 1909, was of longer standing and greater depth. Ellen Crofts Darwin, Frances's mother, had been Jane's closest friend as a Newnham student and a Newnham fellow and lecturer in English literature until her marriage in 1883. Francis (Frank) Darwin, Frances's father, was one of Charles Darwin's sons and "always apt to suffer from fits of depression," especially after the death of his first wife, Amy Ruck, in childbirth. Jane was evidently fond of Frank Darwin, often referring to him as an "old bear," but she loved Ellen Crofts even more.[9]

Gwen Raverat, Ellen's niece, described her as "reserved," observing that "it seemed to be difficult to Aunt Ellen to be warm and open to the ordinary lowbrow inhabitants of the world." She had cut her hair short, always looking "picturesque and charming," and smoked cigarettes with Jane and Alice Dew-Smith. They often played games like "making rhymes about their friends, or comparing them to animals or plants or puddings," and "seemed . . . wonderfully up to date and literary." But Ellen Crofts possessed an air of melancholy that neither her close friends nor her family could explain. Nevertheless, Jane called Ellen "the friend whom I chose for myself" and their friendship lasted until Ellen's death in 1903.[10]

Jane frequently visited Wychfield, the Darwins' Cambridge home, so she watched Frances grow up. Frances recalled,

I can hardly remember a time when "Aunt Jane" was not a part of my existence. It became a custom for her to lunch with my parents almost every Sunday in term. Even as a child I felt she gave roast beef and Yorkshire pudding a particular glow and she went to the head of any intelligent adolescent like champagne.

But, virtually from the beginning, rivalry and competitiveness shadowed their relationship. In her collection of notes on Jane's life, Hope Mirrlees recorded some extraordinary passages from Jane's letters to Frances, the originals of which are not among Jane's correspondence. In one very moving letter, Jane described an incident from Frances's childhood that proved how early in her life Frances began to feel threatened by Jane's ubiquitous presence in the Darwin home.

One afternoon I went in to see your mother when she was reading to you & she told you to wait because it was business—& you went off & lay under the piano & literally glared at me. Your mother took it very hardly, she came out to the door with me & said what *am* I to do Frances is jealous of you—it is terrible—& I laughed (I was very breezy & unmorbid in those days & I said)—It's quite clear what we've got to do, we must never let that adorable little mite suffer on my account—& I never came again at those hours.

This touching excerpt illustrates both Frances's pain and jealousy and Jane's defeat at the hands of yet another family circle that steadfastly refused to revolve continually around her. Ellen reacted to this incident as if both Frances and Jane were her daughters, and Jane may well have designed their relationship that way. She spoke of Ellen Crofts in terms she reserved for descriptions of her own mother. Ellen may have represented the good mother to Jane, and she would be reluctant to share her good mother with Frances. That dynamic had been established before Frances's birth, and it is hard to tell from Jane's memory of the event who felt more jealous of whom. The Darwins provided safe haven for her, as did the Murrays. The main difference is that whereas she felt jealous of Gilbert's wife, in the Darwin case she felt jealous of Ellen's daughter. In the competition for Ellen's affection and attention, her daughter won. Family ties once again proved stronger than intellectual and spiritual ones.[11]

The weekly dinners at Wychfield continued until Ellen's death when Frances was seventeen. The shock proved too much for both Frank and Frances Darwin, who "fled to London to escape a home without her." Frances " 'started vehemently working at an art school.' " The frenetic pace could not divert her attention for long, however, and she suffered a total breakdown that seems to have lasted for four years. Jane bore Ellen's death with a resigned stoicism. She told Gwen Raverat, " 'I could not be sorry when Ellen died, because she was so unhappy; though I don't know why. She loved her husband and child, and had everything she wanted in the world.' " Frances had a much harder time coming to grips with her mother's death, but after several futile remedies and a rest cure, she returned to Cambridge at Christmas, 1906, apparently recovered. With renewed vitality Jane found "almost frightening," she threw herself into the study of Greek as Jane's pupil. While awaiting Frances's return, Jane had written to her:

Very soon you will be back & I shall see you face to face & that will be great joy. . . . What a long bad time you have had—but it is nearly over—I sometimes wonder how much of you, the old you is left, there will certainly be a new you to get to know after all this—but that will be a fresh joy.

Jane, no stranger to depression, understood the trauma Frances had faced, but Frances's return to Cambridge set off a chain of events that culminated in the most profound depression Jane ever experienced.[12]

In the spring of 1907, Jane had given a "small tea-party" to introduce Frances to Francis, whose *Microcosmographia Academica*, a satirical look at academic life, she had read and enjoyed. After Frances's miraculous recovery later that year, the two began to see more of each other. In Frances's memory, "Jane Harrison seemed determined to thrust us together. I was her newest human discovery and plaything and she was delighted that it should entertain him as well." Jane probably did mean to thrust the two together, albeit unconsciously. She sabotaged her relations with men all the more efficiently the more they meant to her, and Francis meant a great deal to her. He also remarked rather bitterly on Jane's propensity for directing other people's lives. "I often thought she did not know what I was really like. Did she ever know what any of her friends were really like, or did she rather see them as symbols and assign them parts in the drama of her life?" Whatever Jane's motivation, she surely had not foreseen her own feelings when the two young people fell in love.[13]

Passages from Jane's letters to Frances Darwin collected by Hope Mirrlees offer the closest look at the actual events leading up to Frances and Francis's marriage in 1909. More letters to Gilbert Murray and other friends provide mostly oblique references to her actual despair, but they offer evidence of how long she suffered with her great unhappiness and its concomitant ill health. For the most part, she remained extraordinarily reticent about the specifics of her love for Francis and the sense of betrayal she felt when he married Frances. Even her letters to Gilbert Murray rarely referred to either of them by name. But Hope Mirrlees's notebook and the extracts of letters to Frances Darwin give concrete evidence that Jane was in love with Francis and felt devastated when he married Frances.

Although the notebook contains only fragments of letters in Hope Mirrlees's own writing and makes no direct mention of their recipient, clearly they were written to Frances Darwin. The letters, despondent, angry, and forgiving by turns, trace the chain of events leading up to the marriage and give a clear idea of Jane's attitudes toward work and love.[14] When Sutherland MacColl married, Jane had convinced herself that she could put aside all emotional and potential sexual attachments to men. She admitted later, however, "When I came back to Cambridge . . . I met a man over my work again & fell deeply in love with him more hopelessly & intensely than ever before." Presumably this statement refers to Neil. The details are murky, but some unnamed "disaster" intervened and "it was more & more imperative I should be separated from the man I did love & more & more I took refuge in the new friendship with ———." This blank must stand for Francis, whose relationship with Jane began as an intellectual friendship. She does not seem to refer here to Neil's death, but perhaps the intervening decades had clouded her memory of the exact order of events. She continues: "Then somehow I drifted into the most beautiful happiness I have ever known—I never consciously fell in love but bit by bit I came to depend entirely on him." He wrote her a letter that "made me feel that things were on a different footing & that he would never marry & that our sort of unmarried-married life would be for always." Hope Mirrlees added that Jane "thought of suggesting they should marry, but just then gossips began to talk & things at Newnham became a little difficult for her—& from sheer pride she wouldn't." One can easily imagine what the Cambridge ladies would have to say about a middle-aged woman nursing a passion for a man nearly twenty-five years her junior. But when Francis fell ill (presumably the appendicitis attack), Jane discovered that her feeling for him was "not friendship but the deepest love." In her words, "I seemed to have found myself married in spirit before I woke up to love."

As Frances and Francis grew closer beginning in early 1908, Jane became increasingly anxious and depressed. Her doctor, Christopher Wheeler, failed to perceive that her poor health resulted from an emotional trauma and advised her "to take more & more exercise," scheduling her for surgery to correct a podiatric problem to facilitate such activity. However, "more & more the frightful nameless nervousness that comes with sclerosis grew on me—till I could sometimes scarcely bear Francis to leave me even to go for a walk." Hope claims that "it was at this stage (i.e., her frightful nervousness soothed by F. [Francis] yet very trying for him) that ——— [Frances] came back [from treatment in Switzerland]."

Jane expected Frances to require a great deal of care because of the long time it took for Frances to cope with her mother's death. But within a year of her return from Switzerland, the rest cure (or rather, an internal psychological process) healed her and allowed her to resume an active life. Jane wanted Frances, in Hope's words, "to be a spiritual daughter to them both," stating, "I felt that F. [Francis] would help me to help you. . . . I always felt as if F. was years older & maturer than I am." The crisis reached a peak when Frances and Francis discovered they were in love.

Hope Mirrlees described the crisis tersely in her own words and with excerpts from Jane's letters to Frances. Jane was to have surgery and "before operation writes letter in case of her death under ether telling him [Francis] F. loves him. After operation destroys the letter & writes another, she feels he must find out for himself that F. loves him." In a letter to Frances, Jane admitted that she "lied even to him & said I did not know whether you cared—I put it on him I said I felt almost sure he cared (which was *not* true) & that he must not let the tie between us ever hamper him." After the operation, Francis escorted Jane to Devonshire, but Jane "gradually feels more & more that his heart is elsewhere & that she is only a duty," as Hope described it. Jane recalled that she "had had the foolish dream that love of one woman need not diminish the closeness of friendship with another." Although Francis "was always about me nursing me & helping me yet he was somehow gone. . . . I seemed to have come back from Death to great weakness just to find the man I always called my 'Rock of Ages' slipping away from me." Once Francis discovered Frances's feelings toward him, Hope asserted, Jane decided to "play providence" as she feared Frances "might go mad." In Jane's own words to Frances, "I was thinking of you then far beyond myself, far beyond him—perhaps as regards him & me I felt we were too closely linked for anything even his marriage to separate us." Jane described her feelings toward Frances: "three parts of one's love is an instinct of protection—a feeling that at all costs one cannot hurt that it is mean to hurt a thing weaker & younger than oneself." As Jane would discover, she herself, although older and unafflicted by an instability so obvious as Frances's, was in reality more vulnerable than the young woman she wanted so desperately to protect.

The final heartbreak occurred when Francis wrote a letter proposing to Frances. After he sent it off, Hope stated, Jane "breaks down & tells him that she herself loves him." No evidence of Francis's response survives, but the hopelessness and fear that drove Jane to make such a futile gesture cannot be overstated. Again, it was uncharacteristic of her to reveal such emotion, and the fact that she actually admitted to a love based not on intellectual compatibility or mutual interest but on genuine passion proves that even she could not deny the strength of her emotions. Up until his engagement, she did not regard the twenty-five-year difference in their ages as an obstacle, for she identified so closely with his generation and had always surrounded herself with younger friends. It was only after the engagement and marriage that Jane began to address questions of age and youth. Along with Francis's rejection, her failing health and her menopause undoubtedly contributed to her finally coming to grips with her age: when Frank Darwin sent word to Francis that Frances would soon be accepting his marriage proposal, Jane suffered her first attack of "pseudo-angina."

Frances Darwin gave her own interpretation of the triangle in 1908. She was a talented artist and presented as a Christmas gift to Francis a drawing modeled on a Greek vase painting (see illustration). The drawing shows four figures, clearly identifiable as Frances, Francis, Frank Darwin, and Jane. The young woman stooping ostensibly to sacrifice a pig is Frances. Francis stands behind her, holding a pig roughly in his outstretched hand. Frank Darwin follows, cuddling a pig lovingly in his arms. Jane brings up the rear of the procession, holding her pig tightly on a leash. All the members of the group would have been familiar with the Greek use of the pig as a symbol for female genitalia, and Frances's drawing provides a wry commentary on each person's attitude toward female sexuality—more specifically, toward her own sexuality.[15]

Hope Mirrlees commented at the beginning of her collection of the letters from Jane to Frances that Jane "had always hoped that Sir F. [Francis Darwin], he [Francis Cornford] & Frances & she would all go off on holidays together, & sometimes he & she alone." In the passage that follows, Jane explained to Frances Darwin how difficult it was for her to comprehend Francis's willingness to relinquish their common work and focus instead on a wife.

Drawing by Frances Darwin, presented as Christmas gift to Francis Cornford, 1908. Courtesy of Christopher Cornford. Reproduced by Michael Manni Photographic, Cambridge.

It was very hard indeed to me at first to realize that there could be anything worth calling a marriage with a community of work—I mean actual specialist work. . . . Even after you were engaged my dream of the solution of the difficulty was to teach you Greek & for us all three to work together.

Jane then wrote poignantly that she felt "that thing after thing had been wrenched from me or offered to me on condition I shared them." This single sentence evokes the image of a much younger Jane, a frightened little girl desolate at her father's second marriage, which required her to share him with a stepmother and, eventually, a large family. Decades later, death had claimed R. A. Neil immediately following their decision to marry. Even her mother had been "wrenched" from her by death: the pattern had persisted from the earliest days of her life.

Frances's response is unknown, but whatever it was, it led Jane to make an uncharacteristically direct attack, incidentally making a striking point about her nature and Frances's.

Of course you understand ———, you & she are by nature birds of prey, you pounce straight down on what you want & eat it up & the devil take the other birds—isn't it so? I knew it was. Well if we are two birds of prey, the Old Eagle, & the Young One shall we try at least not to prey on each other? The Old Eagle would like to try—for she loves her Young One.

In a "later letter," Jane recognized the reality of the situation and steeled herself to become reconciled to the new order.

So we must face both of us, all three of us, the fact that my loneliness may be for life. It isn't I know that I am specially weak in moral cour- age, it [is] just that life is ebbing & with it the power to change & grow new spiritual tissues—One's life lives longest in one's brain & so my only life is really there now. . . . And also tho the loneliness is there & almost always aches, all the bitterness went in that miracle & has never come back—it has tried to once or twice, mechanically I have felt the old misery against you but it goes now directly—& that is due in part to the miracle but also in part to you—to the faith I have in you & your tenderness towards me.

Hope Mirrlees closed this section of her notes with Jane's attempt "to find consolation in work." Jane wrote to Frances that "I began to have horrible nightmares of you dancing with lights & flowers—coming to fetch ———, & me left all broken & desolate." The dream symbolism was wrenchingly clear, but Hope gave the story a happy ending. "After [the] marriage, things improved for her. Once more he [Francis] became interested in work & she felt that he wanted her again . . . & soon *Themis* was under way & things began to open out in the wonderful way they do." Jane's other correspondence tells a different story: one of inces- sant pain and anguish relieved only by driving herself to work more frenetically.

Augustus John divined the full measure of Jane's grief over the Darwin-Cornford marriage and incorporated it in his portrait of her which now hangs in the Senior Combination Room at Newnham Col- lege. Unlike the distinguished founders who appear in traditionally stiff poses and glare ominously from the walls of the Fellows' Dining Room, Jane languishes full length on a sofa with her Wilson Steer painting "Yachts," symbolizing her love for the sea, hanging in the background. It is a sad, tired face that gazes out from the canvas, and Jane is clothed not in her customary blue-greens or shimmering colors but rather in black, with a green shawl draped around her neck and flowing to the floor. John painted the portrait in the summer of 1909, his unconven- tional appearance and personality providing the only highlight in the otherwise unendurable summer of Frances and Francis's marriage. He remembered that, while sitting for the portrait, Jane "smoked innumera- ble cigarettes and talked learnedly with Gilbert Murray." Jane's old friend, Sutherland MacColl, had suggested John as the artist for her portrait, and Jane thanked him for his advice while invoking memories of a time long past. "I remembered how you used to scowl over something that was amiss with the drawing in the corners of my eyes, and so I thought you would know who could best cope with these ineluctable difficulties." She approved of John because "he has seen the vision of the Beauty of Ugliness, and, which is still harder, of Plainness." Even at sixty years of age, Jane was anything but plain, but well-bred modesty combined with great despair made her downplay her own worth. She joked, "I *am* now just what you used to amuse yourself by *making* me into some 20 years ago!"[16]

Later that summer, Jane expanded on her opinion of Augustus John. She "felt spiritually at home with him from the first moment he came into the room." His presence cheered her considerably:

He came to Cambridge in two vans with 6 horses, 7 sons, and I was never quite clear how many wives. I asked the chief one to come and see me, but she couldn't or wouldn't. . . . He was perfect to sit to; he never fussed me or posed but did me just as I lay in the chair, where I have mostly lain for months. I look like a fine distinguished prize-fighter, who has had a vision and collapsed under it. . . . He wanted a background, so I suggested my Steer. He seized it and spent two days working away at it in utter oblivion. I now look as if I was an episode in its career.

She described herself aptly, for despite her striking appearance she was clearly in both physical and psychological pain.[17]

Jane demonstrated her conflicting emotions toward Francis through her difficulty in finding the right name for him. Frances Darwin asserted that his private name was "Zeus," but Jane herself expounded on her inability to arrive at the all-important name. She had tried "Frank," "Comus" (for his role in the 1908 Newnham production of *Comus*), and "Francis," but found all of them unsatisfactory. Before Frances appeared in the picture, Jane had come close to discovering the name that would give her a sense of control over him, but those days were gone. The following letter to Frances Darwin, which dates from late 1908 or early 1909, indicates that Jane had begun to reconcile herself to their engagement.

"Francis" will do quite well as a label for Francis—Comus cannot go on & "Frank" I always flatly declined to call him. I don't like the name *in itself* & all its associations for me are round yr father—tho it expresses him as little as it expresses "Francis." In time I daresay I shall get used to saying the label name, & he had better label me in the family "Jane" tho he has never called me that in his life. Long ago as I daresay he has told you he announced by letter (he always announces everything by letter) that he meant to call me Shvah, which is Hebrew for the Queen of Sheba. It was because . . . but you know yr Bible [*sic*]. So then I fell into calling him Shlomoh (accent on the last syllable) which is Hebrew for Solomon. So if you want to understand our signatures you will have to learn one Hebrew letter . . . he *is* very wise. Long before that when we were in Greece together he got called the Bear—I will show you some-day the photograph that will explain why he was called that—& then Shlomoh became the name of the he-Bear because it is soft & padding & fumbles and shuffles—but these names & great truths are known only to me & him & you.

This touching chronicle of the naming process shows just how far Jane and Francis had drifted apart after such promising beginnings. The transformation from "the Bear" to "Francis" reflects the growing distance between them.[18]

Her difficulty also in finding a proper name for Frances illustrates the extent of her conflicting emotions toward her, which resulted from continual competition for attention from the same people. The tension between them transcended even that between Jane and Francis because, unlike the latter, Jane and Frances had no history of knowing, however briefly, each other's "totemic" names. In the letter to Frances cited above, Jane pursued the logic of naming to its inexorable conclusion:

I think you & I have felt about for names for each other & never found them. Frances doesn't somehow mean much to me. I think that is why I shorten it to F. But it means a remembrance as it was a great deal to yr mother. I shall perhaps some day find the right beast for you but it certainly isn't a bear. You haven't a scrap of one in you, wch is odd because yr father has.

Yet Frances remembered a time when Jane had identified her with bears. Jessie Stewart quotes Frances as saying, "it is odd now to recollect that she very often called me Old One, which was also her nickname for . . . the small endearing woolly bear . . . who lived in a sort of shrine of her mantelpiece." Jane once viewed Frances benevolently, but after she intruded on Jane's relationship with Francis, she quickly replaced past kindly identification with chilling distance.[19]

Jane's relationship with Francis Cornford proved the most spectacular failure of all her complicated attachments to men. The depth of her feeling replicated her emotional tie to Sutherland MacColl, but she acted out the experience on a far grander scale. Moreover, she was much more vulnerable and less resilient in her fifties than she had been in her thirties, and the great betrayal devastated her. Francis compounded the injury of never reciprocating her affection by the insult of marrying the daughter of her closest friend, to whom she had introduced him. Hope implies that Jane experienced her illnesses first and that Francis withdrew from her and gravitated toward Frances because of the strain of caring for Jane. It is just as likely that Jane unconsciously drove him away by engineering his romance with Frances. Her own great passion for him did not prevent her from encouraging his attraction to Frances in order to protect herself against feeling so intensely about him. In fact, she may have deliberately encouraged their relationship in order to destroy her fantasy herself, before Francis had the chance to do so. Regardless, Jane's physical health remained so poor for so long during and after the Darwin-Cornford courtship that her illnesses must have been related to the stress of genuine grief.

Jane counted as her greatest agony the end of her intellectual partnership with Francis. Although she loved him desperately, she knew unconsciously that the strongest bond between them lay in their mutual interest in each other's work. She believed the intellectual bond to be the strongest, and Francis's betrayal shattered the small universe in which she resided at the center and watched her colleagues revolve around her. Nevertheless, the fact remains that Jane ultimately experienced Francis's marriage to Frances as a betrayal less because of their intellectual friendship than because she was very much in love with him herself.

The ultimate reconciliation between Jane and Frances should not be taken as evidence of a final, peaceful resolution of the matter. Betrayed and abandoned, as she thought, and still unconsciously angry over her mother's death, her father's remarriage, and a succession of failed romances, Jane could no longer contain her anger against Francis. To see the extent of that anger, one has only to look at her most impressive work, *Themis*, which she wrote while trying to face up to the reality of her new status as maiden aunt to the man whom she loved so deeply. Letters and reminiscences testify to Jane's conscious attempts to come to grips with the great betrayal; *Themis* offers proof that for Jane, as she had claimed for Phaedra, "there were some facts you must *not* face, still less repent of."[20] Her refusal to face her anger head-on, while causing her almost unendurable anguish, drove her to create her most absorbing work. Turning her anguish into scholarship required prodigious mental effort, but Jane was not yet finished with Francis. *Themis* is not so much a study of Greek religion as a repudiation of the Victorian society that had thwarted her every desire and taken from her every close relationship she had ever had. *Themis* derives its power from the extraordinary energy that infuses every page. The next chapter explores the work itself; for the moment, the complex psychological process that turned personal rage into both chronic illness and innovative scholarship must be examined.

After the vague but unsettling ailments of 1907, Jane began to suffer from more serious complaints in the next year. Jessie Stewart often could not date letters any more precisely than by the year in which they were written, but since Frances and Francis started courting in 1908 it is relatively safe to assume that Jane's illness coincided with the growth of their mutual affection. Early on, she was in high spirits, and she described encounters with doctors and their advice lightheartedly to the Murrays. She made light of her symptoms, warning Gilbert not to "think I am a malade imaginaire or otherwise," but evinced concern by stating her intention "as soon as I can get my head above business to see an *all* round doctor to try [illegible] if he can cure me of extreme shortness of breath &—I believe the two are the same—attacks of abject nervousness. . . . I have leisure to get well in next term if I knew how—talk of egotism."[21]

Gilbert recommended his own osteopathic physician, Christopher Wheeler, to her. She thanked him for the reference, saying she had "to bless your holy name—I did like your Dr. Wheeler." Wheeler suspected a heart ailment, and Jane announced to Gilbert that "it is my heart that is playing the fool—I thought it was—he talks of Nanheim [for a rest cure] but I am to see him in 3 weeks again & then something I suppose will be decided." She confided that "he says I am to drink rather less than more whiskey!" Jane wanted to avoid a visit to Nanheim and had "high hopes I shan't be sent"; the "two drugs" the doctor prescribed enabled her to report that "the last two mornings I woke up *not* fainting," and she expressed hope that the medication would prove effective. It must have done, for Dr. Wheeler did not send her to Nanheim for a rest. Jane told Gilbert, "I *do* like Dr. Wheeler—& I am sure his multitudinous drops & tabloids are doing me good—I am sure he takes extra trouble with me because he has a Murray-cult!"[22]

Dr. Wheeler referred her to a Dr. Robert Jones for the operation on her feet that would enable her to exercise more.

How fierce & violent are the sons of Aesculapius—Mr. Robert Jones
wants my two great toes for his own—I wish they would be content
with just playing on the lyre like your namesake.

It seems I have rheumatoid arthritis in them & the joints are
"cusped"—I swell with pride at this because it shows that in temperament I am like AWV—but it *is* a nuisance because I must either have
them both operated on which means not walking for 6 weeks or I must
have eternal iron bars below all my boots & shoes & even then never be
sure it won't get worse.

By the end of the letter her tone had changed considerably from the eager description of her exotic ills:

I shall have it [the operation] done if Dr. Wheeler will let me but he
rather shook his head over chloroform—I am afraid he is not satisfied

with me. I am "flabby" with a flabby heart—it is disgusting. . . . Well
my vile body *is* disgusting. . . . Do tell me something nice I feel so sodden and depressed.

She frequently expressed such melancholy thoughts over the next four
years. Her increased reliance on medication probably played some part
in her despair, although the root cause appears to have been her emotional turmoil.[23]

In May, Jane's heart had responded to treatment and her improvement
averted the rest visit to Nanheim. Dr. Wheeler pronounced her "heart
performances" as "most creditable & even distinguished" and discovered that her only problem was "an 'area of leakage' in a valve which
makes me have to do most of my work twice over." In a revealing note
to Mary Murray, Jane praised Dr. Wheeler as "the only doctor I have ever
met who took a real interest in making one better when one hasn't
anything very particular the matter. Generally doctors are so bored with
that." She credited him with having "quieted down my heart a bit" and
made her "considerably less nervous—I find that I don't dwell on tire-
some things half as much & I even sometimes forget them!" This passage is noteworthy as a rare instance of Jane's admitting both that her
ailments were subordinate to the general sense of fear and anxiety she
often experienced and that these ailments may have been psychological
as much as physiological in origin.[24]

Jane's growing depression coincided with the production of *Comus* at
Newnham, in the summer of 1908, that drew Frances and Francis together. Francis acted the part of Comus and Frances helped behind the
scenes. This production was the first by a new dramatic society at
Newnham that Jane described as "fathered by Mr. Cornford & maiden-
aunted by me." In June, Jane again thanked Gilbert Murray for sending
her to Dr. Wheeler, reiterating her belief that "he has done something to
stop my heart & nerves playing the fool—I no longer feel that if I am
going out to dinner I must commit suicide before I dress." Although this
letter reveals a precarious mental state, she usually hid the depths of her
despair very effectively.[25]

As she prepared for the operation on her feet during July 1908 by
composing the letter to Francis telling him of Frances's affection for
him, she also wrote to Gilbert Murray of Margaret Verrall's interest in
observing her under anesthesia for purposes of psychical research. "May
Verrall is going to be with me when I come *to*—she is going to suggest
things to me when I am subconscious & see what occurs." She worried
over being anesthetized and told Gilbert she was "steadily remembering
that you said taking ether was your one blissful chance of getting drunk
& I shall see if I can look at it in the same light."[26] Soon after the
operation, after which she destroyed the original letter to Francis and

substituted one in which she disavowed knowledge of Frances's feelings toward him, she admitted to Gilbert that "taking the ether was quite a nice treat, tho' I didn't feel as if I was getting drunk." Francis wrote this letter for her from the hospital, since she was still too weak to write. "I could write today," she asserted, "but they won't let me, because, when I was doing my back hair this morning, I dissolved into floods of tears— not because it was sparse & grey ... but for the sheer pathos of the thing." In addition to her anxiety and uncertainty about Francis and Frances, her gray hair must have reminded her that at her age she could not hope to compete with the young Frances. It is no wonder she could not hold back the tears.[27]

Despite her misery, Jane wrote cheerfully to Jessie Stewart, passing along encouraging words to a friend of Jessie's who faced an operation and also feared anesthesia. With Francis and A. B. Cook working on proofs with her while she was still in the hospital, she appeared content.[28] Francis escorted her to Devonshire to convalesce and Jane wrote a sprightly postcard to Frances Darwin from Braunton. "I know Comus sent you news so this is only one word in my own paw. I wish all day you were here. I can walk from room to room proudly rejecting all proffered paws but upstairs is still a poor business." She was working on a paper on " 'divine dickie birds' for the Oxford Congress. I dictate it to Comus & he sniffs & groans at every other word." Gilbert Murray presented another view of Jane's progress, writing to Jessie Stewart that "Miss Harrison seemed to me at first a good deal pulled down; but since she has begun to get about in a bath-chair she has improved. . . . To-day she seems very bright." Gilbert may have had a better idea of Jane's experience simply because she seems to have confided in him more than in anyone else.[29]

Once again Jane's destruction of her personal papers frustrates the search for her feelings during this period. Her letters to Gilbert Murray tell only part of the story of her despair over the Francis-Frances affair, and her feelings on the matter can only be extrapolated from her somewhat cryptic writings to the Murrays. The letters do reveal, at least, how greatly she suffered and the extent to which anxiety, depression, and rigidly controlled anger damaged her health. As Francis and Frances created their own circle, Jane wrote thanking Gilbert for what must have been a kind response to a sad letter. "I wrote in great despondency, everything seemed crumbling away—but I know you will *not* crumble." She craved work to take her mind off the painful present and admitted that if some unnamed group would request work from her "it would compel me to write & work & I seem only to be able to do it now under compulsion." As the autumn of 1908 approached, Jane had to face the inevitable loss of Francis: in October, he became engaged to Frances Darwin.[30]

Frances described the engagement in a letter to Mary Murray as "the best thing in all the world that could happen to me, it's like suddenly coming to life. . . . I didn't know it was possible to feel so happy or so sure. It is very wonderful." The engagement proved so traumatic to Jane that she fled Cambridge for Yorkshire, which turned out to be a mistake. She "escaped here to a parsonical sister's [Elizabeth Lane's home in the Yorkshire coast town of Bridlington]" as she "felt I could not bear to be a blot on the sunshine—& now they are gone together to Hunstanton [a seaside resort on the Norfolk coast] & all is well with them." However, "for me coming here was a mistake—the feeling that I belong to no-one, least of all to my own kin is so keen." Her only remaining tie seemed to be to Gilbert Murray, to whom she wrote:

I go back next Tuesday the 6th & then to work that is my one hope—
Oh *how* I miss you—coming in twice a day bringing sanity & gentleness
with you & above all the sense of a steadfast friend—I cannot be quite
lonely while the Ther lives on in his chthonic cave & lets me babble of
mimes & magic. . . . I like to have postcards just to make me feel you
are there. I can't *write* about things. I shall worry on.

Once again, Gilbert satisfied Jane's need to belong without making her painfully aware of the distance between them. Distance from Gilbert seemed appropriate and necessary. Visiting her family, though, only reinforced her awareness of how far she had traveled beyond them and Yorkshire.[31]

Jane brooded over the irony of having introduced Francis to Frances and offered two strikingly different interpretations of her role to Gilbert Murray and to Frances's cousin, Ruth Darwin. She wrote as cheerfully as possible to Ruth:

Yes it is a most blessed thing & very blessed to have been cast for the
part of deus ex machina. I don't think my own child could be dearer to
me than Frances & I know now she is safe as human strength & goodness can make her—I know him far better than I know her & of course
the whole thing from his side is ancient history to me as ancient as
Comus himself! that makes it none the less perfect to have it settled.
Of course when they are married they will be lost to this world—that
we must be prepared for—I do hope this my first triumphant appearance
will not turn me into a chronic "deus ex!"[32]

Jane tried to protect herself from her own emotions by distancing herself from Frances Darwin, toward whom she then felt her greatest anger. She had known Frances from her childhood, and she was lying brazenly to Ruth when she denied their long history. She sounded an old theme here, one she revived in later essays appearing in *Alpha and Omega*. Just as her father's remarriage had turned his attention from her because of the "blinding sex delusion," Francis would be lost to her through his marriage.

If Jane managed to put on a good face for Ruth, she let down her guard to Gilbert. "Letters of congratulations begin to pour in upon me & I must take up my role of *deus ex machina*," she wrote; "I never felt it an inspiring part but you will help me to understand it."[33] Needless to say, the confusion and sorrow she expressed more clearly described her true feelings over the dubious distinction of having brought the happy couple together.

A week later, Jane wrote morbidly to Mary Murray: "I am much better for chronic [illegible], but I still shun hot rooms & in fact all evening things. I don't feel as if I could ever face a long proper dinner again & indeed why should one? They are vile inventions." Her only solace lay in bicycling, to which she had returned after recovering from her operation. Resolving to put the past behind her, Jane would the next day "begin interviewing 'first year' archaeologists—& then turn with a clear mind to put things in order for my new book." Despite her ambition, the next month found her still in "constant *slight* physical pain—it is only slight but none of Dr. Wheeler's medicines so far touch it." She was strong enough to visit the Murrays in Oxford, but begged "no dinings out *please* for me."[34]

Jane reacted emotionally to another event of November 1908, when Gilbert Murray decided to forgo the honor of presenting the Gifford Lectures in Edinburgh. He had intended to talk on "Ancient Religion and Modern Anthropology," but his duties as Regius Professor at Oxford demanded too much of his time and he abandoned the plan. Jane, who had been delirious at the prospect of the boost the series would give their common work, was crushed.

What *can* I say? I hoped the Professorship would give you more leisure for other work not less—It is such a crushing disappointment that you should give up the Gifford lectures that I cannot look at it with clear eyes—but that is just rank selfishness just the wish that for a time you should be looking at things more from my angle so as to help *me!* . . . The gist of the disappointment is to me—that I feel you will drift away from mythology & religion & *origines*—you see there are only two people who are scholars & with literary minds who understand that these things are at the back of everything—FMC here for Cambridge—& I hoped you for Oxford—The specialists don't count—they grub up the facts but don't see the relations—& it would have been so splendid that you as Professor should give those lectures.

But again I say I can't see clearly perhaps there are tears in my eyes. Follow your own conviction of what is best for work & I will not uselessly lament.[35]

With Francis rapidly losing interest in their joint work, Jane could barely face the future if Gilbert withdrew from the circle as well. At this bleak juncture, she fell back on a familiar pattern of response to crisis: she fled Cambridge for her beloved coastal retreat of Aldeburgh in Suffolk. During her several months away, she sank into a profound depression and then gathered strength to channel her deep anger at Francis's betrayal, never directly articulated, into the work that was taking shape in her mind.

Judging by her letters to the Murrays, it is astounding that Jane recovered at all. Before leaving Cambridge for Aldeburgh in mid-December 1908, she wrote to Mary that her condition kept her confined to bed. "I am in bed still & am to be till Friday—Rogers [a new doctor] will not let me stir till the last heart pain is gone." Dr. Rogers "diagnosed me exactly the same as Dr. Wheeler," but prescribed instead "rest rest & take a long course of Iodide of Potassium." Jane longed to leave Cambridge, being "sure I want sea." She wrote from the Darwin home at 13 Madingley Road, and without doubt, having Frances Darwin as her nurse exacerbated her illness. Moreover, the "most excellent parlour maid," who was helping to look after her, along with the "equally excellent cook" were "carefully training Frances in housekeeping." Small wonder that Jane could barely wait for Rogers to pronounce her fit enough to travel to Suffolk.[36]

In mid-December, Jane finally escaped to Aldeburgh with her close friend Alys Russell. Jessie Stewart described Jane as retiring "wounded, after physical and mental strain, to Aldeburgh," which understates the severity of her depression.[37] She did not mention the immediate cause, which was the impending marriage. Jane, trying to derive solace from her visit to the usually replenishing Aldeburgh haunt, wrote Gilbert Murray about her discovery of "the Great-good Place—a huge balcony sheltered on 3 sides where I lie all day long." In this idyllic setting even he "would be warm for the sun is shining brightly & white gulls are flapping." She urged him to visit there during the summer, for "there is just room for you & me & Rosalind," obviously the only company she could bear.[38] Despite the fine weather and her propinquity to her "great sea-mother," Jane did not recuperate.[39] Christmas, traditionally an unhappy time for her, found her "ordered another fortnight complete inertia" and "at the bottom of a pit of exhaustion," although she had "no pangs." She ended wearily, "shall I ever get my head up."[40] Her annual birthday letter to Gilbert, written on December 29, 1908, for his birthday on January 2, 1909, touched on the power of work to heal one's soul.

I heard a Darwin story the other day that I liked—the butler was overheard saying to a visiting [illegible] "Master thinks he's ill but it's my opinion if he had something to occupy his mind with he'd be all right."

It is a great thing to be a butler & *have* to clean the silver however sick you feel—but I am feeling less sick—only I seem to have dropped into a pit of exhaustion where there is nothing within reach—that is one's vile body I suppose.

Thankful for his friendship, she closed wistfully, "I believe life for you is pretty full now & I am glad of that," and with the wish that he "live as long as I do & much longer."[41]

Her illness left her time to brood over the abrupt changes in circumstance, and she began to steel herself to the reality of Francis's engagement and his diminishing interest in their work. Still unreconciled to his betrayal, however, she lashed out at him indirectly in a letter to Frances Darwin.

About work. Yes the world *is* a ruthless place & sex the most ruthless thing in it. Thank you for seeing that. I am just now faced by the blank unalterable fact that for more than 6 months Francis has not cared & could not care at all for the work that has been for years our joint life & friendship—but I have faith to believe it may not always be so. While it *is* so it is better that he & I should not be together. I also absolutely believe that you reverence work—tho' you could as yet not understand nor can he how—late in life—work & friendship come to be the whole of life.[42]

At this stage, Jane still clung to the belief that Francis would eventually regain his interest in their work, a necessary illusion. If "work & friendship" were to be the whole of life, she could not face the loss of her closest colleague, even if he had failed at the other roles in which she had cast him.

In an effort to overcome her illness, Jane launched a campaign to convince herself of its physiological root. While apologizing to Mary for her "disgraceful behavior" during a visit to the Murrays' in early 1909, she admitted the strain she had been under but attributed her condition to physical causes. The letter is lengthy but bears close scrutiny, for it demonstrates the supreme effort required to deny the depth of her depression and the force of her anger to transform anxiety into illness.

I wanted to tell you—partly to apologize for my really disgraceful behavior when I was with you—that I am now convinced that the whole business of the heart pain was far more physical than I or Dr. Wheeler thought. What has convinced me is that I had a very bad return of the pain after Alys left me at Aldeburgh—so bad that I was frightened & should have called in a local man only I was so sick of all that I thought for *every* one's sake I had better die if there was a chance—but one night, after not being able to touch food for about 9 hours [illegible] faintness, I felt relief—being hungry in the morning I gulped down my breakfast in a hurry & in about a quarter of an hour back came the old anguish—I can call it nothing else—then at last I said to myself "this is body, not soul" & it must have to do with food & digestion. I halved my meals & ate them like a snail & began bit by bit to get better.

She continued, explaining that "once you have a heart pain there is no distinguishing it from a very bad ordinary heartache—which everyone I should think has to bear sometime in their life." Simultaneously Jane advanced reasons for depression and denied their validity.

Of course the pain was *first set going* by severe mental anxiety, the sort of original attack I had after waiting five days for the telegram [Frances's acceptance of Francis's proposal] was the beginning—but what I mean is that had it been treated physically, rest & care about food from the beginning, I believe, whatever mentally I might have suffered, & for however long the mental pain might have lasted, the *physical* pain would have been over in a few days. The mistake I made was in being too frank. I always feel it is wrong to humbug a doctor—so I told Dr. Wheeler I had had great mental anxiety & he always advised work & going about & getting [illegible] one's general health. He was kindness itself—but after trying various drugs—I think he stopped looking for a physical cause. Rogers to whom I told nothing ordered me instantly to bed. I am eternally grateful to him—it was the first step.... I only slowly began to see that it was the pain (set up by mental misery) that was recalling the mental misery—not the mental misery causing the pain.

This triumph of denial of emotion and the power of depression to cause illness represented the height of Jane's refusal to face the depth of her anger toward Francis. Ironically, the second half of the letter revealed other causes for unhappiness and serves only to emphasize how depressed and abandoned she felt during this crisis.

When I came to stay with you I thought the pain was mentally caused & I thought if anything would distract me & help me get over it, it would be the change & delight of being with you. To my despair it got worse—then when you said & most rightly that I must not go abroad with Mr. Murray I was in desperation because I felt my last hope of relief & distraction was gone. I also felt that you thought I was giving way & *causing* myself pain by useless regrets. I began to accuse myself & feel unfit to live—in reality I know now that I had no more power to stop the pain than Prometheus had to stop the vulture gnawing at his liver.

With a herculean effort, Jane began to submerge the emotions that threatened to get out of control. She accomplished this task by channeling her fury into work. "My despair was that with that gnawing pain I could not work or think except under a fearful strain. Now that the pain is practically gone I *can* work & can think & assuredly, could I have done that before I should never have burdened my friends with my groans. So long as you can *work* life is abundantly worth living." Life is particularly worth living when one has a score to settle. It took time, but the anger that threatened Jane's life, paradoxically, became transformed into the force that saved her.[43]

Believing Cambridge to be "the worst place in the world for me the next 6 months," as she wrote in January 1909, Jane resolved to avoid it. Dr. Rogers foiled her plans by refusing to allow her to travel. Despite occasional setbacks, she slowly began to regain her health, come to grips with the impending marriage, and, most important, start thinking about her next book. Although in February 1909 the "fierce weather" gave her "pains again," Dr. Rogers reported encouragingly that she had "gained ground sclerotically" and advised her "to spend all day lizarding in the sun as soon as there is any sun." In April she decided to go to Aldeburgh for the next term, believing that the sea air would keep her from feeling "the depression that they say is inevitable with iodine so much." Occasionally, though, she could not help but let slip some of the old sadness. Gilbert Murray visited her in Cambridge, and she gratefully acknowledged how much he had cheered her.

It was good of you to come up that last day—I knew it was to help me & I was oh so grateful.

For all this time I cannot say any thanks but I do want to say just this—It *has* helped me—this way—it has made me feel that as long as you let me be your friend I cannot & will not sink lower into any pit of self-abasement.

Jane went to Aldeburgh in the early summer and remained there until after Francis's wedding, which took place in July 1909. She returned to Cambridge later in July and began sitting for Augustus John, who painted the portrait that fateful summer. Upon returning to Newnham, Jane wrote an entirely unconvincing letter to Gilbert Murray, resolving to put the past behind her and focus on the present.

My cave feels very lonely, but it is a good deal less lonely when a letter comes from you—& there is Thursday coming soon. I have resolved to follow your counsel & not to think of the endlessness of the lonely years to come but just to try & go on mending up my life with lots of work from day to day—the thing that helps me most is thinking of the patient lines about the mouths of some people.[44]

Relapses into illness and despair punctuated the next three years, during which Jane worked on *Themis*, but gradually she returned to her usual routine. In October 1909, Dr. Wheeler told her that "having made so much advance I ought to make more." A visit with the Murrays had been "refreshment & delight" that enabled her to "plunge in to work with fresh courage & put thro' my lecture without any undue strain—which shows I must be really strong."[45] But in November she lapsed again into despair, as she confessed to Gilbert Murray: "And here comes your letter. Thank you—did you know O Cheiron how badly I wanted consolation. You see too clearly—I *was* in a good deal of pain—I had been doing rather much I suppose—& a dreadful loneliness was on me at having to go." She asked him to thank John Galsworthy for comments that, although unrevealed, gave her

great inward joy. . . . I did not quite see that Sex was force & that
therein lay not only its strength but its terror & its ignominy—& that
in balance—which I shall never get—lies peace. . . . I am here—& have a
clear fortnight for work—& the stress of the Kouretes is over—& just
because I have no such compulsion I simply can do nothing but sit &
think of the utter loneliness of things—Please send me a word to give
me strength to begin—for I *must* work.

She signed this letter, "your desolate Ker."[46]

The sadness crept into her minor works as well. In December 1909, she delivered a lecture called "Heresy and Humanity" to the Cambridge Society of "Heretics" in which she extolled the virtues of collectivism. Having been disappointed so often in close personal relationships, she became almost strident on the superiority of the communal life. The ferocity of her attack on individualism reached its pinnacle in *Themis*, but she refined her thoughts while brooding over its plot. In this lecture, she provided a glimpse of the pain caused by a close friend's betrayal and offered proof of individual treachery: "A close companionship withdrawn is a wound to our actual spiritual life: if our egotism and self-sufficiency be robust, we recover from it; if weak, we go maimed and halting, with minished personality." During these years, Jane appeared "maimed and halting" despite her inner strength.[47]

April of 1910 found her in rather better spirits. She had heard Gilbert lecture and visited with him. She still worked at her writing, but admitted that "sometimes I do want just to be happy & enjoy myself thro & thro for an hour." She especially welcomed his visit because she had "felt almost sure that old Harpy Providence was somewhere round—she always is nowadays—to snatch the feast from my lips." That summer brought more ill health, and Jane tried escaping to Yorkshire and even a Swedish resort to recover, but other than diagnosing her pain as "intercoastal neuralgia" the doctors could not cure her. Jane's Swedish excursion provided at least temporary diversion, as she went off with Lytton Strachey and his sister, Pernel, in July 1910. Although several weeks at

Saltsjöbaden did not improve Jane's health as it did Lytton's, she still cut a colorful figure. Lytton confided to his mother that Jane and Pernel "both find the place very singular . . . and I should think the place returns the compliment so far as Jane is concerned—she makes a strange figure among the formal Scandinavians, floating through the corridors in green shawls and purple tea-gowns, and reciting the Swedish grammar at meals." The third week of August brought cold weather that proved too much for Jane and Pernel, prompting them to leave and Jane to vow, "this is the last anyone will hear of my health." Despite her resolution, her friends continued to hear of it.[48]

At the same time, the ideas for *Themis* were fermenting in her mind and beginning to take on a life of their own. After a casual conversation in which Jane mentioned some of her ideas on the connection between art and ritual, Gilbert Murray urged her to begin work on what would later become *Ancient Art and Ritual,* but she refused to work on it then. She was "just embarked on the Epileg [her early working title for *Themis*] & it absolutely *must* be done this year." She could not "bear it in my head any longer" and needed to put her thoughts on paper. Three weeks later she sent summaries of chapters and an outline of *Themis* and concluded, "I hope & trust—unless I lapse in my vile body—to get it all written out rather quickly now—I am in the stage now that bad or good I have got to get rid of it before I can think in any other form." Her ideas became obsessions, and she envied Gilbert that "this never happens to you—you always command your material—mine commands me."[49]

Her euphoria did not last long. She added a rather morose postscript to her birthday letter to Gilbert Murray on December 29, 1910, having spent another Christmas alone at Southwold in Suffolk, a town she had often visited with Francis Cornford in happier days. She apologized for a "petulant letter" sent earlier and explained:

I was cross because material blessings were being heaped upon me & a happy healthy Xmas was being organized for me at Littlehampton by telegram & that—when the one thing needful is withheld—exacerbates me—but I broke loose & now I am better. After all tho my measure is much minished it is all laid up in heaven now where neither moth . . .[50]

Once again, the old sorrow crept into her correspondence. Over the next eighteen months, the loss of an old friend prompted further expressions of despair.

Late in October 1910, Henry Butcher suffered a stroke and died on December 29. His death prompted a very sad yet strangely chilling letter from Jane to Gilbert Murray, who had sent his condolences. After the conventional lines about his death's being all for the best under the circumstances, Jane gave her reaction to reading the obituary notices of the man she had loved so many years before.

If ever the present differences resolved themselves into a simple fight with shillelaghs between the scholars and the anthropologists, I should without doubt wield my reluctant weapon on the side of the scholars. Scholarship is the rarer, harder, less popular and perhaps the more permanently valuable work, and it certainly stands more in need of defence at the moment. But in the meantime I can hardly understand how the purest of "pure scholars" can fail to feel his knowledge enriched by the servants who have compelled us to dig below the surface of our classical tradition and to realize the imaginative and historical problems which so often lie concealed beneath the smooth security of a verbal "construe."[26]

Murray focused the argument clearly. Traditional classical scholarship refused to admit the validity of anything other than Homer before the golden age of Greece, and the Ritualists and their allies in other fields challenged this stance. While the exchanges in columns of journals could be scurrilous, the private exchanges could be riotous.

When discussing people who were either not so well known or who were not direct participants in the ideological battle, Harrison could be scathing. After hearing Murray's comments on a "Miss Stawell's screed," Harrison wrote expressing agreement on his disappointment. "She is one of the people who make me hate morality & views & everything I shouldn't: she preaches so insistently that I long to go quietly to hell, but she is a real SS [Sound Scholar]. The only one we ever raised at Newnham." Miss Stawell apparently staged an Oedipal rebellion against her Newnham teachers, and Harrison felt no compunction about criticizing her perfidy. Years later, Harrison asked Murray "how long is 'literature' going to be left to that besotted owl old [John] Sandys—he gives a full page to Professor Seymour's stuffed emptiness & seems to think the only safe thing to say about you is that you 'have been favourably received' by [J. B.] Bury—& this is to guide the young!'[27]

She did not always spare the well known, either. During a 1901 visit to Rome, she complained to Mary Murray back in England that "Mrs. Frazer [J. G. Frazer's wife], (your double!) has been sitting by my bed for two hours, telling me 'who not to know' i.e. who has not paid Mr. Frazer 'proper attention!' This is the price I pay for a few shy radiant moments under the Golden Bough." Although still a "good conservative," she proclaimed herself "ready for any reform in the Game Laws for the preserving of Eminent Husbands." She seemed impatient with both Mrs. Frazer's backstage managing of her husband's career and with Frazer's indulgence of it.[28] Harrison saved her most acerbic comments, however, for her avowed enemies Lewis Farnell, Andrew Lang, and especially William Ridgeway.

Farnell's monumental work *The Cults of the Greek States* in part supported the work of the Ritualists, but Harrison did not think much of his intellectual ability. Faced with reviewing his two volumes on cult practice, she told Gilbert that she longed to be "spiteful—those two huge volumes are just *nil* & now I shall have to try & be kind & Xian just because woe is me—I have the fear of you before my eyes." His kind word on Farnell's behalf prompted her to threaten, "if you say Mr. Farnell is 'important' I should send for my neo-lithic club—he is essentially insignificant." Later, she "had to review Farnell twice" and did not find that he improved with age. "I didn't think it was possible for him to grow duller but with academic officials all things are possible." She defended herself against his harsh review of *Themis* in the *Hibbert Journal* by saying "I don't mind what he says of me a bit" and claiming that "a good deal of the book he simply doesn't understand & never will—& nearly all of it he temperamentally hates which is what one would expect." Her most significant comment on her critics, though, lay in her assertion that "unless I care about people they are quite powerless to hurt me, I suppose that is for worse not for better." She wanted to convince Murray that Farnell did not matter in the least, but his criticism likely hurt more than she cared to admit.[29]

Andrew Lang angered her by writing "enormous screeds to say I am wrong about the All Father. He seems to have reviewed [*Themis*] three times." His behavior at a dinner party also provided her with a charming vignette for her "Reminiscences."

Our hostess brought him up to me and, with a misguided desire to be pleasant, said, "You know Miss Harrison, and I am sure you have read her delightful books." "Don't know Miss Harrison," muttered Andrew, "never read her delightful books, don't want to," etc. (Oh, Andrew, and you had reviewed those "delightful books" not too delightedly!) "Come, Mr. Lang," I said, "we're both hungry, and I promise not to say a single word to you. Be a man." Alas! I broke my word. It was an enchanting dinner. (RSL, 334)

Despite her intellectual differences with Lang, Harrison could ignore them in the interest of a peaceful meal.[30]

By far the most implacable of her critics was the classicist William Ridgeway, whose antics provoked her into a good deal of vituperative rhetoric both in public and in private. Their antagonism dated from her earliest days at Newnham, and Harrison often expressed mock fear that Ridgeway would one day come at her "in full shillelagh." He appears to have been an arrogant, gruff curmudgeon, always ready to take on the Ritualist circle. Ironically, Harrison often quoted Ridgeway's work on early Greece approvingly in her major works, but their basic views diverged and Charles Seltman rightly doubted "very much whether Ridgeway had much influence on her work." In a classic understatement, tolerated Bolshevism largely because conservative Cambridge decried it, but her heart belonged to Old Russia. Her earliest memory, according to her "Reminiscences," was of a family dog symbolically named "Moscow"; her first toy was "a box of bricks and soldiers called 'The Siege of Sevastopol,' given by a patriotic uncle" as a reminder of the Crimean War (RSL, 312). Her father's timber business had brought him into contact with Russian merchants who sent "caviare and cranberries and reindeers' tongues" every Christmas; the tongues had tasted "not only of reindeer, but—but of snow-fields and dreaming forests". These memories formed Jane's vision of Russia that remained intact through the 1917 revolutions and beyond (RSL, 312). This vision probably prevented her from traveling to Russia except for one brief journey to St. Petersburg in 1886 to examine Greek antiquities housed at the Hermitage.[19] She blamed her avoidance of the country on her being too focused on Greece to think about it, but she probably knew that to make a reality of one's ideal would destroy it.

Her romantic view of Russia influenced one of the two significant dreams she claimed to have had in her life. A dream of the Russian forest contained all her favorite images and demonstrated her association of the nation with bears.

One night soon after the Russian revolution I dreamt I was in a great, ancient forest—What in Russian would be called "a dreaming wood." In it was cleared a round space, and the space was crowded with huge bears softly dancing. I somehow knew that I had come to teach them to dance the Grand Chain in the Lancers, a square dance now obsolete. I was not the least afraid, only very glad and proud. I went up and began trying to make them join hands and form a circle. It was no good. I tried and tried, but they only shuffled away, courteously waving their paws, intent on their own mysterious doings. Suddenly I knew that these doings were more wonderful and beautiful than any Grand Chain (as, indeed, they might well be!). It was for me to learn, not to teach. I woke up crying, in an ecstasy of humility. (RSL, 341).

Many years later, Jane delighted in an outing to see "sixteen polar bears" performing in Paris. Although they were "not nearly so clever" as others she had seen, the experience proved to be "just like my dream come true for when the trainer-man tried to make them do their stunts they just shambled past him & went nosing about their own business."[20]

Jane spent the last decade of her life exploring the Russian soul through its language, although she denied being drawn to "the 'Slav soul' " (RSL, 341). After twenty-five years in the tumult of the emotional life, Jane drew back to observe that life from a distance. Language, which expressed the soul of a people and conveyed its perceptions of emotion without entangling one in it, became another means of comprehending the inner essence of a group. At the end of her life, Jane wished she had devoted herself to language: "Life itself may hit one hard, but always, always one can take sanctuary in language. . . . It reflects and interprets and makes bearable life; only it is a wider, because more subconscious, life" (RSL, 341).

The revolution of March 1917 made Jane "so happy" and she believed it to be "the best & biggest thing the war has brought," although her Russian friends remained more circumspect.[21] In 1918, she resented having to prepare that fall's Moncure Conway lecture in religion "lest it should interfere with my real bear-work in term time" and added, "oh those bears I should have been dead long ago but for them, bless them." She idealized the "Czecho-Slovaks" and invoked the image of "John Huss leading those pathetic simple peasants," with whom her sympathies lay; she hoped they would not be "exploited" by the victorious Bolsheviks after the November revolution.[22] Before Gilbert Murray came to Newnham to speak on the League of Nations, which he vigorously supported, Jane warned him to "be pleasant about the Bears (God Bless them) & point out all their spiritualities—or from the Chair I will denounce you."[23]

Although Jane felt an instinctive kinship with Russia, she often took on causes simply to be a thorn in the side of the typical Cambridge intellectual. Her visit with a "real live Bolshevik bear" in 1920 caused a stir in Cambridge, and she enjoyed the controversy as much as the opportunity to speak Russian with a native. She described the encounter to Gilbert Murray.

I loved him so, & to my great joy I understood every word he said (except about two) tho, as soon as he found out I was sympathetic, he poured it all out in a torrent & his accent (as I proudly detected) was not the purest Moscow. . . . I was afraid he might be some scoundrel of a Baltic Junker—playing on their simplicity [he had married the daughter of a College nurse]—so I asked him to tea to spy out the land—& lo! there was a creature who might have been Dostoevsky—pure Slav type—sunken cheeks fanatical dreamy eyes & talking only Russian & Persian. . . . People here say I ought to have turned him out of the College instantly. As if I was likely when I had just caught a real Bolshevik & a Bear at that—Russians do go to my head & make me feel how common we all are—but I wish they didn't have such confusing names. . . . My bear was courteous about England but he couldn't quite hide a certain contempt for our Government. He said very quietly "England does not understand; she believes what the papers say; she did hinder . . . & interfere before she can do no harm now, we are strong now."

Oh dear what is the use of a League of Nations without Russia—

without Germany—I get disheartened—don't you? & civilized women say they "wouldn't sit down to tea with a Bolshevik"—well thank goodness I never asked them.

I asked him, when I said goodbye, how long it would be before one could safely (& economically) go to Russia, adding that I was old & wanted to see both old & new Russia before I died—& he looked me over meditatively & said "Yes you are an old woman, you could not travel privately in Russia now—you might starve, for money is no use— but perhaps you will come as our guest—you will be safe." A frog would have answered "You Mademoiselle are always young and a young woman can travel unprotected in Russia."

Both her disillusionment with the aftermath of World War I and her enchantment with Russia showed in this letter, and clearly Newnham disapproved of the latter. After leaving Cambridge for France, Jane met one of her closest Russian friends during a visit to Pontigny, gathering place for French intellectuals during the 1920s. D. S. Mirsky was a Russian artistocrat who fled after the revolution, and Jane wrote Gilbert from Pontigny that she had lost her "aged heart to a Bear-Prince—why did I not meet him 50 years ago when I could have clamoured to be his Princess."[24]

As much as Jane loved Russia, however, it could not dispel the effects of age and the changed environment of postwar Cambridge. Most of her closest acquaintances had died by 1920. The death in 1916 of Margaret Merrifield Verrall, her closest remaining friend outside the Ritualist circle, left Jane feeling desolate and forced her to consider what to do with her future. Just before Margaret's death, Jane mourned the fact that her "friends seem moving away fast & I begin to feel I ought to be moving on to—but it makes me also feel that one must see the friends left while one can." Shortly before Margaret died in July, Jane wrote to Gilbert Murray and noted "what an empty place Cambridge will seem with that house closed."[25]

Other changes followed the end of the war. Frances Darwin Cornford, who had been so happy in her marriage, nevertheless suffered another breakdown in 1917. Virginia Woolf wrote to her sister, Vanessa Bell, in 1919 that Frances had "a delusion that she must never be tired, and has now spent 2 years in going from rest cure to rest cure," refusing "to see either her husband or children." Frances returned in 1919 on her doctors' advice, but they feared "she may be incurable. . . . All Darwins incline that way." Jane probably sympathized more with Frances's breakdown than with her sudden conversion to Catholicism after the war. Even in 1914, Jane had described her as "very funny now-adays—full of reactions—excited over the empire—& the importance of people being simple & rather stupid & doing their duty at home & having a religion."

She had not then joined the church, and Jane hoped she would reconsider as "it would worry Frank [Darwin]—tho he would stand aside &
yawn heavily." She hoped in vain, however, for Frances did ultimately
join the Catholic church.[26]

Virginia Woolf described Jane's consternation over the wave of conver-
sions sweeping Cambridge in the postwar years. In 1923, she visited Jane
in Paris and wrote to Jacques Raverat, husband of Frances's cousin,
Gwen, about their visit. She described Jane as a "gallant old lady, very
white, hoary, and sublime in a lace mantilla." Jane praised Woolf, Vanessa Bell, and "perhaps Lytton Strachey" as "the only ones of the younger generation" she could "respect." When Woolf baited her by invoking
the name of the Darwins, Jane accused them of being " 'the blackest
traitors of them all! With that name!' she cried, 'that inheritance! That
magnificent record in the past!' " Woolf's appeal that " 'surely . . . our
Gwen is secure?' " elicited the complaint that "Gwen . . . goes to
Church (if not mass, still Church) every Sunday of her life." Jane guessed
that Gwen's "marriage . . . may have weakened her brain," as her husband was "unfortunately French." Woolf promised to break off her long-
standing friendship if this proved true, but reneged when she learned
that Gwen was "a militant atheist." On hearing this news later from
Woolf, Jane "replied, a little inconsistently, 'Thank God.' "[27]

In 1923, in a letter to Gilbert, Jane praised Francis's *Origin of Comedy*, although she "couldn't help laughing at first" over his "Freudian
dramatic hero." She grudgingly admitted that his marriage had not
deterred him from his work as much as she had expected (or perhaps
hoped), and was "specially glad" that the *Origin of Comedy* was "so
fine because it would clearly never have been written but for Frances &
her psychoanalysis complex." She commented further on the nature of
his marriage.

I have always been worried about her reactionary influence on him—(as
is natural enough in the supplanted one!) and I still would rather he had
not repentently taken his four children to the font, but I see now that
he owes a fine bit of work to her & I am relieved—if only he does not
get sodden with domestic bliss! he is a born father as well as husband &
that sometimes makes me anxious—the downward path well worn by
tribal feet is so easy—but as long as she gives him ideas & she is full of
them—all is well.

With Frances's periodic breakdowns, however, her husband was unlikely to become "sodden with domestic bliss." Jane probably felt he had
gotten what he deserved. The betrayal rankled still, but anger had given
way to a resigned bemusement.[28]

The high point of Jane's last decade at Newnham was her relationship
with Hope Mirrlees, which grew stronger during the last few years of

Jane's tenure there. Hope seemed the natural choice of companion when Jane went to Paris in 1922. Some of Jane's close friends blamed Hope for deliberately driving a wedge between them, but Jane herself seemed eager to relinquish the tight grip of those relationships. Gilbert Murray admitted to Jessie Stewart that he "never understood what happened at the end of [Jane's] life" and asked, "did Newnham refuse to continue her Fellowship, and was she greatly hurt? Or did she, for other reasons, determine to leave Cambridge and Greek and her old associations? And what part did Hope play in it?" With the Frances-Francis disaster finally behind her and now facing old age, Jane may merely have wanted to escape Cambridge and its painful associations. But she must have cringed at the gradual change within Cambridge, both in the university as a whole and in Newnham itself. The university, trying to return to normalcy after the war, settled into a renewed intellectual and political conservatism. It still refused to grant women degrees, and the violent protests over this issue occurred just before Jane's departure. The women's colleges, now filled with modern young women who placed more value on a spirited game of field hockey than on intellectual achievement, must have seemed alien to her. She became "depressed because of the queer atmosphere of Truth not mattering which some of the young seem to live in" and felt alienated from the place that had been her spiritual and intellectual home for twenty-five years. She told Gilbert Murray that she wanted to retire gracefully rather than remain at Newnham and be "booted out" at the end of another year. In her letter of thanks for Newnham's parting gift, she said that she was sorry to leave but that "a voice from within said 'Go'" for "a College to my mind is best ruled and taught by the young."[29]

In her "Reminiscences," Jane stated that she left Cambridge with "measureless regret," feeling she had "lived too long the strait Academic life with my mind intently focussed on the solution of a few problems" (RSL, 346). She "wanted before the end came to see things more freely and more widely, and, above all, to get the new focus of another civilization" (RSL, 346). In reality, she needed to get her personal past in order. Every aspect of her life had been challenged in the preceding decade, and she needed to distance herself from her past before she could discern its pattern. At the war's end, she mourned the destruction of the quiet atmosphere that encouraged lively discussion of her beloved archaic age. She wrote poignantly to Gilbert Murray, "shall we ever wrangle again over the horns of Poseidon or the hoofs of Cheiron—I fear not—these lie slain by the war."[30]

Her last significant work of the Cambridge years appeared in 1921. The *Epilegomena to the Study of Greek Religion* briefly recapitulated, without the heated emotion or grand view, the ideas expressed so passionately in *Themis* and the *Prolegomena*. It distilled her views in forty pages, and Gilbert Murray praised its brevity and clarity—qualities never before associated with Jane's work. She reaffirmed the primacy of the group but jettisoned all appeals to the superiority of emotion, calling instead for asceticism. Gilbert Murray called it "a wonderful achievement" that unified all her previous work and made it more intelligible and cohesive. He appreciated her invocation of asceticism, and said it was "almost the most important practical piece of teaching that the world needs nowadays." In this letter, one of only a handful from Gilbert to Jane that survive, he displayed a lack of understanding that helps explain the unbridgeable distance that ultimately lay between them. Jane's conversion to asceticism stemmed from defeat. It represented a graceful but saddening end to a love affair with the irrational. The *Epilegomena* is concise and straightforward but less recognizable as Jane's work precisely because it lacks the passion of her earlier studies. It stands as a monument, however, to how far she had traveled in a quarter-century. For all its disappointing slimness, it still retains a kernel of Ritualist theory and reiterates a belief, albeit a qualified and subdued one, in the power of the group. The *Epilegomena* also represents Jane's closing of the door on her life's work. Having paid final tribute to her theories, she could leave behind that aspect of her life and turn her attention to more intense personal issues.[31]

The *Epilegomena*'s greatest attraction lies in its incorporation of Freudian theory. It bears the imprint of *Totem and Taboo* as much as of Ritualist theory. Jane accepted Freud's description of the killing of the father by the band of brothers, although she attributed their motives to social rather than individual psychological origins. Somewhere between *Themis* and the *Epilegomena,* Jane read Freud and recognized in him a kindred spirit. Indeed, she considered *Totem and Taboo* one of the greatest literary influences on her work. More to the point, however, she intuitively appreciated his work and used it to strengthen her belief in her own theories. Although she was "at first . . . sickened" by "the ugliness of" Freudian theory, she "struggled on, feeling somehow that behind and below all this sexual mud was something big and real" (RSL, 342). *Totem and Taboo* gave her a "sense of release" because Freud seemed to her to understand the "mysteries of sin, of sanctity, of sacrament." She appreciated his contribution to the study of religion but shied away from consciously accepting his emphasis on sexuality. That she unconsciously accepted it, though, becomes clear in the *Epilegomena*.[32]

In spite of her formal denial of the sexual element that Freud placed at the heart of totemic thought, sexual themes run like an undercurrent through much of her work. Noting the obsession with names common to both primitives and neurotics, Freud pointed out that names are preceived as "an essential part of a man's personality" and that knowing or even uttering a name could give one person power over another. The overriding theme in *Totem and Taboo*, however, is the divisiveness of sex, which lies at the heart of all religious impulse, and the uneasiness of modern society in general. "Sexual desires do not unite men but divide them"—Jane expressed that belief almost verbatim. Although the Oedipal conflict that Freud placed at the center of humanity's relation to God is based on a male model, Jane's experience of her father's abandonment made her sympathetic to the inadequacy of the distant, rational projections that replaced group projections and left an emotional void that could never be filled. Although Jane did not read Freud until late in her life and rarely referred to his work, his gloomy vision of a life spent controlling dangerous and ever-threatening forces loomed behind her philosophy and struck a responsive chord. She recognized both the power of his vision and its intimate relation to how she perceived the world around her. His influence affected her on a personal level much more than on an intellectual one.[33]

Writing the *Epilegomena*, however, could not help her totally to reconcile herself to the past. This reconciliation proved much more difficult than she had dreamed. In fact, she fled to Paris in an effort to break resolutely from it. To make the job easier, she burned all of her correspondence before leaving Cambridge. Her friends and colleagues collected three hundred pounds to aid her retirement, and most of Cambridge's classical dons, with the notable exception of William Ridgeway, signed the subscription to demonstrate their gratitude and respect.[34] With nothing remaining to tie her to Newnham and Cambridge, she traveled to Paris with Hope Mirrlees and a few personal possessions to widen her focus in her last years. The past nevertheless went with her, and she used her years in Paris to help heal some of the wounds she had suffered over the course of her long life.

Hope proceeded to Paris first to find them a place to live. In April 1922, Jane wrote from Cambridge with reminders of things to do in preparation for the move. The steadily declining exchange rate meant that lodging would be very expensive and Jane favored "the new furnished flats" as the best bargain. She urged Hope to pay attention to the rate she had to pay for her "excess luggage" on the return trip and also to remember to "reserve [her] seat *well* beforehand as just after Easter is a full time." Recognizing the magnitude of Hope's responsibilities, Jane added, "you poor beast—what a lot of things you have to think of. I wish I was by your side holding your small cold fur-paw & I wish there wasn't such a thing as money!" Nevertheless, in October 1922, they both left for Paris and stayed for several weeks in hotels. Just when Jane despaired of finding a suitable, more permanent home, Alys Russell persuaded the American University Women's Club to take them in.[35]

Jane described their new abode to Mary Murray in December 1922.

This club is an interesting place & has made me revise many anti-American prejudices—I was really at wits' end how to live as our possession of three cases of books made the ordinary hotel keeper look on us almost as criminals. . . . I was afraid at one point we should have to come back to spacious England—space to move and an occasional wash are the only luxuries I ask for—Then—thanks to Alys Russell's kindness this hospitable place took us in—& we are in veritable clover—not to say almost sinful luxury—breakfast in your room . . . hot baths all day long if you like, kind (touched by America) & more than that a personal care & kindness that goes to one's heart. Best of all they have given me—*free*—*as a present* a big studio sitting room—where I can breathe & work & even think if the delights of Paris would leave me a free moment.

Her exposure to Americans did more than make her revise her prejudices. She wrote to Gilbert Murray that because of her stay among American women, she had come to see that her "manners to servants (which I always thought admirable!) are those of the superior slave driver." She liked "their horribly disgustingly opulent student type . . . the clothes these young women wear . . . the number & splendour of them simply abash me." Overall, she judged the American students "the handsomest, best-grown, best-groomed greediest most empty headed crew I ever beheld," and vowed to "try to get at what they think of us." In 1925, Jessie Stewart asked Jane's advice on sending her daughter, Jean, to Paris to study. Jane did not favor the plan, especially if Jean had to stay at the American club, because although "the people are kindness itself," they were "intellectually just no-where."[36]

Despite Jane's sharp criticism of her American benefactors and complaints about "the cold & damp that almost rivals Cambridge," these years proved happy ones. A very subdued courtship with D. S. Mirsky, the exiled Russian aristocrat, amused her in a way unthinkable twenty years earlier. Her "faithful and princely flirt" visited her in the Paris years, and they sometimes traveled together to Pontigny for the "entretiens" hosted by Charles Desjardins. These gatherings, held in August, were devoted to intellectual consideration of various questions. Jane assured Prince Mirsky he would receive a cordial welcome at Pontigny, as "M. Desjardins . . . is very anxious to get intellectual Russians." She did not immediately take to Desjardins but revised her opinion after several meetings.[37] In 1923, she wrote to Jessie Stewart that "the more I see of him the better I like him & I understand now that what put me off at first was a mere trick of manner." She felt especially attracted by his eyes, which were "like a good child's."[38] By the time of her visit to Pontigny in August 1924, however, the discussions had become "horribly metaphysical," and she attended chiefly for the "study they present loses all value and the life of the mind must be subordinated to the life of action. Paradoxically, "this very upset . . . is positively welcomed just by the man who might be expected to resent it: the scholar and thinker." Jane was shocked at how many of her colleagues "went, not reluctantly, but with positive alacrity" (228). She attributed their eagerness to an instinctive recognition that the solitary life of the scholar required the emotional boost that military service, the quintessential experience of brotherhood, would provide. "Into the seething cauldron they stepped as though some healing angel, and not some devil, had troubled the waters, and the cure they found was just the bond of a common fellowship" (231). In this respect, the war could be a positive influence, a compulsory collective experience for those who lived their lives in the rarefied atmosphere of the university. It frightened her that although she perceived it as "a savagery—a setback to civilization," war appealed to the modern imagination (231). She suggested an extraordinary explanation for this phenomenon: the emergence of collectivism as a popular philosophy.

So long as Jane constructed collectivist societies only in the dim past and in the pages of books, collectivism seemed a possible force for good. Once the ideal became reality, however, she turned against it. "The watchwords of my generation . . . were Knowledge and Freedom," and she reproached the young now for favoring "emotion and collectivism" (235). With the dark side of collectivism emerging around her, she no longer wanted to discuss it, saying, "frankly, just now I am rather bored with it" (235). Having "preached collectivism" for "five long years, in season and out," she abandoned it (235). She justified her action by claiming that "Nowadays, collectivism is not only becoming a fashionable dogma; it is—a conquest far more significant—astir in every man's heart. A dogma once boomed is, intellectually, stale, and therefore useless; but a lived experience may remain vital long after the dogmatic death" (235). Still, she longed for a collectivism based on rejection of the exclusivity of sex—the kind of collectivism she had initially created as a model out of her own experience. Her collective ideal had no political basis. In fact, if anything, her conservatism made her suspicious of any political collectivism. She used the vocabulary of her era, but she invested it with entirely different meaning. No one in the larger world could understand her ideal, of course, since it bore such an intimate relation to her personal life. Therefore, her brand of collectivism failed miserably to catch on and was superseded by a vulgar form that led to war.

Jane's wartime letters show a growing disillusionment with the war and its betrayal of her collective ideal. She viewed it as "horribly exciting" at first, but could not "*live* on it—it is like being drunk all day & I want some hot milk clean & feeding."[6] Her heart condition forced her to Paris in October 1914 for treatment. She found it "wonderful to be here

& somehow less unbearable for the nightmare becomes real." Her doctor greeted her as an ally, and she found it "very upsetting to be adored for one's group's sake."[7] She believed so strongly in the folly of war that "down in [her] deepest heart" she felt "we ought . . . to have marched out all of us to meet the German army & said 'we withstand you—shoot us down if you wish.' I wonder if they could have done it."[8] Her long-standing acquaintance with Bertrand Russell also made her sympathetic to pacifism. She asserted that "militarism is the offspring of fear—Germany is brutal because she is frightened—we are humane—as yet, because we are safe." A meeting with a refugee Belgian minister prompted her to accuse her country of being "deep dyed in the spirit of sport," which had led it to "look on war with the same eyes—what we care for is the fair playing of the game."[9] These insights impelled her to write a pamphlet called "War and the Reaction," which elicited some negative response. She even scolded Gilbert Murray for failing to appreciate her sentiments.

Well I never. I don't know what young Thers of forty are coming to, mocking at a respectable old Ker over 60 in a cap & spectacles—Am I really so absurd? Each one of those things was written under dire compulsion, they forced their way out & seemed at the moment of tremendous importance—& even now I feel they have to be said—One thing you ought to remember—till I knew you I never thought or wrote about anything except—Pelasgians. & I suppose I ought to have gone on like that—but you came & muddled me up & made me turn an over focussed mind on practical things.

Like all the other matters on which she wrote, the war had taken hold in her mind and gave her "no choice" but to write about it.[10]

Jane was not totally immune to the war's seductiveness, however, and chafed at her inability to participate in it. She wished "for the first time in my life" that she was "a man and a young one . . . largely because the tension of inaction is almost unbearable, and thinking very difficult."[11] The Scarborough raid of December 1914 particularly upset her because of both the massive destruction of a place in which she had once lived and the death of Joanna, her old servant from the London days. The suffering of animals during the raid deeply touched her, and she cited stories in the Yorkshire Post "about the horses & about one old dog who went out to see how he could help & was lost." Their pathos caused her "a complete nervous breakdown" despite her pride that her "bit of coast has borne some real hurt."[12] She visited Yorkshire because her "native land pulled so hard" at her, and it was then that she learned of Joanna's death.[13]

When the war did not achieve its predicted rapid end, all of Europe dug in for an indefinite period of conflict. On January 1, 1915, with the war only five months old, Jane was "beginning to be bored" by the blackouts and the silencing of clocks and church bells. Still, she could not "hate the Kaiser I can't help loving him a little. I have laughed at him so long & so loud & you know my principles." But Jane's principle of loving anyone who made her laugh could not protect her from the war's effects on both her intellectual work and her health. In 1915, "the world" was "one great disillusionment," and she lamented that she was "dying quietly of want of health. . . . I just have no health." She planned to travel again to Paris for treatment in the spring of 1915, but the war forced the cancelation of her plans. She grew despondent and asked wearily, "oh— will it ever be all over. & will one have any life left in one to live with if it is." Circumstances, however, allowed her to visit her Parisian doctor later that spring, and she announced that his treatment for hardening of the arteries "puts new life into one." He expected "a complete cure now that will be permanent," but she had to continue treatment sporadically throughout the war.[14]

Her recurrent ill health may have resulted largely from the difficulty of working at academic research when the world was so focused on larger and more pressing issues. She blamed herd instinct gone awry for interrupting her work and creating this new, hostile atmosphere. She began to see some justification for the war, but reacted with sorrow and anger that humanity misunderstood and misused the power of the group. Jane wrote to Gilbert Murray:

I think the safe thing for others & perhaps for oneself is *never* to say
this war is right without adding one's deep sense of humiliation as a
human being that war should be—one gains by the herd's power of intense feeling, one loses by its awful stupidity & savagery—& in so far as
one is part of it one has to mourn & repent for that stupidity & savagery. & the test is does one hate Germay—I saw that in France. Even
the civilized men hate Germany & are not ashamed to say so—even my
doctor the best & gentlest of men—said cést la haine Mademoiselle . . .
& I feel in my heart if they came here it would be "la haine" with me.

Jane thanked Gilbert for pointing out in one of his wartime tracts that "to hate Germany was both a stupidity & a sin—for the hate is growing—& is beginning to be made into a herd duty."[15] For decades, Jane had mistakenly assumed that any group would foster only positive, unifying emotions. She had failed to discern until now that hatred and fear could generate new and divisive forces within the group. Her response to another of Gilbert's tracts revealed how irrevocably she had turned against the herd.

It is interesting about the ruthlessness of the really herd creature like
the bee. Their polity makes one cold with horror also I am glad you

show that pack feeling is quite diff[erent] from affection—The *size* of the herd & the relation of the small to the bigger herd is difficult & no one seems to have worked it out fully. . . . of course the more civilization progresses the more intensively a very big herd can act—by telephone etc.

The negative self-feeling of obedience is important. . . . combined with herd feeling it may generate abysses of abjectness. I am very glad you put clearly how much herd emotion *deadens* individual sympathy—people positively use it as a pretext for their own callousness.

Altogether your paper makes me feel more clearly than ever how literally I hate & despise the herd! it is so stupid—so bore-ing—& so idle.

These were not altogether new thoughts, but nevertheless represented a gradual rejection of her old ideals.[16]

Jane considered England's treatment of its conscientious objectors and pacifists the most distressing aspect of collectivism gone wrong. She valued independence of thought above all else and grew angry at the vociferous attacks on those who criticized the war. She was dismayed at the treatment of Gerald Shove, fiancé of her young friend Fredegond Maitland. She also sided with Bertrand Russell in his objection to the war, despite a long period of coolness on her part brought about by his divorce from her friend, Alys Russell, in 1911. On the one hand, Jane defended Gilbert Murray against detractors who abhorred his support of the war, although she did not entirely agree with him; on the other, she supported the right of individuals to oppose the war.

In a 1917 letter regarding Gerald Shove's case, Jane agreed with Gilbert Murray that "a man can have a conscience without belonging to a sect" and criticized the determination of prosecutors to be particularly harsh on the "poor lonely thinker" who opposed the war on philosophical and moral grounds. Fredegond Maitland informed her that "the small lower middle class fanatic too uneducated to state his case" suffered the most from the tribunal that tried Gerald Shove's case. This experience moved Jane to remark, "that awful herd do you remember how I used to enthuse over the herd—give me a hermit crab now."[17]

In order to escape these troubling issues, Jane plunged into the study of languages, especially Russian. This study, along with her contacts with East European refugees, led to a romance with Russia and its language that occupied nearly the rest of her life. She believed that that country cared "more than any other nation for the things of the spirit & that is priceless," and that "the words even seem like Greek to seek for the things of the spirit."[18] The Russians appealed to her from the start of the war because of her romantic association of the country with bears and forests and the Russian soul as seen through its great nineteenth-century authors, and she rejoiced over the March revolution as well. She

& Frances" chapter? They were *certainly* not in the version that you showed me. I am *horribly* distressed that this has been published. Jane would simply have *loathed* it. She was almost morbidly reserved about her past. Moreover it gives an utterly wrong impression of her. She was obviously *not* her real self at that time, but on the verge of a nervous breakdown. She was normally so beautifully just & reasonable & had such splendid self-control. After all I ought to know, seeing that I lived with her off & on for 15 years. It was strictly from her that I learned the importance of justice & reason in the conduct of life, & she despised & detested as the worst form of selfishness any lack of self-control in human relationships. Oh if *only* it could be deleted![4]

Hope's remarkable outburst conveyed much more than despair at Jessie's revelations. She was taunting Jessie with her mention of the years she had lived with Jane, clearly, although perhaps unconsciously, implying that she had been the favored daughter.

Jessie responded reasonably to Hope's accusations. She reminded Hope that the Francis-Frances affair had indeed appeared in the earlier manuscript version. Jessie defended her decision to discuss it by pointing out that Frances Cornford and Gilbert Murray agreed it should be included, and asserted that "it was very important, for understanding Jane's mystic letters & much of 'Alpha-Omega.'" She and Hope both understood that life and work were intricately interwoven, but unlike Hope, Jessie possessed sufficient distance to examine the connections. Later, she wrote to Hope that "I shan't know till I stand before the Judgment Seat whether I did right or wrong!" But even Jessie remained reticent despite her distance, admitting that "there are many things in the letters & in my own experience which a biographer might relish, but which I would not like put in."[5]

Jane's destruction of her letters hampers a full understanding of her life. Jessie faced this problem in her *Portrait*. Gilbert Murray accused Hope of having "a good deal to do" with Jane's decision to destroy her letters and of "weaning Jane from her old friends." Jane's destruction of his letters obviously hurt him, and he asked Jessie to alter her explanation of their destruction in her manuscript. He felt her statement "that Jane burnt my letters" made it look "as if there had been some quarrel between us, which there never was." He asked her to say merely that "they 'were burnt.'" Possibly Hope did encourage Jane to destroy the letters, but I think it more likely that Jane chose that course herself. She was seventy-two when she left Cambridge, bitter and disillusioned. Rather than covering her tracks, she wanted, I think, merely to escape from a painful past. Scraps of paper with familiar handwriting, invoking bittersweet memories, probably seemed better consigned to the fire. The very fact of her reconciliation with her past, played out in Paris in Hope's company, indicated that Jane controlled her own emotions. If Hope had wielded such enormous power, she could have persuaded Jane to live out her life abroad. But having come to grips with her past, Jane insisted on returning home.[6]

Even with the richest resources, however, the full story ultimately remains a mystery. Biographers, like all historians, display selective vision when collecting evidence. Identification and sympathy are difficult to conceal but to some degree essential. Above all one must avoid the temptation of thinking that all can be explained. There is something magical about inexplicable things, as Jane well knew, and this magical quality makes them intriguing and powerful. The fragility and complexity of the individual life can never be fully understood. Perhaps that is for the best.

# NOTES

## PREFACE

1 Recent works analyze this trend. See Susan N. G. Geiger, "Women's Life Histories: Method and Content," *Signs* 11, no. 2 (Winter 1986): 334–51; Elizabeth Kamarck Minnich, "Friendship between Women: The Act of Feminist Biography," *Feminist Studies* 11, no. 2 (Summer 1985): 287–306; and Carol Ascher, Louise DeSalvo, and Sara Ruddick, eds., *Between Women* (Boston: Beacon Press, 1984).

2 Jessie Stewart, *Jane Ellen Harrison: A Portrait from Letters* (London: Merlin Press, 1959), pp. 200–01.

3 Robert Allen Ackerman, *The Cambridge Group and the Origins of Myth Criticism* (Ann Arbor, Mich.: University Microfilms International, 1969); idem, "Some Letters of the Cambridge Ritualists," *Greek, Roman and Byzantine Studies* 12 (Spring 1971): 113–36; idem, "Jane Ellen Harrison: The Early Work," ibid. 13 (Summer 1972): 209–30.

4 Harry Payne, "Modernizing the Ancients: The Reconstruction of Ritual Drama 1870–1920," *Proceedings of the American Philosophical Society* 122, no. 3 (June 9, 1978): 182–92. For a look at the larger implications of the ritual theory, see his "The Ritual Question and Modernizing Society, 1800–1945— A Schema for a History," *Historical Reflections* 11, no. 3 (Fall 1984): 403–32.

5 Walter Burkert, *Structure and History in Greek Mythology and Ritual* (Berkeley and Los Angeles: University of California Press, 1979); idem, *Homo Necans*, trans. Peter Bing (Berkeley and Los Angeles: University of California Press, 1983); idem, *Greek Religion*, trans. John Raffan (Cambridge: Harvard University Press, 1985; originally published Stuttgart: Verlag W. Kohlhammer, 1977).

6 Martha Vicinus, *Independent Women* (Chicago: University of Chicago Press, 1985), chap. 4.

7 JH to GM, 1908, Box 6, JEH.

8 Recently, Carl Degler has urged historians to pay more attention to psychological factors in their study of the past. See Carl N. Degler, "Should Historians Be Skeptical about Using Psychological Methods?" *Chronicle of Higher Education* 33, no. 37 (May 27, 1987): 80. Peter Loewenberg, in *Decoding the Past: The Psychological Approach* (Berkeley and Los Angeles: University of California Press, 1969), gives a lengthy and eloquent defense of the psychohistorical method.

9 J. H. Plumb, Introduction to *Studies in Social History: A Tribute to G. M. Trevelyan*, ed. J. H. Plumb (London: Longmans, Green & Co., 1955), p. xiii.

10   E. M. Butler, *The Tyranny of Greece over Germany* (Cambridge: Cambridge University Press, 1935), p. 8.

## PROLOGUE

1   Virginia Woolf, *A Room of One's Own* (New York: Harcourt, Brace & World, 1929), p. 17.
2   H. Stuart Hughes, *Consciousness and Society: The Reorientation of European Social Thought 1890–1930* (New York: Knopf, 1961).
3   Robert Ackerman, "Frazer on Myth and Ritual," *Journal of the History of Ideas* 36 (1975): 115–34.
4   JH to GM, undated, Box 6, JEH.
5   Perhaps Jane Harrison and James Frazer did not agree on many things, but Stanley Edgar Hyman places them together in a Hebrew class in Cambridge (Stanley Edgar Hyman, *The Tangled Bank: Darwin, Marx, Frazer and Freud as Imaginative Thinkers* [New York: Atheneum, 1962], p. 190).
6   Frank Turner, *The Greek Heritage in Victorian Britain* (New Haven: Yale University Press, 1981) gives a fine analysis of Victorian classicists' perceptions of the ancient world.
7   Ibid., p. 8.

## CHAPTER 1

1   *Dictionary of National Biography*, s.v. "Harrison, Jane Ellen," by Francis M. Cornford.
2   Hope Mirrlees, Notebook, "Marion Harrison," Box 15, JEH. Unless otherwise noted, Mirrlees's material is housed in this collection.
3   Ibid.
4   Stewart, *Portrait*, p. 5.
5   Mirrlees, Notebook, "Marion Harrison."
6   Ibid., "Various Tid-bits from My Own Memories."
7   Ibid., "Marion Harrison."
8   JH to D. S. Mirsky, May 6, 1926, Box 8, JEH. Unless otherwise noted, all of Jane's correspondence is housed in this collection. For an excellent analysis of the loss of the mother, see Nancy Anderson, "No Angel in the House: The Psychological Effects of Maternal Death," *Psychohistory Review* 11, no. 1:20–46.
9   Mirrlees, Notebook, "Lucy (Booty)."
10   Ibid. See also RSL, pp. 317–20.
11   Mirrlees, Notebook, "Lucy (Booty)."
12   Jane Ellen Harrison, "Crabbed Age and Youth," in *Alpha and Omega* (London: Sidgwick & Jackson, 1915; reprint. New York: AMS Press, 1973), pp. 11–12; hereafter cited as *A&O*.
13   Mirrlees, Notebook, "Mrs. Charles Mitchell."
14   Ibid., "Marion Harrison."
15   Deborah Gorham, *The Victorian Girl and the Feminine Ideal* (Bloomington: Indiana University Press, 1982), p. 201. See also M. Jeanne Peterson, "The Victorian Governess: Status Incongruity in Family and Society," in *Suffer*

*and Be Still: Women in the Victorian Age*, ed. Martha Vicinus (Bloomington: Indiana University Press, 1972), pp. 3–19.

16  Mirrlees, Notebook, "Marion Harrison"; Ibid., "Various Tid-bits"; Hilda Lane to Mirrlees, undated, Box 9.

17  Mirrlees, Notebook, "Lucy (Booty)."

18  Ibid., "Marion Harrison."

19  Hope Mirrlees, "Fragments of a Draft Biography," Box 15.

20  Mirrlees, Notebook, "Lucy (Booty)."

21  Ibid. Nevertheless, Charles Harrison managed to leave an estate of more than thirty thousand pounds, largely in property and railroad stock. Most of it went to his widow and his son, Herbert. The three daughters of the first marriage inherited a mere hundred pounds each, as they were already "provided for." The remaining daughters each received a percentage of Charles's railroad stock.

22  Ibid.

23  Ibid., "Marion Harrison."

24  Mirrlees, "Draft Biography."

25  Charles Harrison objected to a substitute clergyman in his Yorkshire parish because "he brought with him leaflets and new hymn-books and new hassocks. . . . He even put a little cross on the Communion Table, but this my father with his own hands swiftly and silently removed" (RSL, 314).

26  Mirrlees, Notebook, "Lucy (Booty)."

27  For a discussion of the rise of Evangelicalism in nineteenth-century Britain, see Ian Bradley, *The Call to Seriousness: The Evangelical Impact on the Victorians* (New York: Macmillan Publishing Co., 1976); and Richard Carwardine, *Transatlantic Revivalism: Popular Evangelicalism in Britain and America, 1790–1865* (Westport, Conn.: Greenwood Press, 1978), especially pp. 85–94. On Evangelical attitudes toward the family, see Elizabeth Jay, *The Religion of the Heart: Anglican Evangelicalism and the Nineteenth-Century Novel* (Oxford: Oxford University Press, 1979). John Clive, in *Macaulay: The Shaping of the Historian* (New York: Alfred A. Knopf, 1973), presents a fascinating study of the Evangelical influence on the formation of intellect. Edmund Gosse, in *Father and Son* (New York: C. Scribner's Sons, 1907), gives an autobiographical account of the same phenomenon. Samuel Butler, in *The Way of All Flesh*, treats it in novel form.

28  Helene Deutsch, *The Psychology of Women: A Psychoanalytic Interpretation* (New York: Greene & Stratton, 1945), p. 439; hereafter cited in the text. I rely on Deutsch partly because she is the only neo-Freudian to draw attention to stepmothers. Her work, however, also conveys a sense of hopelessness about family and interpersonal relationships that more fully illuminates them. Karen Horney, Anna Freud, and the older Melanie Klein emphasized the possibilities of breaking out of old molds. More than any of her colleagues, Deutsch remained Freud's "good daughter" by retaining his gloomy vision of the world. Deutsch also recognized female anger, which constitutes one of her most important contributions to the psychoanalytic interpretation of female personality. Despite her misogyny, or perhaps because of it, Deutsch's work remains critical to an understanding of female psychology. See also Karen Horney, *Feminine Psychology*, ed. Harold Kelmar (New York:

W. W. Norton & Co., 1967); Anna Freud, *The Ego and the Mechanisms of Defense* (London: Hogarth Press, 1937); and Janine Chassaguet-Smirgel, "Feminine Guilt and the Oedipus Complex," in *Female Sexuality: New Psychoanalytic Views*, ed. Janine Chassaguet-Smirgel (Ann Arbor: University of Michigan Press, 1970). Bruno Bettelheim explores the image of the wicked stepmother in *The Uses of Enchantment* (New York: Alfred A. Knopf, 1977), pp. 66–73. For a brief discussion of the emotional state of widowers in the nineteenth century, see Peter Gay, *Education of the Senses*, vol. 1, *The Bourgeois Experience* (New York and Oxford: Oxford University Press, 1984), pp. 236–37.

29   Jane Ellen Harrison, "Homo Sum," in *A&O*, pp. 95–97.

30   JH to MM, August 28, 1909, #395, Box 6.

31   Ibid.; JH to MM, September 17, 1912, #33, Box 8.

32   Cf. Gay, *Education of the Senses*, pp. 71–225. See also the lively debate in many of the reviews of his first volume: David Cannadine in the *New York Review of Books* 31, no. 19 (February 2, 1984), and Neil McKendrick in the *New York Times Book Review*, January 8, 1984, p. 1. Paul Robinson reviewed volume 2, *The Tender Passion* (New York and Oxford: Oxford University Press, 1986), in the *New York Times Book Review*, March 16, 1986, p. 6. Reviewers generally agreed that although Gay's work revealed the experience of a select group, it is difficult to extrapolate from that experience to make judgments about an entire culture.

33   Gorham, *The Victorian Girl*, p. 67. Jonathan Gathorne-Hardy explores the issue of self-control in *The Rise and Fall of the British Nanny* (New York: Dial Press, 1973). He attributes the efficiency of British civil servants in India to their nannies, who instilled in them an almost pathological need for order. He claims that nannies vented their frustrations on their charges as a means of maintaining their sense of self-worth in what was often a demeaning line of work. For a more sinister interpretation of the emphasis on self-control, especially in women, see Peter Cominos, "Innocent Femina Sensualis in Unconscious Conflict," in *Suffer and Be Still*, ed. Vicinus, pp. 155–72.

34   HM to JS, June 26, 1959, Box 14, JEH.

35   Mirrlees, Notebook, Commentary with no heading.

36   Ibid., "Various Tid-bits."

37   Ibid., "Lucy (Booty)."

38   "Fortunately [Charles Harrison] showed appreciation of his exceptional daughter and indulged her passion for education" (Stewart, *Portrait*, p. 5). Robert Ackerman claims that "after some struggle on [Jane's] part, her exceptional gifts caused her to be sent to school" (Ackerman, "The Early Work," p. 210). Both authors ignore the curate episode and, more important, Charles Harrison's promise to his first wife that he would not send her daughters away to school.

39   Mary Paley Marshall, *What I Remember* (Cambridge: Cambridge University Press, 1947), pp. 6–7. Many late Victorian and Edwardian women experienced various degrees of frustration with their early education. They suffered from the relentless boredom that useless lessons inspired. Many also shared Jane's tendency toward psychosomatically induced illness. A few, such as Florence Nightingale, verged on nervous breakdown because of their

stultifying lives. For comparisons, see Beatrice Webb, *The Diary of Beatrice Webb,* ed. Norman MacKenzie and Jeanne MacKenzie (Cambridge: Harvard University Press, 1982), especially vol. 1; Beatrice Webb, *My Apprenticeship* (London: Longmans, Green & Co., n.d.), especially chaps. 1 and 2; Dora Russell, *The Tamarisk Tree: My Quest for Liberty and Love* (New York: G. P. Putnam's Sons, 1975); and Allen F. Davis, *American Heroine: The Life and Legend of Jane Addams* (New York: Oxford University Press, 1973).

40 Cf. Joan Burstyn, *Victorian Education and the Ideal of Womanhood* (Totowa, N.J.: Barnes & Noble Books, 1980); Carol Dyhouse, *Girls Growing Up in Late Victorian and Edwardian England* (London: Routledge & Kegan Paul, 1981); and Gorham, *The Victorian Girl.* Burstyn sees education as a bona fide attempt to challenge traditional views of womanhood, whereas Dyhouse argues that even educational reform was essentially a conservative movement. Gorham focuses on general child-rearing practices designed to inculcate the feminine ideal in young girls.

41 Elizabeth Sewell, *Principles of Education* (London: Longman, Green, Longman, Roberts, & Green, 1865), 1:219; [Montagu Burrows], "Female Education," *Quarterly Review* 126 (April 1869): 238.

42 For a comparison of these two fascinating figures in early educational reform, see Josephine Kamm, *How Different From Us: A Biography of Miss Buss and Miss Beale* (London: Bodley Head, 1958).

43 Many works describe the debate over women's education in the nineteenth century, which seems to have attracted scholarly attention in two waves. One began around the turn of the century and lasted for twenty-five years or so. The other is more recent, having started in the last ten years. Some scholars focus on the political changes, and others on the psychological and social implications of educating women. The works by Burstyn, Dyhouse, and Gorham cited above are recent; there are many other useful and interesting recent works as well. Edward Ellsworth's *Liberators of the Female Mind: The Shirreff Sisters, Educational Reform, and the Women's Movement* (Westport, Conn: Greenwood Press, 1979), is an interesting biography of Emily and Maria Shirreff. He focuses on their efforts to open up educational doors for women. Sheila Fletcher's *Feminists and Bureaucrats* (Cambridge: Cambridge University Press, 1980); Margaret Bryant's *The Unexpected Revolution: A Study in the History of Education of Women and Girls in the Nineteenth Century* (London: University of London, Institute of Education, 1979); and Josephine Kamm, *Hope Deferred: Girls' Education in English History* (London: Methuen, 1965) chronicle the political struggles for women's education. Ann Phillips, eds., *A Newnham Anthology* (Cambridge: Cambridge University Press, 1979), is a collection of students' reminiscences. Rita McWilliams-Tullberg, in *Women at Cambridge: A Men's University—Though of a Mixed Type* (London: Victor Gollancz, 1975), discusses the struggle for the granting of degrees to women at Cambridge. Vera Brittain, *The Women at Oxford* (New York: Macmillan Co., 1960) and Annie M. A. H. Rogers, *Degree by Degrees* (Oxford: Oxford University Press, 1938), study the situation at Oxford. Among the older accounts, Sara A. Burstall, *English High Schools for Girls* (London: Longmans, Green, & Co., 1907), explores secondary education for women. Alicia Percival, *The*

*English Miss To-day and Yesterday* (London: George G. Harrap & Co., 1939), although not a terribly scholarly work, offers some perceptive insights into the influence of the father-daughter bond on a girl's desire for education; see especially pp. 49–50. Alice Zimmern, in *The Renaissance of Girls' Education in England: Fifty Years of Progress* (London: A. D. Innes & Co., 1898), celebrates the efforts of early reformers.

44 Amy Key Clarke, *A History of the Cheltenham Ladies' College 1853–1953* (London: Faber & Faber, 1953), p. 43.

45 Kamm, *How Different From Us*, p. 23.

46 Ibid., pp. 24–28.

47 Clarke, *Cheltenham Ladies' College*, p. 49.

48 R. L. Archer, *Secondary Education in the Nineteenth Century* (London: Frank Cass & Co., 1966), p. 242.

49 Kamm, *How Different From Us*, p. 82.

50 Clarke, *Cheltenham Ladies' College*, pp. 22, 27, 38.

51 Cheltenham: Kamm, *How Different From Us*, pp. 60–62, and Jonathan Gathorne-Hardy, *The Old School Tie: The Phenomenon of the English Public School* (New York: Viking Press, 1978), p. 244; North London Collegiate School: Zimmern, *Renaissance*, p. 65. The silence rule at Cheltenham into the 1970s.

52 Clarke, *Cheltenham Ladies' College*, pp. 49, 89.

53 Kamm, *How Different From Us*, p. 39.

54 Mirrlees, Notebook, "Lucy (Booty)."

55 Ibid. Jane was fortunate that this condition did not lead her family to take her away from school. Many critics of women's education considered amenorrhea a typical side effect of too much intellectual strain. As Deborah Gorham states, "the usual cure recommended by Victorian practitioners for amenorrhea itself . . . was adherence to wholesome living suited to the feminine temperament. . . . An unfeminine lifestyle could . . . be one in which the girl was involved in serious study, or where she sought to escape from the confines of family life. In short, the best safeguard against abnormal menstruation, and the ills that might accompany it, was vigorous conformity to the Victorian ideal of femininity" (Gorham, *The Victorian Girl*, p. 89).

56 Mirrlees, Notebook, Commentary with no heading.

57 Ibid., "Lucy (Booty)."

58 F. Cecily Steadman, *In the Days of Miss Beale: A Study of Her Work and Influence* (London: Ed. J. Burrow & Co., n.d,), p. 18.

59 Mirrlees, Notebook, "Mrs. Charles Mitchell."

60 Ibid.

61 Kamm, *How Different From Us*, pp. 24–25.

62 Mirrlees, Notebook, "Mrs. Charles Mitchell."

63 Hilda Lane to Mirrlees, undated, Box 9.

64 Mirrlees, Notebook, "Lucy (Booty)."

65 Mirrlees, Miscellaneous notes, Box 19.

66 David Friedrich Strauss, *The Life of Jesus Critically Examined*, 2 vols., trans. Marian Evans (New York: Calvin Blanchard, 1860).

67 Mirrlees, Miscellaneous notes, Box 15.

68 Steadman, *Miss Beale*, p. 18.

69   Mirrlees, Notebook, "Lucy (Booty)."
70   Mirrlees, "Outline of Life," Box. 15.


CHAPTER 2

1   [Burrows], "Female Education," p. 242; J. G. Fitch, "Women and the Univer-
    sities," *Contemporary Review* 58 (August 1890), p. 243. For a sampling of
    other contemporary views, see "Feminine Wranglers," *Saturday Review* 18
    (1864): 111–13; "Women at the Universities," *Saturday Review* 43 (1877):
    660–61; Percy Gardner, "Women at Oxford and Cambridge," *Quarterly
    Review* 186 (1897): 529–51; and W. H. Davenport Adams, *Woman's Work
    and Worth in Girlhood, Maidenhood, and Wifehood* (London, 1880).
2   Burrows, "Female Education," pp. 243–48.
3   See, for example, Burstyn, *Victorian Education*; Dyhouse, *Girls Growing
    Up*; and Fletcher, *Feminists and Bureaucrats*, for more detailed discussion.
4   This chapter focuses, of necessity, on Newnham's founding. Barbara Ste-
    phen, *Emily Davies and Girton College* (London: Constable & Co., 1927;
    reprint. Westport, Conn.: Hyperion Press, 1976); M. C. Bradbrook, *That
    Infidel Place* (London: Chatto & Windus, 1969); and B. Megson and J. Lind-
    say, *Girton College, 1869–1959: An Informal History* (Cambridge: Heffers,
    1960), give historical accounts of Girton College. Olive Jocelyn Dunlop,
    *Leaves from a Cambridge Notebook* (Cambridge: Heffer, 1907), and Louisa
    Lumsden, *Yellow Leaves* (London: Blackwood & Sons, 1933), provide stu-
    dent perspectives on Girton life. Annie Edwards, in *A Girton Girl* (London:
    R. Bentley, 1885), reveals the fantasy of those who hoped college women
    would come to their senses after kicking up their heels. Its Newnham coun-
    terpart is Alice Stronach, *A Newnham Friendship* (London: Blackie & Son,
    1901).
5   Blanche Athena Clough, *A Memoir of Anne Jemima Clough* (London: Ed-
    ward Arnold, 1897), p. 175. See also Stephen, *Emily Davies*, chap. 2.
6   Clough, *Memoir*, pp. 172–73. McWilliams-Tullberg, in *Women at Cam-
    bridge*, provides a thorough account of the battle for degrees.
7   Quoted in Barbara Stephen, *Girton College 1869–1932* (Cambridge: Cam-
    bridge University Press, 1933), p. 37; Ibid., p. 64.
8   Ibid., p. 28.
9   Ibid., pp. 145–46.
10  Clough, *Memoir*, pp. 147–49.
11  Henry Sidgwick, "The Theory of Classical Education," in *Miscellaneous
    Essays and Addresses* (London: Macmillan & Co., 1904), pp. 272–75;
    Clough, *Memoir*, p. 175; Henry Sidgwick, "Classical Education," pp. 272–
    75. For more on Sidgwick's life, see Arthur Sidgwick and Eleanor Sidgwick,
    *Henry Sidgwick: A Memoir* (London and New York: Macmillan, 1906).
    Many works have addressed the question of university reform in the Victo-
    rian era. See Sheldon Rothblatt, *The Revolution of the Dons: Cambridge
    and Society in Victorian England* (London: Faber & Faber, 1968); idem,
    *Tradition and Change in Liberal Education* (London: Faber & Faber, 1976);
    Alfred I. Tillyard, *History of University Reform from 1800 to the Present
    Time* (Cambridge: W. Heffer & Sons, 1913); F. M. Cornford, *The Cambridge

*Classical Course: An Essay in Anticipation of Further Reform* (Cambridge: W. Heffer & Sons, 1903); and F. W. Farrar, ed., *Essays in a Liberal Education,* 2d ed. (London: Macmillan & Co., 1869).

12  Clough, *Memoir,* pp. 172, 174–75, 53.

13  Ibid., pp. 181, 169–70.

14  Ibid., p. 155.

15  Ibid., chaps. 1 and 2; p. 182.

16  Percival, *The English Miss,* p. 166.

17  Clough, *Memoir,* p. 153.

18  Ibid., p. 195.

19  Phillips, *Anthology,* p. 1.

20  Quoted in Marshall, *What I Remember,* p. 11; Clough, *Memoir,* p. 232.

21  Stephen, *Girton College,* p. 40; Phillips, *Anthology,* p. 2; Marshall, *What I Remember,* p. 10. Evangelicalism grew up separate from the universities, but "even so, Cambridge became closely associated with Evangelical teaching in the early nineteenth-century and, under the guidance of Charles Simeon, became a forcing-house for Evangelicals lay and clerical. The connection was important, if only because it gave some of the leading Evangelicals a concern for and an interest in scholarship which in general the movement lacked. Although many were unusually successful in business enterprise, they often revealed a deep, and perhaps just, suspicion that secular learning threatened the integrity of the Gospel" (V. H. H. Green, *Religion at Oxford and Cambridge* [London: SCM Press, 1964], p. 222).

22  See Ellen Condliffe Lagemann, *A Generation of Women: Education in the Lives of Progressive Reformers* (Cambridge: Harvard University Press, 1979), for a good discussion of fathers' importance to ambitious daughters. I myself can attest to the validity of this evidence through one small example. In 1977, I took a graduate seminar in Feminist Theory and Method at Sarah Lawrence College. Professor Virginia Yans-McLaughlin, who taught the course that semester, asked us to write brief autobiographies. When she returned them to us, she asked incredulously, "Where are your mothers?" It seems that all of us—in a class of about a dozen women—had written about the influence of our fathers and ignored our mothers.

23  Paley: Quoted in Clough, *Memoir,* pp. 197–98; Anne Clough: quoted in ibid., pp. 200–01.

24  Ibid., p. 205. For other descriptions of women's college life, see Eleanor Field, "Women at an English University," *Century Magazine* 42, n.s. 20 (1890); and Phillips, *Anthology.* Nicholas Pevsner, in *Cambridgeshire* (Harmondsworth, England: Penguin Books, 1970), pp. 194–97, describes Newnham's architecture. For an analysis of the architecture of women's colleges in America, see Helen Lefkowitz Horowitz, *Alma Mater: Design and Experience in the Women's Colleges from Their Nineteenth-Century Beginnings to the 1930s* (New York: Knopf, 1984).

25  Mirrlees, Notebook, "Mary Paley," JEH. Unless otherwise noted, Mirrlees's material is housed in this collection. Marshall, *What I Remember,* p. 22.

26  Ritchie: Mirrlees, Notebook, "Mrs. Herbert Paul (Elinor Ritchie)"; Dew-Smith: Mirrlees, "Draft Biography"; "fickle in her passions": Mirrlees, Notebook, "Mrs. Charles Mitchell."

27   Mirrlees, Notebook, Commentary with no heading; quoted in Stewart, *Portrait*, p. 8; Mirrlees, Notebook, "Alice Dew."

28   Vicinus, *Independent Women*,, p. 140.

29   "An Old Newnham Student," "The Social Life of an Undergraduate," *Girls' Realm* 5 (1902–03): 411, cited in Ibid.

30   Mary Agnes Hamilton, *Remembering My Good Friends* (London: Jonathan Cape, 1944), p. 37–38.

31   Marshall, *What I Remember*, pp. 17, 17–18, 21; Mirrlees, Notebook, "The Greek Play."

32   Marshall, *What I Remember*, pp. 15–21.

33   Ibid., p. 15; Mirrlees, "Fragmentary Notes on Early Newnham Days," Box 14.

34   Mirrlees, "Fragmentary Notes."

35   Ethel Sidgwick, *Mrs. Henry Sidgwick: A Memoir* (London: Sidgwick & Jackson, 1938), p. 37.

36   Phillips, *Anthology*, p. 53.

37   Mirrlees, "Fragmentary Notes."

38   Ibid.

39   Mirrlees, Notebook, Commentary with no heading; Clough, *Memoir*, pp. 194, 196.

40   Mirrlees, Notebook, "Mrs. Herbert Paul."

41   Ibid.

42   Ibid., "Alice Dew."

43   Ibid., "Mrs. Herbert Paul."

44   Ibid.

45   Marshall, *What I Remember*, pp. 8–9, 10–13; Janet E. Courtney, *Recollected in Tranquillity* (London: William Heinemann, 1926), p. 93.

46   Dyhouse, *Girls Growing Up*, pp. 33–35.

47   Jonathan Gathorne-Hardy briefly addresses the surrogate family issue in *The Old School Tie*. He studied secondary schools, but his comments apply to women's colleges as well. In his research, he "found a number of teachers (particularly at girls' schools) saying that in the boarding house the public schools had created the ideal substitute-family unit." He labels this assertion "rubbish," asking "who ever heard of a family unit with sixty children and one parent?" He claims that the "house system . . . like boarding itself . . . was an accident" (pp. 29–30). It seems to me that Gathorne-Hardy misses the point. The boarding system may indeed have been an accident. If it evolved into a surrogate family, however, it must be examined as such. Whether or not the founders wanted to establish a surrogate family is immaterial. It seems likely that they did not. But Gathorne-Hardy fails to see that although the family structure found in women's schools does not replicate the nuclear family they came from, women students restructured it to suit their needs. They needed the emotional sustenance associated with parents, but not parental authority and control. Thus, the students provided each other with support and validation of their experience while escaping parental control.

48   Woolf, *A Room of One's Own*; Dorothy Sayers, *Gaudy Night* (London: Victor Gollancz, 1935). Woolf's classic plea for female intellectual autonomy voiced

the desires of a specific group of women. She addressed the desires that concerned a small group of highly educated, upper-middle-class female intellectuals, but her work nevertheless captures an important concept: the individual's right to independent thought and creative expression. Dorothy Sayers infused her mystery story with an underlying theme. In essence, she portrayed a female community as fundamentally healthy. The academic women turn out not to have committed the crime—a solution that challenged public perceptions of their nature. Whether academic women could be assimilated into the larger culture remained debatable. Lily Briscoe in Virginia Woolf's *To the Lighthouse* (New York: Harcourt, Brace & World, 1927) represents the female intellectual as perennial outsider. For a look at the significance of women's education and the female intelligentsia in other European settings, see Karen M. Offen, "The Second Sex and the Baccalaureat in Republican France, 1800–1924," *French Historical Studies* 13, no. 2 (Fall 1983): 252–86; Samia Spencer, "Women and Education," in *French Women and the Age of Light*, ed. Samia Spencer (Bloomington: Indiana University Press, 1984); and Barbara Alpern Engel, *Mothers and Daughters: Women of the Intelligentsia in Nineteenth-Century Russia* (Cambridge: Cambridge University Press, 1983). In Jane's case, and I would argue generally, the female intelligentsia served a specific purpose: it provided emotional sustenance for women's forays into the world of male scholarship. Despite Jane's reliance on female support, she never lost sight of her complex and conflicted connection to male intellectual culture. I thank Elizabeth Fox-Genovese for an enlightening discussion on the issue of the female intelligentsia and intellect as power. See Elizabeth Fox-Genovese, "Culture and Consciousness in the Intellectual History of European Women," *Signs* 12, no. 3 (Spring 1987): 529–47.

49  Christine de Pisan, *The Book of the City of Ladies*, trans. Earl Jeffrey Richards (New York: Persea Books, 1982); Mary Astell, *A Serious Proposal for the Ladies* (1701; reprint. New York: Source Book Press, 1970). Both of these authors stressed women's need to free themselves of obligations to family, especially to men, in order to learn. Much of the recent debate over female culture centers on the nature of women's relationships. Young women frequently shared intense friendships in the nineteenth century. In the educational setting, I am inclined to attribute them to women's emulation of patterns set by their brothers, the rigidly enforced sex segregation that formed the basis of women's admission to universities, and the need for companionship less troubled by disagreements over social roles and expectations. Cf. Martha Vicinus, " 'One Life to Stand Beside Me': Emotional Conflicts of First-Generation College Women in England," *Feminist Studies* 8 (Fall 1982): 603–28; Nancy Sahle, "Smashing: Women's Relationships before the Fall," *Chrysalis* 8 (1979): 17–27: Leila Rupp, " 'Imagine My Surprise': Women's Relationships in Historical Perspective," *Frontiers* 5, no. 3 (1980): 61–70; and Lillian Faderman, *Surpassing the Love of Men: Romantic Friendship and Love between Women from the Renaissance to the Present* (New York: William Morrow & Co., 1981).

50  Unfortunately, not all women were able to break from their families and survive the alienation education caused. Jane broke successfully from her background, but many of her contemporaries stopped short of total rejection

and settled for redefining their roles as women. The most tragic case of the failure to form a surrogate family and its consequences is found in Victoria Glendinning, *A Suppressed Cry: The Life and Death of a Quaker Daughter* (London: Routledge & Kegan Paul, 1969). This wrenching true account tells the story of a young woman, Winnie Seebohm, whose family's opposition to her desire to be educated literally suffocated her.

51    Mirrlees, Notebook, "The Half-Sister, Jessie."
52    Ibid., "Mrs. Charles Mitchell"; Mirrlees, "Outline of Life," Box 15; *Dictionary of National Biography*, s.v. "Butcher, Samuel Henry."
53    Mirrlees, Notebook, "Mrs. Paul's Answers"; Elinor Ritchie Paul to HM, June 13, 1934, Box 14; Mirrlees, Notebook, "Outline of Life."
54    Mirrlees, Notebook, "Jessie."
55    Ibid., "Helen Salter (Helen Verrall)."
56    Mirrlees, "Draft Biography"; JH to JS, June 1900, Box 10.
57    Mirrlees, "Draft Biography."
58    Mirrlees, Notebook, "Outline of Life."

## CHAPTER 3

1    Jane Ellen Harrison, *Introductory Studies in Greek Art* (New York: Macmillan and Co., 1882), p. vii; hereafter cited as *ISGA*.
2    Mirrlees, Notebook, "Helen Salter," JEH. Unless otherwise noted, Mirrlees's material is housed in this collection.
3    Alice Dew-Smith, *Newnham College Roll Letter*, January 1929, pp. 64–65.
4    Mirrlees, Notebook, "Hope Malleson." See Claire Richter Sherman and Adele M. Holcomb, eds., *Women as Interpreters of the Visual Arts* (Westport, Conn., and London: Greenwood Press, 1981), p. 35, for a brief discussion of Jane as a model for Eugenie Sellers at the beginning of Sellers's career.
5    Mirrlees, Notebook, "Mrs. Paul on the Homeric Theatricals"; ibid., Commentary with no heading; ibid., "Alice Dew."
6    Ibid., "Alice Dew"; JH to Hope Malleson, December 7, 1881, Box 8, JEH. Unless otherwise noted, all of Jane's correspondence is housed in this collection.
7    JH to Hope Malleson, October 20, 1881, Box 8, JEH. For a more detailed discussion of the association between classical study and male identity, see chap. 4.
8    *Pall Mall Gazette*, 1891, p. 2; undated clipping in the Newnham College Archive, Cambridge. Only the year it appeared in print has been marked.
9    Ibid.
10    Mirrlees, Notebook, "Lucy (Booty)."
11    Dew-Smith, *Roll Letter*, pp. 64–65; Mirrlees, Notebook, "Alice Dew-Smith."
12    Mirrlees, Notebook, "Professor Myres."
13    Dew-Smith, *Roll Letter*, p. 64.
14    Mirrlees, Notebook, "Homeric Theatricals."
15    Mirrlees, "Draft Biography."
16    Elinor Ritchie Paul to Mirrlees, June 13, 1934, Box 14.
17    Mirrlees, Notebook, "DSM."
18    Mirrlees, Notebook, "Hope Malleson." Hope Mirrlees wrote to Jessie Stew-

art that, on reflection, she thought Jane had grown "bored with sharing a house with Miss Get Wilson," who "had become a complete invalid, and couldn't do her share of the housekeeping, and often had to be nursed. And though Jane was quite fond of her she was not one of her *dear* friends" (HM to JS, March 4, 1951, Box 14).

19   Vicinus, *Independent Women,* pp. 1–9. See also Lee Holcombe, *Victorian Ladies at Work: Middle-Class Working Women in England and Wales, 1850–1914* (Hamden, Conn.: Archon Books, 1973).

20   For Jane's description of the Sesame Club, see Stewart, *Portrait,* pp. 39–40. Jane may have felt comfortable in a mixed club like the Sesame, which allowed both male and female members, because of her academic career. The club's "list of members . . . includes much that is best in the literary and educational world" (Eve Anstruther, "Ladies' Clubs," *Nineteenth Century* 45 [1899]: 601).

21   Dora Greenwall, "Our Single Women," *North British Review* 36 (1862): 35.

22   Alice Zimmern, "Ladies' Dwellings," *Contemporary Review* 77 (1900): 96–104.

23   Evelyn March-Phillips, "The Working Lady in London," *Fortnightly Review* 58 (1892): 193–203.

24   Anstruther, "Ladies' Clubs," pp. 598–611.

25   Harrison mentions Joanna's years of service in a letter to Gilbert Murray, December 31, 1914, Box 6; also quoted in Stewart, *Portrait,* pp. 158–59.

26   JH to Hope Malleson, April 30, 1882, Box 8.

27   Mirrlees, "Draft Biography."

28   Mirrlees, Notebook, "Notes on Jane's Early Life."

29   *Dictionary of National Biography,* s.v. "MacColl, Dugald Sutherland."

30   Augustus John, *Chiaroscuro* (London: Jonathan Cape, 1952), p. 49.

31   In her *Portrait,* Stewart discreetly refused to address the possibility of a love affair, and Ackerman dismissed Jane's attraction to Sutherland in a brief footnote (see Ackerman, "The Early Work," p. 213n14). Both acknowledged his influence on her work, and Stewart quoted some fairly revealing passages from Jane's letters to him during this period, but neither devoted much attention to his role in her life. The unpublished letters and notes tell a much more interesting story than has yet come to light.

32   Mirrlees, Notebook, "DSM."

33   Mirrlees, Notebook, "Alice Dew." Hope Mirrlees admitted late in her life that Jane "was frightfully shattered by Sutherland's marriage, tho' she had refused to marry him herself" (HM to JS, March 4, 1951, Box 14).

34   See Stewart, *Portrait,* pp. 121–22; Ackerman, "The Early Work," p. 213.

35   JH to DSM, February 6, 1887, Box 8. These letters are typescript copies of the originals, apparently done at Jessie Stewart's request.

36   Ackerman, "The Early Work," p. 223.

37   JH to DSM, undated; undated; January 13, 1887, Box 8.

38   JH to DSM, February 6, 1887, Box 8.

39   Mirrlees, "Notes for a Draft Biography"; Mirrlees, Notebook, "The Letters."

40   JH to DSM, undated, Box 8.

41   JH to DSM, undated; undated, Box 8.

42  JH to DSM, November 13, 1887, Box 8; Mirrlees, Notebook, "DSM's List of Dates"; Ibid., "DSM."

43  Jane Ellen Harrison and D. S. MacColl, *Greek Vase Paintings* (London: T. Fisher Unwin, 1894), p. 5.

44  Ackerman states that *"Mythology and Monuments of Ancient Athens* (1890) might be called the first book of the Cambridge Ritualists, even though Miss Harrison had at this time not even met Murray, Cornford, or Cook, because it indicated the general direction to be taken by the group later" (*The Cambridge Group,* p. 142). I believe the roots can be traced back even further, to *Myths of the Odyssey* (1882). Jane was a Ritualist long before she knew it.

45  Jane Ellen Harrison, *Myths of the Odyssey in Art and Literature* (London: Rivingtons, 1882), p. ix; cited hereafter in the text.

46  Harrison, *ISGA*, pp. v–vi; cited hereafter in the text.

47  JH to DSM, undated, Box 8.

48  Stewart, *Portrait*, pp. 107, 5.

49  "Extracts from DSM's letters from Greece," Box 8.

50  D. S. MacColl, "Diary of Greek Journey, 1888," Box 8.

51  Ibid.

52  Ibid.

53  Ibid.

54  Some women, of course, were forced by circumstance to travel alone or went off as wives to wild and unfamiliar territory. See Joanna Trollope, *Britannia's Daughters* (London: Hutchinson, 1983), and A. James Hammerton, *Emigrant Gentlewomen: Genteel Poverty and Female Emigration, 1830–1914* (London: Croom Helm, 1979). Studies of women who traveled for more personal reasons are Catherine Stevenson, "Female Anger and African Politics: The Case of Two Victorian 'Lady Travellers,' " *Turn-of-the-Century Women* 2, no. 1 (Summer 1985): 7–17; Katherine Frank, *A Voyager Out: The Life of Mary Kingsley* (Boston: Houghton Mifflin Co., 1986); and Susan Goodman, *Gertrude Bell* (Leamington Spa, England, and Dover, N.H.: Berg Publishers, 1985).

55  JH to Hope Malleson, June 6, 1888, Box 8.

56  JH to DSM, undated. There is no heading or date on this letter, but clearly it was meant for MacColl.

57  Mirrlees, Notebook, "DSM."

58  The travel information in this paragraph comes from Hope Mirrlees' Notebook, either "DSM" or "DSM's List of Dates." The papers also include a notice of D. S. MacColl's lecture series. According to Ethel Sykes, she and Sutherland taught Jane "dance-steps" during those years (Mirrlees, Notebook, "Ethel Sykes"). In addition, "Jane was one of the first people to encourage Isadore Duncan. I. D. began by dancing in Sargent's and other painters' studios, to Greek poetry read aloud" (Mirrlees, Notebook, "Margaret Marshall").

59  Mirrlees, "Outline of Life."

60  DSM to JS, November 1, 1943, Box 10.

61  Mirrlees, Notebook, "DSM."

62  JH to MM, March 15, 1902, #42, Box 6.

63   JH to DSM, August 15, 1909; January 27, 1903, and July 3, 1914; dated 1905; May 30, 1909, Box 8.

64   Even Hope Mirrlees admitted that "not getting the Chair at London University (Ernest Gardner was the successful candidate, a man whom she personally disliked, and whose approach to archaeology she detested) was a very bitter disappointment" (HM to JS, March 4, 1951, Box 14). But during her lifetime Jane kept her bitterness to herself. She may well not even have recognized until very late in her life how angry Ernest Gardner's appointment made her.

65   JH to Edmund Gosse, October 24, 1888, Edmund Gosse Papers, Brotherton Library, University of Leeds.

66   Stewart records Jane's memory of Margaret Merrifield's appointment as classical lecturer. Margaret flew into a "generous rage when she was preferred before her friend," and Jane recalled that she "came immediately to London to see me and blindly stamped about the room thereby healing her friend's hurt vanity." That was the only time Jane ever saw her "thoroughly irrational" (Stewart, Portrait, p. 10).

## CHAPTER 4

1   "Note on the Award and Tenure of the Fellowship and on the Work Done by Fellows," JEH.

2   JH to GM, September 27, 1903, #151, Box 6, JEH. Unless otherwise noted, all of Jane's correspondence is housed in this collection.

3   Several biographies fill out the picture of early twentieth-century Cambridge. See, for example, Paul Levy, Moore: G. E. Moore and the Cambridge Apostles (New York: Holt, Rinehart & Winston, 1979); Victor Lowe, Alfred North Whitehead: The Man and His Work, vol. 1 (Baltimore and London: Johns Hopkins University Press, 1985); and Ronald Clark, The Life of Bertrand Russell (New York: Alfred A. Knopf, 1976).

4   Noel Annan, "The Intellectual Aristocracy," in Studies in Social History, ed. Plumb, pp. 241–87.

5   Raverat: Gwen Raverat, Period Piece: A Cambridge Childhood (London: Readers Union, Faber & Faber, 1954), pp. 30, 2; Jebb: Mary Reed Bobbitt, With Dearest Love to All: The Life and Letters of Lady Jebb (Chicago: Henry Regnery Co., 1960), p. 173; Glover: T. R. Glover, Cambridge Retrospect (Cambridge: Cambridge University Press, 1943), pp. 105–07. Countless Cantabridgians wrote their memoirs, but Raverat's is the most engaging. It is also one of the few that gives a female perspective on Cambridge culture. For others, see Marshall, What I Remember; Hamilton, Remembering My Good Friends; Dunlop, Cambridge Notebook; and Lumsden, Yellow Leaves. For a faculty wife's perspective, see Mrs. Ernest C. Roberts, Sherburne, Oxford and Cambridge (London: Martin Hopkinson, 1934). The women's memoirs contrast sharply with the men's. Cf. Charles B. L. Tennyson, Cambridge from Within (Philadelphia: George W. Jacobs & Co., n.d.); T. G. Bonney, Memories of a Long Life (Cambridge: Metcalfe & Co., 1921); T. Thornely, Cambridge Memories (London: Hamish Hamilton, 1936); and Glover, Cambridge Retrospect.

6   Mirrlees: Notebook, "V. de Bunsen," JEH; Malleson: Mirrlees, Notebook, "Hope Malleson." Unless otherwise noted, Mirrlees's material is housed in the JEH collection. In 1951, Hope Mirrlees wrote to Jessie Stewart that Jane's "return to Cambridge was a rather battered ship's return to port. She always talked about Newnham and communal life as something wonderfully peaceful. And I think coming back to Cambridge was what they call now an 'escape.' " Nevertheless, Hope also remembered "her telling me she was terrified in case she should loose [sic] touch with things, and from a sort of superstitious feeling she kept some rooms in London for the first few years she was at Cambridge" (HM to JS, March 4, 1951, Box 14).

7   Mirrlees, Notebook, "V. de Bur sen."

8   Virginia Woolf to Violet Dickinson, October 22, 1904, *Letters of Virginia Woolf*, ed. Nicholson and Trautmann, vol. 1, *1888–1912*, p. 145. Jane reciprocated Mrs. Maitland's lukewarm feelings. When the widowed Florence Maitland became Sir Francis Darwin's third wife, Jane wrote that she "couldn't marry Mrs. Maitland myself she is too fly away" (JH to GM, February 2, 1913, #599, Box 6).

9   V. H. H. Green, *The Universities* (Harmondsworth, England: Penguin Books, 1969), pp. 291–94.

10  Cf. Ackerman, *The Cambridge Group*, p. 150. He adheres to the view that when Jane returned to Newnham, she "rejoined the academic world, in which she felt at ease." I contend that she found the adjustment far more difficult than that.

11  Rothblatt, *Revolution of the Dons*, pp. 88, 21. For further discussion of class and status, see Charles Anderson and Miriam Schnaper, *School and Society in England: Social Backgrounds of Oxford and Cambridge Students* (Washington, D.C.: Public Affairs Press, 1952); Hester Jenkins and D. C. Jones, "Social Class of Cambridge University Alumni of the Eighteenth and Nineteenth Centuries," *British Journal of Sociology* 1, no. 2 (June 1950): 93–116; J. P. C. Roach, "Victorian Universities and the National Intelligentsia," *Victorian Studies* 3 (December 1959): 131–50; and Peter Musgrave, *Society and Education in England since 1800* (London: Methuen, 1968).

12  Rothblatt, *Revolution of the Dons*, p. 148. For discussion of the influence of the classical curriculum, see also Rothblatt, *Tradition and Change*: Q. D. Lewis, "Henry Sidgwick's Cambridge," *Scrutiny* 15 (December 1947); Martin L. Clark, *Classical Education in Britain 1500–1900* (Cambridge: Cambridge University Press, 1959); and Green, *The Universities*.

13  The question of classical education as indicator of social status is discussed in many comparatively recent works. In addition to those cited above, see also Turner, *The Greek Heritage*, chap. 1; Jenkins, *Victorians and Ancient Greece*, chap. 4; and Paul Bloomfield, *Uncommon People: A Study of England's Elite* (London: Hamish Hamilton, 1955).

14  A. H. Halsey and Martin Trow, *The British Academics* (Cambridge: Cambridge University Press, 1971), p. 40. See also Rothblatt, *Revolution of the Dons*.

15  Raverat, *Period Piece*, p. 163; JH to MM, December, 8, 1912, MM #34, Box 8.

16  Dyhouse, *Girls Growing Up*, p. 76; Burstyn, *Victorian Education*, p. 27.

17  Dyhouse, *Girls Growing Up*, p. 77; Mirrlees, Notebook, "V. de Bunsen." Robert Ackerman offers an explanation of Jane's attraction for both students and colleagues. "One of the keys to understanding Miss Harrison's life and achievement is perfectly obvious, but bears naming nevertheless— she was a woman. That is, if we may deal in generalizations, as a female she had not been brought up to stifle feeling or the expression of emotion, as had the majority of her male colleagues. . . . likewise she was not constrained as were her fellows by existing models of proper scholarly behavior. . . . Because she was a woman I am sure (without being able to prove it) that to some extent at least her world found her behavior charming where the same behavior in a man would have been thought childish or bizarre" (Ackerman, *The Cambridge Group*, p. 125). Jane's experience at Newnham proves this statement false. Newnham's administration particularly feared Jane's uniqueness and allowed her to return, much against its better judgment, only because of her reputation. She was undoubtedly more constrained than men by "models of proper scholarly behavior," but her unconscious decision to challenge those models enabled her to conduct herself the way she did.

18  "Our most brilliant resident don": Hamilton, *My Good Friends*, p. 60; Brown and Wilson: Phillips, *Anthology*, pp. 50, 67.

19  Phillips, *Anthology*, p. 45; Ethel Sidgwick, *Mrs. Henry Sidgwick*, p. 33; Ethel Sidgwick to JS, January 8, 1958; Hilda Lane to MM, undated, Box 9; Clark, *Bertrand Russell*, p. 144. Jane set herself a "daily allowance" of 30 cigarettes (JH to GM, July 21, 1902, #79, Box 6). Russell may have had reason to hold a grudge against Jane, who was a good friend of his first wife, Alys. Russell says that when he and Alys separated, few people knew the reason for the split. But "if there was a gap in the story it was soon filled in by rumour, at least in Cambridge, where it was borne along by Jane Harrison." He recorded that she professed to have " 'heard, on very reliable authority, that the real cause of his leaving Alys was a married woman in Cambridge, name unknown' " (Clark, *Bertrand Russell*, p. 144). In his biography of Alfred North Whitehead, Victor Lowe names Whitehead's wife, Evelyn, as the woman with whom Russell was in love, although it appears that they never actually had a sexual relationship (Lowe, *Alfred North Whitehead*, 1:246). Jane probably knew as much as Alys did. Like everyone else, despite his bravado, Russell hated to admit that other people might have suspected the truth.

20  Phillips, *Anthology*, pp. 47, 68.

21  Stewart, *Portrait*, p. 187.

22  Phillips, *Anthology*, p. 97.

23  Hilda Lane to HM, undated, Box 9.

24  Victoria de Bunsen in the *Newnham College Roll Letter*, January 1929, p. 66; Phillip, *Anthology*, p. 86; Mirrlees, Notebook, "V. de Bunsen"; Francis Cornford in the *Newnham College Roll Letter*, 1929, p. 72, quoted in Stewart, *Portrait*, p. 20.

25  de Bunsen, *Roll Letter*, p. 66; Mirrlees, Notebook, "V. de Bunsen"; JH to GM, undated, #32A, Box 6; JS to Mrs. Crum, undated, Box 10 ; JH to JS, JGS #22, July 1901, Box 10.

26   JH to MM, June 22, 1902, #70, Box 6; Mirrlees, Notebook, "Helen Salter"; JH to D. S. Mirsky, February 27, 1925, Box 8.

27   Dora Russell, *The Tamarisk Tree*, p. 40; Vera Brittain, *Testament of Youth* (New York: Macmillan Co., 1933); Josephine Kellet, *That Friend of Mine: A Memoir of Marguerite McArthur* (London: Swarthmore Press, 1920).

28   JH to JS, 1909, JGS #45, Box 10.

29   de Bunsen, *Roll Letter*, p. 67; JH to MM, April 19, 1902, #46, Box 6.

30   Stewart, *Portrait*, pp. 14, 12; JH to MM, June 15, 1900, #14A, Box 6.

31   JH to JS, June, 1900, JGS #14, Box 10.

32   JH to MM, June 15, 1900, #14A, Box 6.

33   JH to JS, September 28, 1900, JGS #3, Box 10. As with most of Jane's letters, Stewart has added the date in her own writing. She dated the letter 1899, but since the Greek trip occurred in 1901, it is more likely that the letter actually dated from 1900.

34   JS to Mr. Crum, March 27, 1901, Box 10.

35   JS to Mr. and Mrs. Crum, April 2, 1901, Box 10. For a similar encounter between Jane and classicist Andrew Lang, see chap. 5. English scholars, enamored of the alleged serenity of the classical age, considered Jane's work outrageous. Continental scholars, however, especially the German archaeologists, shared some of her feelings. See Butler, *The Tyranny of Greece*; Turner, *The Greek Heritage*; and Jenkins, *Victorians and Ancient Greece*.

36   JH to JS, 1901, JGS #27, Box 10; JH to Edith Crum, undated, Box 10; JH to JS, January 1, 1905, JGS #52, Box 10; JH to GM, 1902, #69, Box 6.

37   JH to JS, May 5, 1908, JGS #62, Box 10.

38   JH to JS, undated, JGS #45, Box 10; JH to JS, September 16, 1904, JGS #43, Box 10; December 1902, JGS #33, Box 10.

39   Mirrlees, Notebook, "Margaret Marshall"; JH to JS, April 12, 1904, Box 10.

40   JH to MM, September 3, 1904, #223, Box 6; JH to JS, Box 10. In *All Creatures Great and Small*, Yorkshire veterinarian James Herriot tells of his visit to a lorry driver who "kept a pig at the bottom of his garden for family consumption," but couldn't bear to see it slaughtered. Harriot stopped by on "one of these occasions" and the man "seized my hand in his and sobbed at me 'I can't bear it, Mr. Herriot. He was like a Christian was that pig, just like a Christian' " (James Herriot, *All Creatures Great and Small* [New York: St. Martin's Press, 1972], p. 277). In her "Reminiscences," Jane described Yorkshire as "a Paradise for dogs. . . . I have seen them crowding the platform at York station about the Twelfth of August, waited on assiduously by eager porters while their masters went neglected" (RSL, 326–27). Only in the north of England can sheepdog trials become one of the most popular televised sporting events. Jane came by her love of animals naturally.

41   JH to JS, September 5, 1905, JGS #55, Box 10.

42   Stewart, *Portrait*, p. 69.

43   Jane Ellen Harrison, "Scientiae Sacra Fames," in *A&O*, p. 18.

44   Stewart, *Portrait*, p. 18; JH to JS, November 1901, JGS #26, Box 10; Mirrlees, Notebook, "Outline of Life"; JH to JS, 1901, JGS #26, Box 10. Cf. Ackerman, "The Early Work," p. 211n5; idem, *The Cambridge Group*, p. 120.

45   Mirrlees, Notebook, "V. de Bunsen"; JH to JS, October 20, 1924, JGS #13, Box 10.

46  Mirrlees, Notebook, "Margaret Marshall."

47  Mirrlees, Notebook, "Outline of Life."

48  Vicinus, *Independent Women*, p. 331n100. Cf. Faderman, *Surpassing the Love of Men;* Carroll Smith-Rosenberg, "The Female World of Love and Ritual," *Signs* 1, no. 1 (Autumn 1975): 1–29; Nancy Cott, *The Bonds of Womanhood* (New Haven, Conn.: Yale University Press, 1977).

49  Mirrlees, Notebook, "Hope Malleson"; Virginia Woolf to Clive Bell, September 24, 1919, in *Letters of Virginia Woolf*, ed. Nicolson and Trautmann, vol. 2, *1912–1922*, p. 391.

50  JH to HM, July 3, 1910, Box 9; undated, Box 9; JH to Lina Mirrless, undated, Box 9; JH to HM, undated, Box 9.

51  JH to HM, undated, Box 9; undated, Box 9.

52  JH to HM, undated; undated; August 4, 1914, Box 9.

53  JH to HM, April 2, 1912; undated; December 25, 1914, Box 9.

54  JH to HM, November 10, 1913; September 2, 1913; undated, Box 9.

55  JH to HM, undated, Box 9; Mirrlees, Notebook, "The Letters."

56  In the Harrison family, "post-cards were an innovation and all innovations anathema" (RSL, 321).

57  JH to HM, May, 1914; July 13, 1915; July 15, 1915, Box 9.

58  JH to HM, March 26, 1918, Box 9.

59  JH to Lina Mirrlees, undated, Box 9.

60  JH to MM, August 28, 1904, #220, Box 6; JH to JS, September 30, 1901, JGS #23, Box 10.

61  Harrison, "Scientiae Sacra Fames," p. 117; hereafter cited in the text.

62  Zimmern, *Renaissance,* provides a contemporary account of the struggle for both women's colleges and degrees up to 1898 while glorifying the pioneer reformers. Bryant, *The Unexpected Revolution,* is a social history of the same movement that touches on universities throughout Great Britain. For the story of the Cambridge experience, see McWilliams-Tullberg, *Women at Cambridge;* Mary Agnes Hamilton, *Newnham: An Informal Biography* (London: Faber & Faber, 1936); and Stephen, *Girton College.* For Oxford's struggle, see Rogers, *Degree by Degrees;* and Brittain, *The Women at Oxford.*

63  See McWilliams-Tullberg, *Women at Cambridge.*

64  JH to GM, Spring, 1907, #295, Box 6.

65  JH to GM, October 30, 1912, #590, Box 6; JH to GM, March 19, 1922, #830, Box 6. The first underlined phrase occurs in a clipping from the London *Times,* October 30, 1912, p. 11, which Jane enclosed in her letter.

66  JH to GM, undated, #242, Box 6; March, 1919, #802, Box 6.

67  JH to GM, October 23, 1920, #815, Box 6; JH to GM, December, 1920, #816, Box 6.

68  JH to GM, December 25, 1920, #822, Box 6.

69  JH to GM, October 1921, #829A, Box 6; also quoted in Stewart, *Portrait,* p. 186. In a postscript, Jane added that "FMC [Cornford] says he feels it is his obvious duty to strangle his newborn son as belonging to a sex unfit for civilized life!" One can appreciate the sentiment yet cringe at its expression in such terms.

70   Rothblatt, *Revolution of the Dons*, p. 133; JH to GM, October 1921, #829A,
     Box 6.

CHAPTER 5

1   In his recent biography of Gilbert Murray, Francis West emphasizes Gil-
    bert's criticism of Jane and the differences in their work, citing Murray's
    comment that her *Prolegomena* sounded " 'like Aunt Fanny trying to be
    naughty,' although 'in many ways she is so clever' " (p. 133). West relied on
    Murray's personal correspondence, housed at Oxford, for his evidence, and I
    fully believe that Murray made that comment. Since West does not include
    footnotes and neither cites the recipient of the letter nor explains the con-
    text in which it was written, however, I hesitate to devote much attention
    to the conflicts between them. All friendships that span nearly thirty years
    contain elements of tension and disagreement, especially when the friends
    are as passionate about and absorbed in their work as Jane and Gilbert were.
    Certainly Gilbert was not the saint that Jane imagined him, but the fact that
    she created this image is more interesting than a concrete understanding of
    his character. The overall serenity of their long friendship attests to their
    genuine respect and admiration for each other, regardless of specific in-
    stances of conflict. See Francis West, *Gilbert Murray: A Life* (London and
    Canberra: Croom Helm, 1984), especially pp. 132–38. His analysis of Mur-
    ray's marriage (chap. 3, "A Whig Marriage"), while not directly applicable
    here, makes interesting reading.
2   Woolf: *The Diaries of Virginia Woolf*, ed. Anne Olivier Bell (New York:
    Harcourt Brace Jovanovich, 1977), vol. 1, *1915–1919*, p. 210; Dodds: Jean
    Smith and Arnold Toynbee, eds., *Gilbert Murray: An Unfinished Autobiog-
    raphy, with Contributions by His Friends* (London: George Allen & Unwin,
    1960), pp. 18, 17; Berenson: Bernard Berenson to Bertrand Russell, March 22,
    1903, *The Autobiography of Bertrand Russell* (Boston: Little, Brown & Co.,
    1951), 1:291; Thomson: J. A. K. Thomson to JS, December 6, 1957, Box 11,
    JEH.
3   Smith and Toynbee, *Murray*, pp. 13–14, 33–34, 25.
4   Ibid., pp. 87–88.
5   Dodds: Ibid., p. 16; Ridgeway: Glover, *Cambridge Retrospect*, p. 79.
6   See *Dictionary of National Biography*, s.v. "Cornford, Francis Macdonald;
    Ibid., s.v. "Cook, Arthur Bernard."
7   Ackerman, *The Cambridge Group*, pp. 122–23, 120–21, 121.
8   Ibid., p. 120. Ackerman later states emphatically that "we must de-
    emphasize sentiment" as a factor in Jane's central position in the group
    (Ackerman, "The Early Work," p. 211). He ultimately attributes Jane's
    closeness to her male colleagues to her belief that "she was never as
    competent in her philological scholarship as she would have wished," and
    adds that "she suffered (or claimed she did) throughout her life from hav-
    ing begun the study of Greek relatively late" (Ibid., p. 210). Although it is
    true that Jane occasionally deprecated her philological skills, this self-
    deprecation should be seen as false modesty more than as a serious evalua-

tion of her shortcomings. For one thing, long before the "impostor syndrome" received its sociological name, women of keen intelligence played down their abilities in order to facilitate personal relations in a male world. Jane remained insecure throughout most of her academic life not so much because of real intellectual inadequacies as because of her sense of not belonging to the scholarly fraternity. Second, Jane's greatest work of scholarship depended more on her interpretation of ritual ceremonies than on strict philological studies. Relying on other scholars for assistance in translations would not necessarily invalidate her theories or indicate great weakness on her part. Finally, in her heart Jane believed her view of the ancient world was right and cared little, if at all, about other scholars' opinions.

9  Harrison, "Scientiae Sacra Fames," p. 139; hereafter cited in the text.

10  Harrison, "Homo Sum," in *A&O*, p. 111.

11  GM to JS, April 23, 1952, Box 17; October 26, 1953, Box 17.

12  Jacquetta Hawkes, Review of Jessie Stewart, *Jane Ellen Harrison: A Portrait from Letters, New Statesman*, June 20, 1959, p. 871; Patricia Meyer Spacks, *The Female Imagination* (New York: Avon Books, 1972), p. 6.

13  JH to GM, May 24, 1902, #65, Box 6.

14  JH to GM, August 24, 1900, #1, Box 6; December 1900, #2, Box 6; Mirrlees, Notebook, "V. de Bunsen"; JH to GM, December 24, 1900, #7, Box 6. Not everyone agreed with Jane's assessment of Gilbert's *History*. See Herbert Paul, "The New Learning," *Nineteenth Century* 42 (December 1897): 928–39. In this scathing review, Paul reproaches Gilbert for his lack of reverence toward classical authors. A round of what Jane would have called "langwidge" ensued: see Gilbert's response and Paul's defense in "Letters to the Editor," *Nineteenth Century* 42 (January 1898): 165–68. Unless otherwise noted, Mirrlees's material is housed in the JEH collection.

15  JH to GM, December 1900, #6, Box 6; JH to MM, February 1901, #11, Box 6.

16  JH to MM, July 8, 1903, #144, Box 6. For more on Mary's jealousy of Gilbert's many female friends, see West, *Gilbert Murray*, chap. 3.

17  JH to MM, March 28, 1903, #135, Box 6. For more on the Murrays' health, see West, *Gilbert Murray*, chap. 3.

18  JH to GM, January 1902, #25, Box 6; JH to MM, January 1902, Box 6.

19  JH to GM, September 1904, #227, Box 6; September 1911, #485, Box 6.

20  JH to MM, March 23, 1904, #197, Box 6.

21  JH to MM, September 17, 1911, MM #23, Box 8.

22  JH to GM, February 1, 1902, #31A, Box 6.

23  JH to GM, January 1902, #28, Box 6; February, 1902, #33A, Box 6.

24  JH to GM, May 15, 1902, #139, Box 6; November 20, 1902, #111, Box 6.

25  JH to MM, February 27, 1903, #132, Box 6.

26  JH to GM, November 30, 1909, #408, Box 6.

27  JH to GM, May, 1909, #385, Box 6.

28  JH to MM, March 15, 1902, #42, Box 6; February 27, 1912, MM #25A, Box 8.

29  JH to GM, July 1906, #290, Box 6; JH to MM, July 8, 1903, #144, Box 6.

30  JH to JS, June, 1909, JGS #70, Box 10; JH to Ruth Darwin, undated, Box 8.

31  JH to GM, 1906, #288, Box 6.

32 JH to GM, April 1906, #284, Box 6. Like Jane, Gilbert Murray frequented rest homes and clinics for the "cure" of real and fancied ailments.

33 JH to GM, 1915, #725, Box 6.

34 JH to MM, January 30, 1902, #30, Box 6; JH to GM, March 19, 1902, #43, Box 6.

35 Mirrlees, Notebook, "DSM."

36 JH to GM, October 11, 1903, #157, Box 6. As Jane noted in the *Prolegomena*, Keres "were, if not exactly evil spirits, certainly spirits that brought evil" (*PSGR*, 165). That she took her nickname from this malevolent creature seems interesting, if only because it highlights a darker side of her personality, which she hid so successfully otherwise.

37 Mary Murray: JH to MM, October 15, 1903, #158, Box 6; Eleanor Butcher: Mirrlees, "Draft Biography."

38 JH to GM, November 8, 1903, #161, Box 6.

39 JH to MM, April 19, 1904, #199, Box 6; JH to GM, February 1906, #282, Box 6; September 26, 1911, #489, Box 6; January 30, 1910, #418, Box 6.

40 JH to MM, December 10, 1901, #21, Box 6.

41 JH to GM, June 16, 1902, #68, Box 6; Ibid.; JH to MM, January 2, 1903, #121, Box 6; September 9, 1903, #147, Box 6; JH to GM, March 15, 1908, #330, Box 6; JH to MM, July 19, 1911, MM #22, Box 8; January 25, 1913, MM #35, Box 8.

42 JH to GM, 1913, #616A, Box 6; undated, #560, Box 6.

43 JH to GM, September 3, 1914, #686, Box 6; JH to MM, October 1914, MM #45, Box 8.

44 JH to GM, December 28, 1903, #174, Box 6; December 29, 1910, #465, Box 6.

45 JH to GM, Spring, 1912, #549, Box 6; JH to Frances Darwin, November 14, 1908, quoted in Ackerman, "Letters," p. 121.

46 JH to GM, 1905, #275, Box 6; 1908, #347, Box 6.

47 JH to GM, November 24, 1901, #18, Box 6; April 22, 1902, #49, Box 6; August 18, 1910, #445, Box 6.

48 JH to GM, November 24, 1901, #18, Box 6; GM to JH, September 30, 1906, Box 9; JH to GM, January 26, 1911, #472, Box 6.

49 JH to GM, May 18, 1909, #384, Box 6.

50 JH to GM, 1908, #351, Box 6.

51 JH to GM, February 1907, Box 6.

52 JH to GM, October 29, 1902, #102, Box 6.

53 JH to GM, September 17, 1909, #398, Box 6; December 22, 1902, #117, Box 6; September 17, 1909, #398, Box 6. For Jane's discussion of the Skiraphoria, see *PSGR*, pp. 134–35. Walter Burkert, who has reopened the debate over the meaning of *skira*, favors the translation of "white earth" that Jane used. He admits, however, that modern scholars have not made any more strides toward understanding the term than did ancient commentators, who expressed confusion themselves. See Burkert, *Homo Necans*, pp. 143–49.

54 JH to GM, April 27, 1902, #52, Box 6; May 2, 1902, #58, Box 6.

55 JH to GM, September 7, 1902, #86, Box 6.

56 JH to GM, September 9, 1902, #87, Box 6.

57 JH to GM, September 10, 1902, #88, Box 6.

58   JH to GM, October 11, 1902, #98, Box 6.
59   Harold Nicolson, Review of Jessie Stewart, *Jane Ellen Harrison: A Portrait from Letters*, *Observer* (London), June 21, 1959; GM to JS, September 16, 1928, Box 17.

## CHAPTER 6

1   Gilbert Murray, "Francis Macdonald Cornford," *Proceedings of the British Academy* 29 (1943): 421–32.
2   Frances Darwin, quoted in Stewart, *Portrait*, p. 20; Mirrlees, Notebook, "Helen Salter," JEH. Unless otherwise noted, Mirrlees's material is housed in this collection.
3   JH to JS, July 10, 1904, JGS #42, Box 10; JH to GM, September 2, 1905, #263, Box 6; April 1, 1905, #239, Box 6, JEH. Unless otherwise noted, Jane's letters are all in this collection.
4   JH to GM, July 1906, #290, Box 6.
5   Margaret Verrall to MM, February 14, 1907, Box 6.
6   JH to GM, May 14, 1907, #301, Box, 6; Cornford, *Newnham Roll Letter*, p. 76.
7   JH to GM, May 14, 1907, #301, Box 6; June 1907, #305, Box 6; FMC to GM, June 18, 1907, quoted in Ackerman, "Letters," p. 120.
8   FMC to JS, June 8, 1907, Box 10.
9   Raverat, *Period Piece*, p. 191.
10   Ibid., p. 193; JH to Frances Darwin, December 1908 or early 1909, quoted in Ackerman, "Letters," p. 123.
11   Frances Darwin, quoted in Stewart, *Portrait*, p. 105; Mirrlees, Notebook, "The Letters."
12   Stewart, *Portrait*, p. 105; Raverat, *Period Piece*, p. 164; Stewart, *Portrait*, p. 105; JH to Frances Darwin, undated, CDP.
13   Frances Darwin: Stewart, *Portrait*, pp. 107, 106, 107; Francis Cornford: Cornford, *Newnham Roll Letter*, p. 75. Paul Delany, in *The Neo-Pagans: Rupert Brooke and the Ordeal of Youth* (New York: Free Press, 1987), calls Jane the "éminence grise of the Cornford-Darwin courtship." He states that the "match between Frances and Francis was of her making, and proved a credit to her insight" (p. 51). Evidence from Jane's private papers suggests otherwise.
14   The letters to follow are found in Hope Mirrlees's Notebook. They are copied in her handwriting and undated, but it seems reasonable to assume that because of her close relationship with Jane she had access to the originals at one time. The extracts are accompanied in the Notebook by Hope's own commentary.
15   The figure that prompted this drawing, a young woman sacrificing a pig, can be seen in *PSGR*, p. 126, fig. 10. For discussions of the meaning of the *khoiros* as vulva, see Jeffrey Henderson, *The Maculate Muse* (New Haven: Yale University Press, 1975), p. 131, par. 110 (cf. 111); Froma I. Zeitlin, "Cultic Models of the Female," *Arethusa* 15, nos. 1–2 (1982): 129–57, with a remark on "piglets, a well-known gloss for the vulva," on p. 144; and Walter Burkert, *Homo Necans*, trans. Peter Bing (Berkeley and Los Angeles:

University of California Press, 1983), pp. 258–59. I thank Thomas Africa for drawing my attention to the symbolic significance of this drawing.

16  John, *Chiaroscuro*, p. 64; JH to DSM May 30, 1909, Box 8.

17  JH to DSM, August 15, 1909, Box 8.

18  Stewart, *Portrait*, p. 107; JH to Frances Darwin, late 1908 or early 1909, quoted in Ackerman, "Letters," pp. 121–22.

19  JH to Frances Darwin, quoted in Ackerman, "Letters," p. 122; Stewart, *Portrait*, p. 107.

20  Scholars writing on Jane Harrison's life have ignored the full effect of her personal relationships on her life and work, especially in the case of her relationship with Francis Cornford. Jessie Stewart and Robert Ackerman scarcely comment on Francis, although for different reasons. Stewart knew something of the true story but discreetly withheld direct discussion of all its implications, instead relying heavily on Francis's and Frances's memories of Jane's ill health to excuse her behavior and emphasizing their genuine affection for her. She also avoided making connections between Jane's personal unhappiness and her poor health, choosing rather to laud Jane's scholarly achievements in the face of such physical sufferings. In fact, perhaps out of a desire to protect Jane and throw future historical hounds off the scent, Stewart blamed Jane herself, stating that "Jane felt resentment that she was no longer getting the same poetic inspiration from his mind" (*Portrait*, p. 112). Stewart thus implied, as might have been the case if there were not another side to the story, that this demand for inspiration constituted an unreasonable expectation. As one of Jane's closest friends, Stewart's refusal to discuss the situation in detail is understandable. Ackerman devotes even less attention to Jane's passionate attachment to Francis, his only reference to him being that Jane "seems to have been in love" with both him and, earlier, Sutherland MacColl. Furthermore, he claims that "in a sense . . . the Cambridge group may be seen biographically speaking, as a particularly happy time in Jane Harrison's life, when her emotional energies were most closely bound up with those of its three other members" (*The Cambridge Group*, p. 120). Cf. Stewart, *Portrait*, chap. 9; and Ackerman, *The Cambridge Group*, chap. 3.

21  JH to GM, 1908, #322, Box 6.

22  JH to GM, 1908, #335, Box 6; 1908; #332, Box 6; March 15, 1908, #330, Box 6.

23  JH to GM, 1908, #344, Box 6.

24  JH to GM, May 1908, #341, Box 6; JH to MM, May 14, 1908, MM #4, Box 6.

25  JH to GM, Spring, 1908, #327, Box 6; June 1908, #345, Box 6.

26  JH to GM, July 1908, #353A, Box 6.

27  JH to GM, August 2, 1908, #354, Box 6.

28  JH to JS, August 2, 1908, JGS #63, Box 10.

29  JH to Frances Darwin, August 2, 1908, CDP; GM to JS, September 3, 1908, Box 10.

30  JH to GM, 1908, #315, Box 6.

31  Frances Darwin to MM, October 4, 1908, CDP; JH to GM, September 30, 1908, #357, Box 6.

32   JH to Ruth Darwin, October 4, 1908, Box 8.
33   JH to GM, October 1908, #358, Box 6.
34   JH to MM, October 11, 1908, MM #6, Box 8; November 1908, MM #7, Box 6.
35   JH to GM, November 8, 1908, #364, Box 6.
36   JH to MM, December 1, 1908, #364A, Box 6.
37   Stewart, *Portrait*, p. 115.
38   JH to GM, December 16, 1908, #365, Box 6.
39   JH to DSM, May 30, 1909, Box 8.
40   JH to GM, December 26, 1908, #366, Box 6.
41   JH to GM, December 29, 1908, #368, Box 6.
42   JH to Frances Darwin, December 1908 or early 1909, quoted in Ackerman, "Letters," p. 123.
43   JH to MM, January 30, 1909, MM #11, Box 8.
44   JH to GM, January 8, 1908; February 26, 1909; April 1909; 1909; July 19, 1909, Box 6.
45   JH to MM, October 24, 1909, Box 6.
46   JH to GM, November 1909, Box 6.
47   Jane Ellen Harrison, "Heresy and Humanity," in *A&O*, p. 36.
48   Murray: JH to GM, April 4, 1910, #427, Box 6; August 12, 1910, #444, Box 6. Strachey: Quoted in Michael Holroyd, *Lytton Strachey: A Critical Biography* (New York: Holt, Rinehart & Winston, 1967), 1:457.
49   JH to GM, October 8, 1910, #450A, Box 6; October 27, 1910, #457, Box 6.
50   JH to GM, December 29, 1910, #465, Box 6.
51   JH to GM, January 4, 1911, #466A, Box 6; January 1911, #493, Box 6.
52   JH to GM, January 1911, #493, Box 6.
53   JH to GM, April 18, 1911, #480, Box 6; September 1911, #487, Box 6; JH to MM, December 25, 1911, MM #25, Box 8.
54   JH to GM, January 1912, #504A, Box 6; JH to MM, March 12, 1912, MM #26, Box 8.

## Chapter 7

1   See Hughes, *Consciousness and Society*.
2   Friedrich Nietzsche, *The Birth of Tragedy from the Spirit of Music*, trans. Francis Golffing (New York: Doubleday, 1956), hereafter cited in the text as *BT*; J. J. Bachofen, "Mother Right," in *Myth, Religion and Mother-Right: Selected Writings of J. J. Bachofen*, trans. Ralph Manheim (Princeton: Princeton University Press, 1967); Harrison, *TH*, 125n2, and S. C. Humphreys, *Anthropology and the Classics* (London: Routledge & Kegan Paul, 1978), p. 96; *TH*, p. xxiin1. "The discovery [of the social origin of religion] was first formulated by the genius of Emil [sic] Durkheim in his brief paper, 'De la définition des phénomènes religieux,' in *L'Année sociologique* of 1898 [2 (1897–98): 1–28]. His theory has been since expanded in his *The Elementary Forms of the Religious Life...*"; Henri Hubert and Marcel Mauss, "Essai sur la nature et la function du sacrifice" appeared in *L'Année sociologique* 2 (1897–98): 29–138, and is cited on p. 137n1; Durkheim's "Prohibition de l'inceste et ses origines" appeared in *L'Année sociologique* 1 (1896–97): 1–

70, and is cited on p. 139n1; Henri Bergson, *Creative Evolution* (*L'Evolution créatrice*), trans. Arthur Mitchell (New York: Henry Holt & Co., 1911).

3   Jane owed a considerable debt to these scholars, for she drew heavily on their work for supporting evidence in both the *Prolegomena* and *Themis.* Frazer's *The Golden Bough* (1880s) and *Totemism* (1887), Robertson Smith's *Religion of the Semites* (1889) and E. B. Tylor's *Primitive Culture* (1878) and *The Early History of Mankind* (1873) appear frequently in her notes. For an analysis of Frazer's influence on the Ritualists, see Ackerman, "Frazer on Myth and Ritual," and Hyman, *The Tangled Bank*, pp. 187–291.

4   GM to JS, February 6, 1945, Box 17, JEH.

5   Jane Ellen Harrison, *Ancient Art and Ritual* (New York: Henry Holt & Co., 1913), p. v; hereafter cited in the text.

6   Turner, *The Greek Heritage,* examines Victorian British scholars' interpretations of the ancient world. See especially chap. 3, which discusses George Grote's *History of Ancient Greece.* See also Jenkyns, *Victorians and Ancient Greece,* chap. 8.

7   Harrison, *ISGA*, pp. 178, 263–64.

8   Ibid., pp. 178–80.

9   A useful recent survey of the origins and impact of *The Birth of Tragedy* is M. S. Silk and J. P. Stern, *Nietzsche on Tragedy* (Cambridge: Cambridge University Press, 1981). Euripides foreshadowed modern consciousness by facing at least the possibility that there are no gods. In his *Iphigenia in Aulis,* for instance, Clytemnestra, speaking of Achilles, says, "If gods exist, you, being an upright man, will taste / Their kindness; if not, nothing further's to be done" (Philip Vellacott translation, 11:1034–35). His sense of hopelessness and loss even touched Gilbert Murray and must certainly have appealed to Jane. In all fairness to Nietzsche, his precarious mental state probably heightened his awareness of the need for reason to balance emotion. Had Jane ever come so close to the abyss, she might have changed her tune as well. Her disillusionment with society at large after World War I is as close as she ever came to applauding reason (see chap. 8).

10  Harrison, *PSGR*, p. 262n1; Bachofen, "Mother Right," p. 79. Claude Levi-Strauss, in *The Raw and the Cooked,* trans. John Weightman and Doreen Weightman (New York: Harper & Row, 1969), offers an analysis of primitive connections between women and nature. Sherry Ortner, in "Is Female to Male as Nature Is to Culture?" in *Woman, Culture and Society,* ed. Michelle Rosaldo and Louise Lamphere (Stanford, Calif.: Stanford University Press, 1974), offers another view. Jane's interest in matriarchy connected her to theorists as diverse as Engels, who adapted Lewis Henry Morgan's work on the Iroquois in North America, and mainstream anthropologists such as E. B. Tylor, whose "The Matriarchal Family System" appeared in the *Nineteenth Century,* July 1896. See also Joseph Campbell's introduction to the collection of Bachofen's writings. Jane responded to the general climate of opinion on the question of matriarchy, but infused it with her own spirit.

11  Bachofen, "Mother Right," pp. 91, 75. See Jane Ellen Harrison, "The Influence of Darwinism on the Study of Religion," in *A&O*, pp. 143–78.

12  Harrison, *PSGR*, p. viii; hereafter cited in the text.

13   JH to GM, September 1905, #270, Box 6.

14   "Review of *Prolegomena to the Study of Greek Religion*," *Cambridge Review*, March 10, 1904, p. 245. For another reaction, see Lewis Farnell, "Review of the *Prolegomena to the Study of Greek Religion* by Jane Ellen Harrison," *Hibbert Journal* 2, no. 8 (1903–04): 821–27.

15   Gilbert Murray, *Five Stages of Greek Religion* (Oxford: Clarendon Press, 1925), pp. 48–49.

16   Harrison, "The Influence of Darwinism," pp. 144, 152, 161.

17   Cornford, *Newnham College Roll Letter*, p. 75. Other writers have produced their works in similar fashion. For an interesting study of this process in a little-known but highly talented British woman novelist, see Gladys Mary Coles, *The Flower of Light: A Biography of Mary Webb* (London: Gerald Duckworth & Co., 1978), especially pp. 139–42. Mary Webb resembled Jane in many ways, not the least of which were her provincial background and her attempt to assimilate into London literary circles.

18   Harrison, *TH;* hereafter cited in the text.

19   JH to GM, 1908, #347A, Box 6; June 1908, #345, Box 6; Easter Eve, 1914, #671, Box 6; October 1911, #495, Box 6; JH to DSM, May 30, 1909, Box 22.

20   See Payne, "Modernizing the Ancients."

21   Mirrlees, Notebook, "Mrs. Charles Mitchell," JEH. Unless otherwise noted, Mirrlees's material is housed in this collection. Paul Delany is mistaken about Jane Harrison's attitude on nude bathing. He quotes Rupert Brooke's statement regarding "bathing naked by moonlight," in which Brooke asserted that he was "with Jane [Harrison] in these matters" (Delany, *Neo-Pagans*, p. 93). Brooke was probably invoking the authority of Jane's philhellenism, which included approval of Greek athletics but not necessarily nude bathing at Cambridge.

22   Arnold van Gennep paid homage to Jane's research in his 1909 *Rites de Passage* but criticized her for not recognizing the importance of the order in which the initiation ceremonies occur. See Arnold van Gennep, *The Rites of Passage*, trans. Monika B. Vizedom and Gabrielle L. Caffee (Chicago: University of Chicago Press, 1960), pp. 88–89.

23   See also her article s.v. "Mountain Mother," in *Hastings' Dictionary of Religion and Ethics*.

24   I thank Thomas Africa for identifying Lewis Farnell as the likely author of this review. Farnell did not review *Themis* any more kindly in the *Hibbert Journal*. See Farnell, "Review of *Themis: A Study of the Social Origins of Greek Religion*," *Hibbert Journal* 11, no. 42 (1912–13): 453–59.

25   JH to GM, May 5, 1904, #203, Box 6.

26   Gilbert Murray, *Four Stages in Greek Religion* (New York: Columbia University Press, 1912), p. 7.

27   JH to GM, October 1903, #155, Box 6; February 1908, #323, Box 6.

28   JH to MM, February 24, 1901, Box 8.

29   JH to GM, April 1907, #300, Box 6; 1908, #350, Box 6; 1921, #821, Box 6; 1913, #607, Box 6.

30   JH to GM, April 3, 1912, #548, Box 6.

31   JH to GM, January 28, 1911, #474, Box 6; Charles Seltman to JS, October 15, 1943, Box 14.

32  JH to JS, September 1901, JGS #24, Box 10; September 12, 1902, JGS #30, Box 10.

33  Review: JH to GM, January 28, 1911, #474, Box 6; Lecture: JH to GM, February 16, 1911, #479, Box 6. Ackerman briefly touches on a central factor in Jane's aversion to her critics. He relates the Cambridge group's view of the world at large to its view of its critics, likening it to the Eniautos-Daimon always threatened with extinction by its enemies. In his words, "[Jane] and her friends must have thought of themselves as incarnations of the Eniautos-Daimon engaged in the recurrent and necessary battle with the force of the past, the forces of death." He adds that "admittedly such thoughts must have been felt to be as fanciful as they in fact are, but it is impossible for persons as imaginative as Miss Harrison and Murray not to have seen their lives in these mythic terms" (Ackerman, *The Cambridge Group*, p. 214). The fact that the group did indeed view itself in these terms helps account for the appeal of its work.

34  JH to GM, Summer, 1907, #303, Box 6; 1908; #328, Box 6; February 1910, #422, Box 6.

35  JH to GM, May 30, 1901, #13, Box 6.

36  JH to GM, December 1912, #583A, Box 6.

37  JH to GM, 1912, #555, Box 6.

38  Jane Ellen Harrison, "Crabbed Age and Youth," in *A&O*, p. 21 For an updated psychoanalytic interpretation of this relationship, see Peter Lowenberg, "Emotional Problems of Graduate Students," in his *Decoding the Past*, pp. 48–58.

39  Stewart, *Portrait*, pp. 109, 112.

40  JH to Frances Darwin, April 29, 1912; CDP; JH to GM, Easter Day, 1912, #551, Box 6.

41  JH to GM, April 16, 1913, #604, Box 6; JH to MM, July 10, 1913, MM #36, Box 8; JH to GM, Summer, 1913, #614, Box 6.

42  JH to GM, December 27, 1913, #634, Box 6; JH to MM, June 3, 1914, MM #42, Box 8.

43  Cornford, *Newnham College Roll Letter*, p. 75.

44  Ibid., pp. 77–78.

CHAPTER 8

1  Jane Ellen Harrison, "Unanism and Conversion," in *A&O*, pp. 71–73.

2  Harrison, "Heresy and Humanity"; hereafter cited in the text.

3  Harrison, "Crabbed Age and Youth"; hereafter cited in the text.

4  JH to GM, August 1914, #684, Box 6, JEH. Unless otherwise noted, all Jane's letters are housed in this collection.

5  Jane Ellen Harrison, "Epilogue on the War," in *A&O*, pp. 221–59; hereafter cited in the text.

6  JH to GM, September 17, 1914, #687, Box 6.

7  JH To GM, September 1914, #688, Box 6.

8  JH to GM, November 1914, #693, Box 6.

9  JH to GM, November 1914, #694, Box 6.

10  JH to GM, November 17, 1914, #697, Box 6.

11  JH to DSM, December 14, 1914, Box 8. See Sandra Gilbert, "Soldier's Heart: Literary Men, Literary Women, and the Great War," *Signs* 8, no. 3 (Spring 1983): 422–50; Roland Stromberg, *Redemption by War: The Intellectuals and 1914* (Lawrence: Regents Press of Kansas, 1982); and Paul Fussell, *The Great War and Modern Memory* (Oxford: Oxford University Press, 1975), for discussion of the effects of World War I on high culture.

12  JH to GM, December 19, 1914, #704, Box 6.

13  JH to MM, December 31, 1914, MM #47, Box 8.

14  JH to GM, January 1, 1915, #709, Box 6; 1915, #711, Box 6; April 1915, #718, Box 6; Spring, 1915, #719, Box 6.

15  JH to GM, 1915, #726, Box 6.

16  JH to GM, 1915, #726A, Box 6.

17  JH to GM, August 22, 1917, #764, Box 6.

18  JH to GM, October 1914, #688, Box 6.

19  Mirrlees, Notebook, "Outline of Life." Unless otherwise noted, all Mirrlees's material is housed in this collection. See also RSL, 341.

20  JH to D. S. Mirsky, February 27, 1925, Box 8.

21  JH to GM, March 18, 1917, #763, Box 6.

22  JH to GM, August 2, 1918, #775, Box 6.

23  JH to GM, November 3, 1918, #771, Box 6.

24  JH to GM, December 1920, #816, Box 6; August 1923, #849, Box 6.

25  JH to MM, May 31, 1916, MM #54, Box 8; JH to GM, June 28, 1916, #749, Box 6.

26  *Letters of Virginia Woolf*, ed. Nicolson and Trautmann, vol. 2, *1912–1922*, p. 377; JH to GM, August 27, 1919, #685, Box 6.

27  *Letters of Virginia Woolf*, ed. Nicolson and Trautmann, vol. 3, *1923–1928*, pp. 58–59.

28  JH to GM, January 1, 1923, #838, Box 6.

29  GM to JS, April 23, 1952, Box 11; JH to GM, August 1, 1921, #803, Box 6; 1921, MC; JH to Agnes Conway, January 1923, Box 17.

30  JH to GM, March 25, 1919, #803, Box 6.

31  GM to JH, July 30, 1921, #827, Box 6.

32  Jane Ellen Harrison, *Epilegomena to the Study of Greek Religion*, 1st Amer. ed. (New Hyde Park, N.Y.: University Books, 1962; originally published Cambridge: Cambridge University Press, 1921). See pp. xxiii–xxx.

33  Sigmund Freud, *Totem and Taboo*, trans. James Strachey (New York: W. W. Norton & Co., 1950), pp. 56, 144. In the preface to the second edition of *Themis*, Jane attributed her change of heart in the *Epilegomena* to Freud, whose work had taught her "that the full-blown god, the Olympian, has a biological function which could never be adequately fulfilled by the *daimon*."

34  JS to GM, September 28, 1922, Box 17.

35  JH to HM, 1922, Box 9.

36  JH to MM, December 25, 1922, Box 8; JH to GM, January 1, 1923, Box 6; JH to JS, May 12, 1925, Box 10.

37  JH to JS, January 24, 1923, JGS #103, Box 10; JH to HM, undated, Box 9; JH to D. S. Mirsky, undated, Box 8.

38  JH to JS, March 1923, JGS #104, Box 10.

39  JH to D. S. Mirsky, August 23, 1924, Box 8.
40  JH to Mirsky, May 9, 1925, Box 8.
41  Mirrlees, "Draft Biography."
42  JS to GM, June 1902, #68, Box 6; Mirrlees, Notebook, "D. S. MacColl."
43  Harrison, "Crabbed Age and Youth," p. 16.
44  Mirrlees, Notebook, Commentary with no heading.
45  GM to JS, October 26, 1953, Box 17; Victoria de Bunsen to JS, undated, Box 10.
46  JH to GM, January 8, 1928, #863, Box 6.
47  Holroyd, *Lytton Strachey*, p. 673.
48  *Diaries of Virginia Woolf*, ed. Bell, vol. 3, *1925–1930*, entry for April 17, 1928, p. 180.

## APPENDIX

1  JS to HM, August 16, 1959, Box 14; Scrap, Box 14; HM to JS, March 29, 1943, Box 14, JEH. Unless otherwise noted, all their correspondence is housed in this collection.
2  HM to JS, June 11, 1950, Box 14; GM to JS, June 28, 1944, Box 16.
3  HM to JS, May 1946, Box 14; July 18, 1954, Box 14.
4  HM to JS, June 26, 1959, Box 14. Stewart quoted Virginia Woolf verbatim. Cf. Stewart, p. 200, and *Diaries of Virginia Woolf*, ed. Bell, vol. 3, *1925–1930*, p. 180.
5  JS to HM, June 28, 1959, Box 14; August 16, 1959, Box 14.
6  GM to JS, October 26, 1953, Box 16.

# Index